THE FEELING OF GREATNESS

"THE FEELING OF GREATNESS"

The Moe Norman Story

Tim O'Connor

▣ Eyelevel Videos Inc.

Published 1995
Printed and bound in Canada

Canadian Cataloguing in Publication Data pending.

ISBN 0-9680064-0-X

Published By:
Eyelevel Videos Inc., and Eyelevel Products International
1380 Matheson Blvd. East, Suite #5, Mississauga, Ont., L4W 4M1
55 Newton Sparta Road, Suite #107, Newton, NJ 07860

For Sandy, whose love and support allowed me to follow a dream.

Contents

Preface and Acknowledgments

I cannot pretend to understand Moe better than people who've known him for decades, but I can only hope this book will help people understand him better than they did. I also hope to bring greater recognition and appreciation for a vastly undervalued and misunderstood legend.

It was also a goal to set the record straight on many erroneous stories that have persisted for years, to unearth some new tales and dust off old favourites. My rule for this book was that in pursuit of accuracy, all significant anecdotes are based on first-hand accounts, although I made some exceptions for some stories that are relatively harmless and too much fun not to tell.

First off, I want to say "Thanks Moe" for putting your trust in me, allowing me into your inner-circle and to pester you with so many questions.

A great deal of thanks must also be extended to Jim Walker, my publisher — thanks for giving me the opportunity of a lifetime to write this book — and to editor Jon Kieran.

There are many other people who greatly assisted me and for whom I am eternally grateful. The time and effort expended by so many people is further proof of the love and admiration they have for Moe.

A number of people were especially helpful: Nick Weslock, everyone should be so lucky as Moe is to have such a great friend; Irv Lightstone, what a storyteller, what a memory; Herb Holzscheiter, another great pal and ally; Moe's lifelong buddies John Czarny, Gus Maue and Ed

Woroch; and Gary Slatter, who always made time to return my calls.

I owe a big thanks to Mark Evershed, who introduced me to Moe, arranged many of our early meetings and helped me gain his trust.

A special thanks to Lee Trevino, for the assistance he gave me and Moe.

I was touched by the help of Moe's brothers and sisters, Ron, Rich, Doreen, and especially Marie Kelly, for her time and photographs.

And no writer can give enough thanks for librarians. I especially owe a great debt to Karen Hewson, curator of the RCGA museum and library, who went to all kinds of trouble for me; Kathryn Murphy, executive secretary to the Masters tournament at Augusta National; Grace Schmidt of the Kitchener Public Library; the women of the Toronto Sun library; and the folks at St. Thomas Golf and Country Club.

A number of other people were great to me: Ernie Hauser, Bert Turcotte, Craig Shankland, Jerry Magee, Jim Suttie, Paul Bertholy, Gerry Kesselring, Tony Matlock, Lloyd Tucker, Ken Venturi, Tom Stewart, David Colling, Sam Snead, Ken Girard, Jack Marks, Gary Menaul, Stan Leonard, Doug Ford, Ken Venning, Ken Tucker and Keith Kirkpatrick.

I also must thank my mentor: John Gordon, executive director of the Ontario Golf Association, who brought me into this great world of golf writing when he was the editor of Score. And thanks to Lorne Rubenstein, one of the world's great golf writers and talents. You've been an inspiration more than you'll ever know.

I am especially grateful to Peter Carter, who published my first magazine story on Moe and got this book rolling, and to Bob Weeks, editor of Score, whose support and talents have been of immeasurable assistance and a great source of encouragement.

And finally, thanks to my mother and father for introducing me to golf and sharing this magnificent obsession.

Foreword
By Lee Trevino

The simple fact is that when people talk about the great ball-strikers, Moe Norman's name always comes up.

Of course, people always seem to revert back to Ben Hogan because he won four U.S. Opens. Heck, I've won a couple of U.S. Opens and was as good a ball-striker as Hogan had ever seen.

It's not something that you're born with, that you just wake up with in the morning and have. Ball-striking comes from a tremendous amount of confidence. And confidence comes from working extremely hard.

If you were going to give a speech in front of 5,000 people and you didn't know what you were going to say, it wouldn't be a very good speech. You'd be nervous and unable to execute. If you did your research, organized the content and practiced the delivery, you would be able to give the speech without any flaws.

I think ball-striking follows the same principle.

Moe Norman, Lee Trevino and Ben Hogan probably spent most of their youth on the practice tee hitting golf balls — and sacrificing many other things in the process.

So why did we do this? Ben Hogan was a little better educated than Moe Norman and myself. Lee Trevino left school at 14. I didn't have any other choice. Sacrifice was part of my personal development as a golfer. I had to practice a tremendous amount and do it with a very unorthodox swing. Moe Norman also didn't have the most classic swing in the world — but it has always worked for him!

Ben Hogan was not an accomplished golfer in the very beginning. He learned to become one. And after the bus accident crushed his legs, he made his comeback by hitting golf balls 10 to 12 hours a day. But then, Hogan had a classic swing. It probably wouldn't have mattered whether he practiced hard or not — though he did.

The point is, Ben Hogan could fall back on better fundamentals than either Moe or myself. In this way, I think Moe and I were a lot alike. I think that's why we appreciated each other, not only in ball-striking but in how much we accomplished with what we had. Perseverance is the crucial reason why Moe became such a good ball-striker.

He didn't have the greatest technique in the world. Moe and I were perfect examples of people not being able to come up with classic golf swings and the right instruction. We actually developed and invented our own golf swings and we're living proof that if you work hard enough and sacrifice enough, you can be successful.

I don't think Moe ever reached his potential. Perhaps in the beginning he had a label. I heard the pros talking at Royal Oak (Golf Club in Titusville, Florida, owned by the Canadian Professional Golfers' Association) about him being "disturbed" and "eccentric." But I've always liked Moe personally. He was my kind of guy. I could relate to him. I could see the pain he was going through because people appreciated him for his ball-striking, but not for his qualities as a person.

There's no question in my mind that Moe Norman would have made it anywhere. In Europe, in the U.S. and beyond. And the reason is simple: he was dedicated to the game of golf. He practiced extremely hard, day in and day out.

I only have a positive attitude about Moe. I can't think about him in any other shade. I've heard a million stories about him and I never believed any of that hogwash for one second.

I thought the man was very smart and very intelligent. He wouldn't have been the golfer he was otherwise. You not only have to hit the ball on the course, you need to have course management and that's something a lot of college graduates can't get. So don't give me that baloney that Moe Norman wasn't a smart individual. Maybe not book-smart, but street-smart — yes sir! He knew exactly what the heck he was doing. And I think that's one reason he had the success that he had.

Moe sure had a funny way of striking the golf ball, but it worked! I remember him standing by the range at The National (Golf Club of Canada, north of Toronto) when I won the Canadian PGA (Championship in 1979). I remember George Knudson came by and we were hitting five irons.

I said "Hey Moe, these people want to know how good you can hit it." I gave him my club and Moe said, "This is a matchstick, nothing, nothing. The grip's too small, the shaft's too limber, the head's too light."

But I said, "Moe that's what I play with. Forget that business and just hit the ball."

Well, the first one he put the club behind the ball about six inches and he hit the prettiest little draw out about 170 yards. Then another ball with the same amount of draw maybe a foot away from the first. He hit five golf balls and they were in a five-foot circle. I mean Moe could cover the balls he hit with a blanket. I turned and said, "Give me my club back. Matchstick my foot."

He said, "It took me a little while to get used to it."

I was very curious why he was putting the club six inches behind the ball. And he looked at me and said, "What do the instructors tell you? 'Keep the club low going away.' By starting six inches behind the ball that's as low as I can get the club."

It made a heck of a lot of sense. No one's ever taught that. It was his way of doing something that's not in the instruction books. He went back low in one piece, which I thought was very clever.

He was a tremendous ball-striker, but again that came from hard work. He wasn't born with it. He did it because he loved the game and he sacrificed everything to play.

I'm not one to judge Moe Norman and his peers to see if he got a fair shake or not. But I certainly love the man, enjoy being around him and I think he's very comfortable being around me.

To me he didn't have a picturesque swing, but he's the best ball-striker I ever saw come down the pipe. I haven't seen them all, but I don't know how anyone could hit the ball better than Moe Norman.

And I'm glad to be his friend.

Chapter One
You Have to See It to Believe It

He moved into his rigid stance, legs spread wide and ramrod straight, his arms reaching way out from his body, the clubhead a foot behind the ball. He took one peek at the distant green, swung with trademark haste and watched his drive rifle down the centre of the fairway.

Moe Norman held his follow through for a second — arms and club extended as one above his head, like he was trying to poke a hole in the clouds. Some members of the gallery at the 1971 Quebec Open laughed incredulously. Some hooted "All Right Moe!" Others uttered little sounds of amazement and shook their heads as in disbelief. They'd been watching this performance all day. Every shot the same. Perfectly straight. As if the ball were running along the edge of an invisible ruler in the sky.

Gary Slatter, a struggling pro, had watched his buddy and playing partner do this all day too. Moe was leading the tournament as they teed off the 16th hole at Summerlea Golf Club in Vaudreuil (near Montreal). Tired of saying "good shot," Slatter sniffed "Well, not bad Moe."

Moe's head turned around like he'd been slapped, his eyes wild. "Not bad! Not bad!" Moe stomped over to Slatter, waving his arms and nearly shouting: "If you could hit it like that you'd have lotsa money!"

Just then, Moe reached down, wrapped his thick arms around Slatter's thighs in a bear hug and flipped him upside down. The fans were shocked — the Quebec Open had turned into a heavyweight wrestling match with two 200-pounders in polyester and Banlon. In a startling demonstration of strength, Moe hoisted Slatter off the ground, turned him upside down, started shaking his legs and barked: "OK, let's see how much money you got in your pockets. Let's see how much!" Slatter was helpless, strung up like a fish, his arms flailing in the air. The crowd was in hysterics.

Moe let go after a few seconds and Slatter clambered to his feet. The two friends shared a good laugh, but Slatter's concentration was shot for the rest of the back nine.

When they got to the 18th tee, Moe was leading the tournament by a shot. The hole, which has since been changed, was a long par-four of about 440 yards that plunged down into a valley and rose back up to the green, which was guarded on the left-front side by a small lake. Moe bombed a drive and then cracked a three-wood onto the green. As he approached the green, the gallery surrounding the green was fairly quiet. Moe asked a marshall if anyone else had made it home in two shots that day. "No sir, you're the first."

Moe grimaced like he'd just been punched in the stomach. He looked down at the grass, shaking his head from side to side, then grabbed his putter. As he walked to his ball, he asked Slatter plaintively: "Why didn't they clap?" He didn't even seem to stop walking as he putted the ball. It wasn't even close. Again, he looked at Slatter. "Why didn't they clap? I'm the first one to hit the green in two and they didn't clap." Again, he missed. Now he had a three-footer for bogey to remain tied for the lead. Again, he asked Slatter the same question. His putt missed. The gallery gasped as if they'd just seen someone fall in front of a subway train. Slatter went white.

Moe tapped in his fourth putt. He'd just given the tournament to American Jay Dolan. As he walked up to Slatter, he said, "I can't believe they didn't clap."

Slatter recalls: "It was as if he didn't care about the tournament. The cheers were more important than the putts."

The next day, Moe and Slatter were playing together in a practice round for the Canadian Open at the Richelieu Valley Golf Club just outside Montreal. As they approached the 10th tee near the clubhouse, a group of reporters began to pester Moe with sarcastic questions. "How's the putter today Moe? Any four-putts?" The scribes chuckled gleefully. Moe tromped past them, not saying a word, and walked on the tee of the monster par-three, a 233-yarder. Moe grabbed his driver and bashed the shot.

Moe watched the ball in the air for two seconds, then turned around, crossed his arms and announced: "I'm not putting today."

The ball landed on the green soft as a wedge inches from the cup and rolled into the hole. A hole-in-one! "He called it in the air!" Slatter shouted.

The crowd of reporters stood in shocked silence as Moe, smiling his great Halloween grin of crooked teeth, strode off the tee, chattering away to Slatter just like always.

***

Moe Norman is certainly not your garden-variety sports legend. A reporter cannot just walk up to Moe and ask for a few minutes of his time. If he doesn't know you, he'll just walk away. Press him and he might turn the air blue to make you go away.

There's only one way to meet Moe Norman: get gently introduced by someone in his inner circle of friends. If Moe knows his friends trust you, and he detects a sincere interest and a good heart, he might open up.

"I'm the best striker of the ball the world has ever known," he says matter-of-factly. "That's not me saying it. Ask all the pros who's the best. Not the best player, the best striker of the ball. Ben Hogan and I are in a different world, which doesn't exist for anyone else trying to hit it pure - dead straight, every time."

An extraordinary thing happened to one reporter a few years ago at Royal Oak Golf Club in Titusville, Florida, near Cape Canaveral. After being introduced to the legend, he was invited to play a round of golf. As the tee time approaches, Moe disappears. His partners wait on the first hole, hoping. They're becoming too disappointed to play. Just then Moe re-appears, strides up on the tee, says "Hi guys" and in one continuous motion extracts a driver from his bag, pokes a tee in the ground and bashes his ball.

It surges into the sky like a rifle shot and floats down on the other side of a palm tree beside a lake. It looks like he's put his drive in the water. The ball has just disappeared over the tree when he launches another one over the same tree. Hell, over the same palm on the same branch.

As Moe hustles down the fairway, his trademark blue long-sleeved turtleneck hugs a powerful chest and a thick linebacker's neck, the back of which is crisscrossed by deep lines. His wide jaw is a mixture of crimson and brown skin, some peeling off in little hunks. The red sunburn on his face looks like it hurts. His teeth are snaggled and sore looking. When he listens, his thick grey eyebrows arch upwards while his soft blue eyes widen like he's constantly surprised. His grey hair is clipped short at the sides, but longer untamed tufts stick out in various directions on top. In his mid-60s, Moe looks fit enough to give a Florida gator a good wrestle.

When Moe gets to his golf balls, they're about four feet from each other, and about six feet from the water. He aimed for this spot! He's taken the shortest route to the hole by playing as close to the water as possible.

Without hesitation, he reaches out and places his wedge about 12 inches behind one ball and pulls the trigger. The ball arcs in the air and lands softly six feet from the flag. He hits the other ball. Four feet away.

At the 220-yard fifth hole, a long par three, Moe lashes a four-wood. From the clubface, the ball is locked on to the flag and lances into the green within two inches of the hole. "Ooh, missed again, missed again. Tap-in two, tap-in two. Almost unplayable lie on the green," he says in a light sing-songy voice, reminiscent of Pooh Bear.

As the group walks to the green, Moe spreads his arms and laments: "I hit it close every time and I get nothing. Freddie Couples can't hit it this good and he gets $200,000."

***

It seems cruel. A shame. That Moe Norman — a man as gifted as Wayne Gretzky or Michael Jordan — couldn't take full advantage of his extraordinary skill and talent. That golfers with far less skill have made millions, and yet he has lived largely hand-to-mouth. That he's so misunderstood, so unappreciated — perennially outside the ropes in the game of life. That as Moe gets older, he might end up poverty stricken, alone and forgotten. That his vast knowledge of golf is still untapped, and he may never receive the official recognition that he richly deserves. That Moe Norman never became a household name like Ruth, Howe, Montana or Nicklaus.

The cognoscenti of the golf world certainly know Moe Norman. It seems there are hundreds, thousands, of Moe Norman stories.

He's the eccentric who speaks rapidly and repeats himself, the amateur who sold his prizes and hid from trophy presentations, the pro who hit balls off eight-inch tees on the PGA Tour. The masochist who hit 800 balls daily until his hands bled. The unofficial world-record holder for the total number of golf balls hit in a lifetime — something like five or six million. The maverick who bucked the authorities seemingly at every turn. The fastest player in the world.

On and on it goes.

Many stories are pure myth or greatly embellished, but many of the wildest stories are indeed true. That's the beauty of Moe. He makes you sad one second and laugh the next. He wearily acknowledges that he's often felt like golf's buffoon: "If you want a laugh in golf, you talk about Moe Norman."

And do the stories make him mad? "No, if it bothered me, I'd be dead long ago."

Unfortunately, the yarns often overshadow his incredible record of 54 victories in tournaments two days or longer, including two Canadian Amateur championships. At last count he's set 33 course records. Three of those records are in that rarely visited universe of 59. Four are at 61. He calls a hole-in-one a fluke. He's had at least 17.

Despite Moe's incredible ability, his is a bittersweet story. He's been estranged from his family for decades and faced poverty more than a few times. He rents rooms but only a few close friends know where. Most of his possessions are in his car trunk. He doesn't have a phone. He's never smoked, had an alcoholic drink, or a date. He distrusts strangers, but loves kids.

Moe is certainly famous and respected around the world, including by the likes of Lee Trevino. "The public doesn't know Moe Norman. But you ask any golf professional — whether in Australia, the U.S. or Great Britain — and they'll say, 'that's the Canadian guy who hits it so damn good, isn't it'. I mean he is that good," Trevino said in a Canadian Broadcasting Corporation documentary.

Author Scott Young said his famous son, singer Neil Young, was playing golf in Tahiti with a local club pro, when he hit a weird looking shot. "That's a Moe Norman shot," Young said. The pro was very impressed. "You know Moe Norman?"

Tom Stewart played the PGA Tour and around the world in the 1970s. Wherever people talked about great ball-strikers, Moe's name was spoken with reverence. "My caddie in the Australian Open in 1980 was the president of the club and one of the first questions he asked me was whether I had ever watched Moe Norman play. I had a caddie in Manila who had undying respect for Moe. I was at the Royal Calcutta Golf Club for a luncheon and Moe's name came up.

"The greater the appreciation you have for the game, the more respect you have for Moe Norman," Stewart said.

Ben Crenshaw is one of those people. Crenshaw has been a witness a number of times to Moe's annual ritual at the Canadian Open, when he hits balls on the driving range in his street shoes and all the pros gather around to watch in awe. "Remarkable. Remarkable," Crenshaw gushes. "People who've never seen him wouldn't know from someone's description how good he is. You have to see it to believe it. He's slightly unorthodox, but the only thing you have to see is the ball going to the target, every time, every time."

How remarkable? Moe was playing early one morning at Tomoka Oaks in Daytona Beach, Florida, with buddy Ken Venning. Moe hit three drives on the 10th hole. As they walked, Venning said he saw a big mushroom growing in the middle of the fairway. The mushroom turned out to be Moe's three balls — touching. "You could see the lines in the dew where they rolled up against each other."

During a clinic on a range, Venning put a shag bag about a 100 yards away and told Moe he'd donate $5 to charity every time he hit the bag. "He hit the bag with everything from wedges to drivers. At $100, I said, 'Stop!'"

Stewart relates a tale about a clinic Moe gave after a tournament at his Adios Golf Club in Deerfield Beach, Florida. "Moe announced 'The clinic will begin.' We have a practice green about 85 yards away. He hit his first shot into the hole. On the fly! These guys had been all anxious to get inside and start drinking, but he held them all spellbound for an hour and a half."

Paul Azinger was about 19, playing on the Brevard Junior College golf team in Florida, when he first met Moe on a practice tee with his teammates. "He got out of his car and (coach) John Redman said, 'Boys, there's the greatest ball-striker who ever lived right there.' I looked over at this guy and went 'Yeah, right.' It was about 120 degrees and he's wearing a long-sleeve turtleneck.

"He started ripping these drivers right off the ground at the 250-yard marker and he never hit one more than 10 yards to either side of it and he hit at least 50. It was an incredible sight. When he hit irons, he was calling how many times you'd see it bounce after he hit it — sometimes before he hit it — and he'd do it. It was unbelievable."

Stan Mikita, former all-star centre with the Chicago Black Hawks, was about 20 when he met Moe at a club in St. Catharines, Ontario. "We were on the 9th tee. It was a 400-yard par four. Moe says 'What's this hole?' I said it was a drive and a wedge. He proceeded to hit a wedge about 130 yards and then knocked a driver about three feet from the hole."

Trevino is one of the game's greatest shot-makers, and he's seen many of the game's best, but he's said many times: "Moe Norman is the best ball-striker I ever saw."

A respected shot-maker in his own right, 1964 U.S. Open winner Ken Venturi played often with Moe and Ben Hogan. In fact, Venturi is acknowledged as the world's expert on Hogan's swing. So, Mr. Venturi, is Moe Norman the best ball-striker who ever lived? "It would be pretty hard to dispute that. A lot of people might dispute that, but I don't think they've seen Moe at work."

Such an assertion could be debated forever, because many people could argue Bobby Jones, Byron Nelson, Hogan and Sam Snead won majors — they got the ball in the hole in golf's biggest events. Arguing who's the best is beside the point. The key is that Moe is ranked in the same league.

He also developed a homemade swing that defies every convention and sacred tenet of golf instruction, but it is recognized in many quarters as the simplest and most repeatable swing in the game. The jury is out, however, whether anyone else can master it or whether it's like Moe himself — impossible to bottle or harness.

The obvious question is that if Moe Norman was such a brilliant ball-striker, how come he never made it big on the PGA Tour or on golf's world stages? The answer lies in his personality.

Moe Norman is one of the most complex characters in the history of the game. Golf has had its share of eccentrics — Walter Hagen the playboy, Tommy Bolt and Lefty Stackhouse of hair-trigger-temper fame, Ky Laffoon who was said to have dragged his putter behind his car to teach it a lesson, Mac O'Grady the ambidextrous maverick — but none was as fascinating as Moe Norman. One of the most common exclamations, from fans, players and friends who've known him for 30 years is, "I don't understand Moe."

***

The purpose of this book is to enable fans of the game to better understand Moe Norman as a ball-striker and person. In the process, it is hoped that readers will come to appreciate his talent, technique and accomplishments. It's also hoped the book will increase the game's respect for Moe and steer people toward the same conclusion — that Moe Norman is a treasure, that golf is far richer because of him and that we as golf fans are blessed to have him around.

While Moe's story is bittersweet and poignant, he has given hundreds of thousands of people a great deal of joy by being different — by simply being himself. Ultimately, Moe has surmounted many obstacles and prejudices to achieve greatness.

And, frankly, Moe's story is a great one to tell.

Chapter Two
Incubator Avenue

Murray Irwin Norman and his twin sister Marie were born July 10, 1929, in Kitchener, Ontario.

Mary and Irwin's family was growing quickly. Just 10 months earlier, Mary had given birth to her first child, Ron. And after the twins, she delivered Doreen a year later — her fourth child in three years. Shirley came along a few years later, and Rich in 1942 was the last of six children for the short and attractive, round-faced woman.

Mary kept a spotless home and loved to sew, cook and make jam and preserves. As in most big working-class families, the kids wore hand-me-downs, but their clothes were always clean, neatly patched and mended.

Irwin Oscar Norman was a reserved, stern-looking man who often appeared deep in thought. He had very wavy brown hair that stood straight up. He didn't much like his hair and would often stick his head under the tap to wet it and try to comb out the waves.

The Norman children were much like their father — a bit shy and quiet. "We all have a shy streak. We're not bold," says Marie. Her brother Rich describes Irwin as a "great dad," who was generally happy and not much of a disciplinarian. "He never hit, just hollered."

Irwin was a furniture upholsterer by trade, but with automation he finished his career as a shipper. The Normans were very fortunate that he kept a job throughout the Depression.

Irwin and Mary were devoted Roman Catholics, as were most of their neighbours. Irwin's heritage was Scottish and Methodist, but he converted to Catholicism before his marriage to Mary Bisch. Like the majority of Kitchener residents, Mary was of German ancestry and spoke some German. Her parents, Jacob Bisch and Mary Eisenmenger, were born in Canada. The Bischs were farmers near the town of Linwood just north of Kitchener.

Kitchener and its twin city Waterloo are in the rolling countryside of southern Ontario — about 90 minutes drive southwest of Toronto — and home to some of the province's richest farmland. In the early 1800s, the area was settled by Mennonites from Pennsylvania, followed by a massive wave of Germans, including furniture makers and farmers. The village of Berlin was the centre of commerce and trade in the area and it grew quickly during the century. It was renamed Kitchener in 1916 during the First World War when Berlin became synonymous with the enemy. The city was named after Lord Horatio Kitchener, an English war hero who died in action.

The wide range of skills that German immigrants brought to Kitchener created a broad economic base. J.M. Schneider started making sausages, the Seagram's distillery opened and Electrohome set up operations, as did a number of small breweries, furniture manufacturers and insurance companies. An excellent road and rail system — and proximity to the Toronto and American markets — drew automotive and rubber companies to the area. B.F. Goodrich, Uniroyal and Dominion Rubber established factories that belched black smoke in the air.

An ashen haze and the acrid smell of rubber often hung over the city, especially in the dog days of August. The Norman family home was a block and a half from the gigantic Uniroyal factory, which now sits closed, black and dead, an eerie monstrosity that takes up an entire block. "There were days we couldn't sleep on the back porch (in summer) because you'd get covered in soot," Marie said. "There were certain days you couldn't put out the wash. It would just get black."

Many of the workers lived in working-class Westward, where homes sat cheek by jowl with the factories and plants. Westward straddled the side of a hill dominated by colossal Kitchener Collegiate Institute, a sombre grey high school. Westward borders on Westmount, where the business elite and plant managers lived in fancy homes and fraternized at the Westmount Golf and Country Club. The Westmount crowd also socialized at the ritzy Granite Club, which was in Westward. Canadian figure skater Barbara Ann Scott, who went on to win the gold medal and the women's figure skating title in the 1948 St. Moritz Olympics, boarded next door to the Normans while she trained at the Granite Club. Rich remembers watching Scott and other skaters stretching in the neighbour's backyard.

The modest homes of Westward were built close together, sturdy and basic, huddled down as if to maintain their balance on the rolling streets. The Normans lived on Gruhn Street, a quiet, narrow road that winds its way up the hill toward busy Glasgow Road. They lived in No. 57, a two-story red-brick home, set into the hillside.

Although six kids and two adults squeezed into three bedrooms, it was not a chaotic household. Like their parents, the Norman kids were generally a quiet group, and Irwin didn't put up with much noise or bedlam.

The front wooden steps led up to a porch covered in cedar shakes, a plain door and a large living room window. Two smaller windows upstairs allowed the kids to see down into the King Edward Public School playground across the street. The entrance to the school, an opening in the eight-foot chain link fence at a sharp curve in Gruhn Street, was only about 100 feet from their front door.

You could cut the small front yard with a pair of scissors, but Irwin would sit on the porch and admire his patch of green that sloped sharply to the sidewalk. Irwin was a fanatical green thumb. The grass front and back was dense and always neatly trimmed. "We couldn't touch the grass," Rich deadpans.

The family never missed mass at St. John's Roman Catholic Church, where they took up an entire row. Otherwise, Irwin and Mary spent their entire weekends in the small L-shaped backyard, their private oasis, fussing over an elegant garden alive with flowers and neatly pruned shrubs, pear and cherry trees. The centrepiece of the garden — and Irwin's pride and joy — were roses intertwined on six white trellis archways.

The garden had the calm, regal ambience of a rich country gentleman's estate, rather than the backyard of a working stiff in Westward. So much so, the Normans won third prize in a city landscaping contest one year. In spring, the garden was ablaze with about 400 tulips. In summer, Rich said "it was a bee's paradise," exploding with pinks, reds and yellows.

Irwin came by his passion for horticulture honestly. His father William had run Norman's Flower Shop in the nearby village of Elmira. He had died in his greenhouse when, in his old age, he fell and hit his head.

William emigrated from Scotland, along with wife Lydia, whose maiden name was Proudlove. Rich said his paternal grandfather was apparently "the black sheep of the family and a rebel" in Scotland. But old photos showed him with two or three stripes on the arm of his Royal Navy uniform. In Elmira, he was highly regarded as a wise man whose advice was frequently sought.

After groceries, household bills and gardening, there wasn't much money left over, but Irwin was fastidious in maintaining his house in tiptop shape at all times with a fresh coat of paint nearly every year. He attended to all repairs — pronto.

Irwin, who loved to play hockey in his younger days, and son Ron, were keen followers of the Toronto Maple Leafs hockey club. They enjoyed huddling together in the living room on Saturday nights, listening to the shrill play-by-play of legendary broadcaster Foster Hewitt on radio. Ron said Murray got along well with his father, although he didn't share in their Saturday night ritual.

At times the family barely made ends meet, particularly during the Depression, but they never went without food or proper clothing. Like many families at the time, there was the occasional fiscal crisis. When Irwin couldn't make the $72 mortgage payment one month, the trust company threatened to foreclose. But a local alderman successfully intervened, saying "You can't throw the Normans on the street."

Five of the six children remember the family home as a happy place anchored by two supportive and loving parents. Mary sold the house after Irwin's death in 1971 at age 71. She died at age 85 in 1985.

Murray's memories of home were different.

***

The hill at Kitchener Collegiate Institute was the favourite tobogganing run for miles around. It's levelled out now, an arena sits where the hill used to be. But in 1934, it was steep and smooth, and you could really scoot down the hill. It was so steep, little tykes trying to climb back up would slip and slide, weighted down by a wooden toboggan or sleigh.

Busy Glasgow Road loomed ominously at the bottom. But there was about a 100-yard flat at the bottom of the hill leading to the two-lane road. There was no fence separating the schoolyard and the road. For most parents and kids, the distance between the road and the bottom of the hill seemed far enough. There wasn't any danger. "You didn't think about the road," said Ed Woroch, one of Murray's closest childhood friends. But there was also a six-foot bank that dropped sharply from the schoolyard to the road.

Five-year-old Murray Norman was a freckle-faced kid with rusty red hair and a brush cut that cruelly accentuated his ears, which stuck out from the side of his head. He and his friend Jimmy were warned not to take their sleighs on the hill. Mary and Irwin thought it was too dangerous. But the pull of the hill was too much to resist.

And on this particular day, it was very cold. Powdery snow was falling. Marie said the hill was already covered with "sheet ice," so the kids were zipping down the hill. It was crawling with kids from "Incubator Avenue," as the locals called Gruhn Street. Some families had 10 to 12 kids. Children were laughing and screaming as they blazed down the hill.

Marie remembers standing at the top of the hill and watching Murray and his friend Jimmy zoom down the hill on their wooden toboggan. The toboggan reached bottom at a tremendous speed and hurtled across the flat area. Then, there was a car. Marie gasped.

The toboggan was starting to lose speed when it reached the bank at the edge of Glasgow Road, but the toboggan, Moe and Jimmy went over the edge and into the path of the car.

The little toboggan vanished under the front wheels.

"Then we saw no one," Marie recalls. "We saw the car swerve. The driver lost control and the car went right up the steps unto the veranda of a house on the street."

Marie stared in disbelief, her heart in her throat. For what seemed like forever, nothing happened. "We thought they were dead." Just then, two little figures crawled out from underneath. Pulling themselves to their feet, they put their heads down, and with little legs and arms pumping, they ran down the street toward the Norman home, tears streaming down their faces. Marie, hysterical, ran home.

Marie recalls seeing Murray, crying, his face puffy and red, in Mary's arms. Other than that, thankfully, he seemed OK. In no time, he was roaring around again like usual.

The driver, a man, was at the Norman home. He was badly shaken. Marie remembers two police officers, the motorist, and Irwin and Mary, who were both very upset. They were all talking in the family living room. The man insisted on taking Murray to the hospital. The agitated couple fretted and debated, but ultimately decided against it.

This was about 30 years before Canada's national health insurance program, which pays for medical care and hospital treatment through taxes and premiums. Before medicare, you paid for all treatment. And this was the Depression. Canadian parents were far less prone to rush a child to hospital for every nick and cut. Marie says the attitude about Murray's injury was practical. "You can walk. There's no broken bones. Life goes on."

"We were poor and couldn't afford to take him to the doctor," Ron said. "My parents didn't worry too much. They thought he was alive, and that was the main thing."

***

Although far less so today, Moe Norman has always been an extremely sensitive individual. If you try to give him a compliment, or make a seemingly innocent comment, there's a chance he can take it the wrong way. And then he may unleash a verbal volley that would make a linebacker blush. Or just walk away. Or both.

It is with great trepidation, therefore, that the subject of the car accident is broached. The inference, of course, is that it caused some kind of brain injury that would explain Moe's eccentric personality. And asking Moe Norman if he suffered brain damage from a bonk on the head 50 years ago can be considered just a wee bit delicate.

When, eventually, the subject comes up, Moe visibly stiffens. When asked for his memories of the car accident, Moe looks at the carpet and says, "yup, yup, yup."

In a slow, measured voice, he adds quietly: "There were three of us on a toboggan. We went across the (Glasgow) road into a driveway."

The toboggan stopped right behind the car, facing the same direction. Moe was sitting in the front.

"He wasn't moving at first, but then he backed up. He was backing up slowly and struck me. I remember the tire rolling over my face, just over the side of my face," he says, brushing an open right hand across his right cheek up toward his ear to demonstrate. He moves his hand at a sharp angle, explaining that the right rear-wheel grazed him, rather than hit him flush. The tire pushed his right cheekbone up. "Just a shade higher than the other one. You can hardly notice." Moe says he remembers crying and being terrified, but not much else.

At the right moment, a delicate question: "Do you think it had any, uh, effect on you?"

"I was only five," he says matter-of-factly. "That's something no one would know."

***

His brothers and sisters were so young at the time, they can't remember what — if any — effect the accident may have had on their brother. Echoating — repeating yourself — and rapid speaking are common traits of brain injury. But Ron always remembered his brother speaking quickly and repeating.

After the accident, Ron said Murray would occasionally turn very pale and have "little spells similar to convulsions. He wasn't properly treated. I always thought that had something to do with the way he was. I think that caused a lot of his problems."

In addition to his rapid speech, Moe always seemed nervous and anxious. The family attributed these qualities to the accident. "We always thought something was wrong," said Sister Doreen Norman, a Roman Catholic nun in Newmarket, Ontario. "I know from talking to my mother that she regretted there was no treatment. She was sorry they couldn't have looked after him. They thought there was some damage."

Ron said the other siblings were close, but not with Moe. "Moe didn't bother much with the family. He was a complete loner. He did his own thing. He was never very close to anyone. Moe is Moe."

While Moe shared a room with Ron and also later with Rich, they were more like roommates than brothers. There were few fights. There wasn't much brotherly talking after the lights went out. Moe would just jump into bed, roll over and go to sleep.

In the mornings, he'd roar downstairs, wolf down breakfast, and without saying a word, fly out the door. When it was his turn to help with the dishes, Doreen remembers that he would "run like a deer." It wasn't laziness that made him run. Co-existing was a struggle. He always seemed to be in a big hurry, not for the sake of speed, but to escape.

And yet, Moe loved to play. He was a rambunctious kid, seemingly possessed of an inexhaustible source of energy. His siblings say he was extraordinarily gifted with athletic talent and anything to do with numbers.

He was brilliant at Chinese checkers and smashing chestnuts on strings. Doreen says his hand-eye coordination was astounding. "He'd hit your chestnut right on and break it. We played a lot of games together. He'd always win. He was so quick. In marbles, he always seemed to be lucky. He was so good at that. We didn't like to play with him because he'd always win. He was a good shooter. He was so direct."

Moe's first exposure to golf was breaking branches off trees with Ron and fashioning their own clubs. "We had no money," Ron said. They dug a hole at each end of the playground behind the collegiate. "That's how we started — just kids hitting a ball."

Moe loved anything physical — sports, climbing trees, running around, wrestling on the ground with friends, tickling and laughing. He immersed himself completely in any kind of play. He was also a daredevil. Childhood friend John Czarny remembers going out to a railway underpass just outside Kitchener one winter. There had been lots of snow and there were deep snow banks underneath the tracks. And Moe jumped off — 30 feet down into a snowbank.

And no tree was too high or difficult to climb for Murray was a skinny kid, agile and fearless. "I'd go right to the top and get that ripe apple." At around nine years old, Moe was a good swimmer. "I could lie on my back in the water and read a funny book. Read away, Donald Duck, Pluto or whatever I had," he says in a sing-songy carefree way.

With his excellent hand-eye coordination, Moe was a brilliant batter in baseball. Moe says one season he hit .341, but Czarny says Moe once hit .610. He could place the ball around the field almost at will. "As soon as it came out of the pitcher's hand, I could see whether it was going to curve right to left or left to right."

Ed Woroch, who is the same age, says that when Moe came up to bat, he'd taunt outfielders. When the left fielder would start moving right because Moe was a left-handed batter, he'd yell to the fielder that he would hit to the spot just vacated. And then he would do it. "Moe wasn't a showoff. He was a real tough competitor. He could just place it wherever he wanted. He didn't swing hard — he'd just meet it."

On temporary rinks in city parks and schoolyards, the kids would play shinny for hours and hours. Moe said he couldn't skate "worth a nickel" because of weak ankles, but he had a great wristshot. Moe would often rifle the puck from one end of the rink — and it would sail over the foot-high boards at the other end. "I'd scare all my friends. I had such a hard shot. When I'd get the puck, everyone else would jump over the boards," he says, laughing.

At St. John's Roman Catholic elementary school, Moe was the undisputed head of the class in arithmetic. His talent with numbers was extraordinary. He worked out math problems so fast, teachers and classmates were dazzled. "I was a wizard at math. I wore a hole through my teacher in math with my concentration."

Despite his skill, Moe didn't automatically shoot his arm up to every question or volunteer to go the chalkboard, says Woroch, who first met Moe in Grade 3. "He thought he'd be showing off." It could be argued that Moe was too shy, but Woroch says Moe did his fair share of participating. His buddy adds that Moe was a quiet, well-behaved boy.

"You didn't notice him at school. He didn't cause any commotion. He was like everyone else."

Moe focused on arithmetic, eager and confident. What seemed difficult for many kids was a snap for Moe. Arithmetic suited his nature. In many ways, he never liked sorting things out. He just reacted. Moe either liked something or he didn't. He always was a black-or-white thinker. And with math, there were no shades of grey. The answer was right or it wasn't.

Not only was he extremely quick with numbers, his memory was astounding. One reason he did so well in arithmetic was that once he solved a problem, he remembered the sequence of numbers and the answer. He memorized times-tables and could recite them in rapid succession.

Oddly, Moe excelled in arithmetic, but struggled with every other subject. "I was always the smartest in my room in math, but the dumbest in everything else." Phonics, science, history, languages — he found them all too difficult to understand so he'd give up and stop paying attention. Moe felt inferior to his schoolmates. He couldn't tell a story, explain why it rains or say who invented the telephone. "I thought everyone else was smart and I wasn't. I felt out of place."

For an anxious kid, already riddled with doubt, this attitude was a disaster. He called himself "dumb Moe." As he got into the middle grades of elementary school, he stopped asking or answering questions. He was afraid he'd say something ridiculous and confirm what he thought everyone already knew — that Moe was slow.

When Moe was playing games (and he played everything very well), he would find a level playing field in his own mind. Whether he was knocking balls over the third baseman's head or winning at alleys, Moe was no longer the kid a notch below everyone else.

Moe felt different, and he was. He spoke so fast, other kids often couldn't understand him. He had a high-pitched, sing-songy voice that went up in pitch as he talked. He ended sentences on a high note, as if he were asking a question. And he would repeat phrases: "Moe's a shmo, Moe's a shmo.... batter's out, batter's out."

Other kids didn't talk like this. And kids — being kids, direct and uninhibited — would be cruel. They would mimic his Gatling-gun speech and repeat the words in his face.

He also fuelled the abuse because everything Moe did was exaggerated. He would antagonize other kids. If there was a race, he'd run the hardest to win. In road hockey, he'd check with furious enthusiasm, battering shins with his stick. But Moe often didn't know when he crossed the line from rough-housing to too rough.

Moe was also a pincher. He'd grab a little bit of skin between his thumb and forefinger, give it a quick twist and laugh. "Geez, it hurt," says George Hillebrecht, who is four years younger. "We got mad at him. I don't think he realized that he was hurting you." Brother Ron said: "A lot of people didn't like that. It was a nervous reaction he had."

Often rebuffed and afraid, Moe stayed away from kids who challenged him, kids he didn't know, new places, situations he'd never been in. Anything and anyone that was unfamiliar and might cause him pain, he avoided.

Moe was an anxious bundle of nerves, exceedingly self-conscious, timid, distrustful, cautious and afraid. In other words, excruciatingly shy. On top of that, he had a brutal inferiority complex.

Inadvertently, Moe created a cocoon to protect himself. Unless he was comfortable with other kids or the situation that he was in, he preferred to be alone. As such, he appeared morose and serious. And some kids, like sharks smelling blood, would exacerbate Moe's fear and make fun of him. Moe says they would taunt him with: "Here comes the shy baby! Here come's the shy baby!"

Chapter Three
Golf Takes Hold

In the early 1940s, the dominant player in golf was a moon-faced, angular Texan whose humble demeanour and name made you think more of a poet than a cowboy. Byron Nelson was in his prime, winner of the 1937 and '42 Masters, '39 U.S. Open and '40 PGA. Lord Byron possessed a modern upright swing and a shy smile that looked like a straight line. Nelson was a haemophiliac so he was rejected for military service.

In 1945, he won 18 tournaments — including 11 in a row, a record that will likely never be broken. The winning stretch included the PGA Championship and climaxed at the Canadian Open. His season-scoring average was an unbelievable 68.33.

Nelson's rival since childhood in Fort Worth had been the strangely quiet Ben Hogan. A small man with a powerful motion, Hogan was well known for his wide stance and long backswing, which detonated a whirl of arms and legs through the ball. In his characteristic uniform of a white shirt and grey slacks, Hogan had won a few tournaments — but he battled the occasional duck hook.

Ben Hogan's best buddy was the polar opposite in demeanour and dress. Jimmy Demaret was a fancy dan who strode around like a proud peacock in radiant hues: blinding yellow, robin's egg blue, torrid pink, topped off with berets in coordinating shades. Winning the 1940 Masters transformed Demaret into a star.

But the most popular golfer was Slammin' Sammy Snead, the long-hitting Virginian with the effortless, fluid swing that reflected the man himself — buoyant, confident and snappy in a white long-sleeved cotton shirt, tie and straw fedora. Snead was also Canada's favourite golf star, having won the Canadian Open in 1938, '40 and '41. He cemented his stature with the PGA crown in 1942, his first major.

Although Snead was as American as a corncob pipe, the shirts and ties reflected the British and Scottish pre-occupation with decorum and deportment. To Snead, golf was a gentleman's game.

To the working-class folk of Westward in Kitchener, Ontario, golf was a rich man's game. The dandies who drove cars, strode around with wives in mink coats and occupied stately homes with pillars and manicured hedges in Westmount, they played golf. Many of Kitchener's finest — the Seagrams and the Schneiders, the factory executives, the store owners, judges, bankers and lawyers — frolicked behind the stone gates at private Westmount Golf and Country Club.

While the short-sleeved golf shirt was starting to gain favour, ties were still de rigueur at Westmount. Many men still wore knickerbockers, or plus-fours. Like most of Canada's wealthy country clubs, the core of Westmount's membership was British. And along with their tweed caps, pleated shorts and knee socks, the gentry of Westmount appeared like overgrown private school brats to the folks of Westward. The attire, the atmosphere, the game, all appeared pretentious and about as manly as croquet, crumpets and tea.

Besides, the Second World War was raging. Canadian boys were getting crippled and killed. With gasoline rationing, many tournaments across Canada were cancelled. Memberships at clubs nosedived. Rubber was in short supply, and so were golf balls. According to historian Jim Barclay, the manufacture of golf clubs and equipment ceased in Canada by October of 1942.

With the entry of the United States into the war after Pearl Harbor, the PGA severely reduced its schedule from 1942 to '45. It was a grim time. Many people stopped playing golf. It didn't seem appropriate. But many others tried to make the best of things, especially those who could afford to, and keep a stiff upper lip. Kitchener's barons of industry and commerce played their genteel game at Westmount and socialized in the lavish, English-Tudor-style clubhouse.

The course itself was another marvellous creation by Stanley Thompson, Canada's most prolific and famous golf architect. Thompson brought an artist's flair and strategic intelligence to his courses, including Banff Springs in the Alberta Rockies and St. George's in Toronto. He carved Westmount out of heavy forests of maple, oak and conifer atop the wildly heaving landscape, so there's little room to spray the ball and few flat lies.

To 12-year-old Murray Norman, however, the most important thing about Westmount was the opportunity it afforded him to caddie — and supplement his 10-cents-a-week allowance. Nine holes fetched a flat rate of 30 cents, 18 earned 50 cents, usually with a nickel or dime tip. Occasionally, if you were good and had a nice, rich golfer, you might get 75 cents.

Westmount was only a 10-minute bicycle ride from Gruhn Street. Murray began to caddie whenever he could, every day after school, on weekends and all day during the summer. He was slight, but could shoulder heavy bags all day. He was driven — Murray loved the sound of change in his pocket.

Westmount pro Normie Hines, onetime New York Americans hockey star, constantly reminded his caddies to keep their mouths shut, and their ears and eyes open. But Ed Woroch said that quite often when they were in the same group, Murray would look at his golfer, then at Ed and whisper, "I can play better than that."

John Czarny also caddied at Westmount. He tells what is likely the first Moe Norman golf story. And suitably, it's a tale from the caddie yard. Czarny says the small wooden caddie pen was attached to Hines' pro shop near the driveway. But John and Murray would hide in bushes beside the shack and watch the cars drive in. "You'd run in when you saw a good bag come in," Czarny said.

"One day we're in the bush and we see this millionaire come in, but we stayed in the bush because this guy was really cheap." But Hines yelled for them and Murray got stuck with Mr. Cheapskate.

Czarny picks up the tale: "After caddying 18 holes, he gave Moe two quarters. Moe took both quarters and flipped them in the air and said 'You need them more than I do.' Then he took the man's clubs and started throwing them up in a tree. The man was livid."

Moe said three of the clubs stayed in the tree. "How he got them down I don't know." Hines was furious and suspended Moe for one month.

Despite that misadventure, Murray enjoyed most of the members, and they liked the skinny redhead kid who talked so fast. He was an excellent caddie. He hurtled down the fairways, always ready with a club or to hold the flag. Murray was a pleasurable companion who chattered eagerly when spoken to, an expert on rules and any sports statistic you needed. Being a numbers hound, Murray devoured the sports page of The Kitchener Record newspaper.

He was also an amazing ball-hawk who could find a ball launched into the deepest jungle. With furious determination, Murray would claw his way into any tangle and rescue a ball — no matter how deeply entombed — to spare his golfer a lost-ball penalty.

Westmount was heaven for Murray. He was impressed by the self-assured men, their splashy clothes, big cars, the camaraderie and good golf. Since it was a great test of golf, Westmount drew a fair number of decent players. When he got a good bag in a tournament, Murray got caught up in the game and rode the roller coaster of emotions with his golfer. Non-golfers thought it was just a game to while away the time. To Murray, it was sport, just as exciting and athletic as belting a home run.

He learned to appreciate well-struck shots and to read wind and greens. Before his golfer was finished saying, "What do you thin ...," he'd blurt out his prognosis. And invariably, he was right.

For an anxiety-ridden kid, being appreciated as a great caddie was a tremendous ego stroke. Westmount was also a beautiful, peaceful place — an escape from the noise and smells of Kitchener's dirty factories. The sweet smell of fresh-cut grass replaced the acrid stench of rubber. Tall trees hid industrial stacks belching black smoke into the air.

Murray also played his first games of golf at Westmount, feeding his growing fascination for the game. He began to play hooky from school on Thursday mornings — caddie's day — so he could play the course. Caddies enjoyed this privilege at clubs across North America; it introduced kids to the game on quality courses they could never afford to play. Caddying was a stepping stone into golf for many kids from the other side of the tracks, including Nelson and Hogan.

Many of Westmount's caddies couldn't afford clubs, so the members often lent them to the kids. Woroch said there was only one left-handed member at Westmount, and the grouch didn't lend his clubs. So Ed and Murray, both lefties, were forced to become righties. Besides, left-handed clubs were in chronic short supply, and thus, expensive. Woroch said they each bought their first golf club from Hines — a $1.50 five-iron with a steel shaft painted a cream colour to resemble hickory, which was fading from use. Each time they caddied, they paid Hines a dime until they retired their debt.

It was at Westmount that Murray earned the nickname "Moe." A couple of guys starting calling him "Moe the Shmo." Soon it was shortened to Moe — and stuck.

Murray wanted to play more than just Thursday mornings. That was impossible at Westmount because his father wasn't a member. So he ventured over to Rockway, a public course owned by the City of Kitchener. Rockway was at the city's eastern edge, a two-cent ride at the end of the King Street streetcar line. There he played with kids such as Eddie Woroch, John Czarny and Tony Matlock, who lived on the farm next door.

The green fee was 10 cents for 18 holes. With a mismatched set consisting of his five-iron and battered hand-me-downs given to him by Westmount members, Murray sped around Rockway. He'd play 18, 36, 54, and sometimes 72 holes a day. It became his merry-go-round of golf. In the summer between Grade 8 and 9, he'd spend entire days at Rockway.

"I just wanted to play morning, noon and night," Moe said. "I was so comfortable. I didn't want to go to bed. I didn't want to go home and eat. I'd rather starve than not play golf. And I did."

One attraction of golf was that size didn't matter. While other boys were getting taller and thicker in his later grades, Murray was still a shorty. "I was always so small and light, I couldn't play big sports with body contact."

He was feeding his competitive appetite with golf. Besides, Murray wasn't much of a team guy. Golf suited his loner nature. No one telling you what to do. No one else to rely on. You could play by yourself. And even when playing with others, you were still in command of your score.

"As a kid, Moe was a loner," said Czarny, who is about three years older than his friend. "He just shied away from everything. He was very serious. He never associated with other kids much. He was shunned in school. He never got involved. That's why the game of golf became so important to him. He didn't need support."

His increasing obsession with golf was puzzling his parents, and getting him into considerable hot water. One day he teed up a ball on the front lawn and drove it right between two houses — 200 yards away. He caught hell. Marie remembers Murray making a horrendous racket hitting balls against a neighbour's garage. "He got in trouble for that."

And despite warnings not to, he'd drive balls off the lawn over the 10-foot chain-link fence into the playground of King Edward elementary school just across the street. Irwin was ticked about the divots in his immaculate lawn.

Murray and Eddie Woroch also hit balls on the school grounds, but sometimes back toward Gruhn Street. Every once in a while Moe would really connect. The ball would rocket out of the schoolyard and bounce dangerously off the sidewalk or road.

His growing proficiency in propelling a golf ball resulted in 11 broken windows in two years. "It got to a point where people knew it was Moe," Woroch deadpanned. The aggravation of dealing with irate neighbours and forking out up to $1.25 to replace a window fuelled Irwin's anger about his son's fixation. "I'd hit the ball with this end," Moe recalls, touching the clubhead, "and he'd hit me with this end," he says, then touching the grip.

"I broke two in one day. The cops found me at four in the morning. I was hiding. People would come running to my house. 'Your son broke my window again!'

"I'd bounce it off the windows and bumpers of their cars, and run it right into their driveways. After a while I didn't run because they knew it was me. Twice my friends tried to put the blame on me, but I could prove where I was at that time."

As Murray became more consumed by golf, school became more boring and frustrating. Except arithmetic, of course. His lowest mark ever was 78, but he never scored higher than 61 in anything else. "The only homework I'd do was math. I always knew I needed to know about money. With other things I didn't care. I didn't need to know who discovered this or that. What do I care about spelling, adjectives and pronouns. It used to drive me crazy," he said, slapping his forehead with an open palm.

Mary had always talked about her son going to university and excelling in math. But as Moe got older, he realized that his family could never afford it.

In Grade 8, Murray also wanted to escape the crowd at school. He felt picked on occasionally and snubbed by many of the "in-crowd" at St. John's. His clothes were often wrinkled and dirty.

The in-crowd were caught up in wearing the right clothes, dancing to big-band music, sneaking their parents' liquor or smokes. Not Murray Norman. He was an innocent. Astonishingly naive. Other kids were making their first steps into the adult world. Murray Norman didn't know who Benny Goodman or Artie Shaw were. He preferred Daffy Duck comic books to Superman. Girls were a complete mystery. He didn't get jokes and had no interest in hanging out. Play golf or cards, bowl or shoot pool — yes. Make the scene — heck no!

Murray was building his own little world with golf and numbers at the centre. If something didn't fit in his world, he didn't make any attempt to understand it. It didn't exist. Growing up in this way, he was building a wall around himself. "Golf and math were the only two things that I figured mattered to me in my life."

His fascination with golf was leading to fireworks at home. To Mary and Irwin, golf was leading their son away from school. Golf had taken over their son's mind like a raving evangelist, promising wealth and happiness.

Coming home and facing his father after playing golf became nerve wracking. Murray would wonder, "What's he going to say to me this time?" Irwin didn't hit his son, that wasn't his style, but Murray was still afraid of his father's outbursts.

By Grade 9 at St. Jerome's high school, he was skipping school regularly. Mary begged with him to stop devoting so much time to golf and to go to school. "I wouldn't do my homework. I wouldn't go through school like other kids. She wanted me to live like they did. I said 'Mom, not everyone lives the same. Mom, everyone is different.' And I was a different type of kid.

"I said, 'Mom, don't take away my happiness.'"

The truant officer petitioned the Normans a number of times to order their son to attend school. Despite their hectoring, he stayed away. Moe said he was finally expelled, and his mother's dreams for her son, the math genius, died.

Marie said, however, his departure from school was caused mainly by a quarrel with a teacher. "He got into a tiff with a teacher. Murray left and never went back." Marie couldn't remember what the tiff was about (Moe says it didn't happen) but her story foreshadows Moe's reactions to conflict: cross him once and he may never talk to you again.

Brother Rich said Mary was concerned this golf mania would just lead her boy to a life of disappointment. She was still racked by guilt that they never had Murray checked by a doctor after his car accident, and she wondered if they were somewhat responsible for his behaviour. She'd try to reason with Murray, but "he'd snap off and be out the door," Rich said.

"It bothered her that she couldn't get through to him. He had his own way of doing things and he didn't like anyone prying into his life."

When Murray left school, he got a job doing piece work at Merchant's Rubber. Golf consumed his off-hours. "Golf, golf, golf, that was it," Marie said. "When he got into golf, that became his life. When he was 12, Murray said to me 'Someday I'll be richer than all of you put together.'

"He wasn't like the rest of us and sit around the table and talk. He'd eat his dinner and be gone — back to Westmount, Rockway or to hit golf balls around. We didn't see him much anymore."

While he worked at Merchant's and later at Kaufman's factory, his mind was on a golf course, seeing himself making the big shot to win a championship and getting rich. Golf was making Murray feel good about himself and fuelling some big dreams.

The Normans couldn't understand their son's fixation. This was well before Arnold Palmer and television teamed together in the early 1960s to expand golf to the general public. In the '40s, golf was a rich man's game. And here was Murray gallivanting around with golf clubs, hobnobbing with the high brows. What was next? Polo?

Irwin was outraged by his golfing obsession, Moe said. His father didn't want to hear about golf or see any clubs in the house. For fear that his father would break his clubs, Moe said he would hide the clubs in a hole that he dug under the front porch. "My dad was fat so he couldn't get into the hole and reach them." He said Irwin became so enraged one time his father buried the clubs in the family's backyard.

Golf was his life, but he resigned himself to the belief that his family considered it a silly fantasy. What he held dear, they ridiculed. The young lad turned inward and away from his family. Home was just a bed. His teenage years were tense at 57 Gruhn.

"We all played baseball and hockey and we asked, 'Why do you play that sissy sport?'" Rich said. "He just loved golf. Why? We didn't know. He was obsessed. It wasn't a working man's game."

"He was fanatical about golf," Czarny said. "The family would say, 'What's he doing?' There was some animosity. He couldn't care less. He just hit balls and played. He shut off his mind."

As a teenager, he spent as much time out of the house as possible. He got home late at night when every one else was asleep, got up and zoomed out the door in the morning.

His real home was Rockway Golf Club.

Chapter Four
Home Course of Champions

While Westmount was the hoity-toity private club, Rockway Golf Club was built by, and for, the average guy.

Rockway's origins are rooted in the Great Depression of the 1930s. With about one in three people unemployed, Canada suffered tremendously during the worldwide economic collapse.

Canada was hard hit because more than a third of its income was from exports. Kitchener, a city of factories, was especially vulnerable. Many of the rubber, auto parts and manufacturing plants that shipped products out of the country were closed. Although Irwin Norman managed to stay working at local furniture stores, many families had to scrape by on monthly government relief payments of about $20 to $30. Bankruptcy, scurvy, alcoholism, depression and suicide were common.

Like many cities, Kitchener devised make-work projects that paid about 20 cents a day. City engineer Stanley Shupe had an idea to make use of an abandoned sewer farm on the city's eastern boundary. In previous years, the collecting ponds in this low-lying area had corralled excess water when rainfall filled city sewers to their limit. By the late 1920s, however, more efficient sewers had made the sewer farm unnecessary.

Shupe convinced municipal officials to transform the area into a city-owned public golf course as a make-work program for hundreds of men. This was before bulldozers. The workers used picks, shovels, hand scrapers, teams of horses and wagons to move earth used to build Rockway's greens and tees.

Rockway Golf Club opened in 1935. Shupe is credited as the club's designer, but he's believed to have been assisted by C.E. "Robbie"

Robinson, one of Canada's great early golf architects. The cream-coloured, stucco clubhouse is charming, resembling a quaint family home with a couple of gabled windows poking from the pitched roof and thick ivy covering the east end. Suitably, it sits on the highest point of the property, allowing a beautiful view of the 18th green from the lounge and its great granite fireplace (at least, until an addition was tacked on years later).

Rockway's starting and finishing holes are on high ground, while the heart of the course is built into the side of a hill and the lowlands where the collecting ponds used to be. The dinky trees that were planted to define the holes have since grown into tall poplars, thickly trunked maples and oaks, dense conifers and gigantic willows that weave in the wind. At about 5,900 yards, with its undulating fairways and tiny greens, Rockway is a good test. Many players have arrived thinking they'll scorch it, but leave humbled and respectful.

Rockway is a pay-as-you-play course, but it also has members. In the 1940s, 18 holes cost about 50 cents. A junior membership was about $10, while adults were tagged for about $20. "Rockway people were down-to-earth golfers — the bread and butter crowd," said Tony Matlock, who was about seven years old and living on a farm next door when the course was built.

It was an unpretentious and relaxing place, and kids were welcome. On summer days, kids with half sets of rusty clubs and ratty canvas bags would spend all day there. "If adults needed a fourth, they'd ask a junior to join them," said Matlock, a lifelong member. "They just enjoyed the camaraderie. They were instrumental in helping juniors that way. It gave us all a competitive edge."

The greatest help a junior could ever have was in Lloyd Tucker, Rockway's head pro from 1937 to 1959. While many pros treated juniors as nuisances to be tolerated, Tucker took great interest in the youngsters, many of whom also caddied at the club.

A short man with glasses and a bright, toothy smile, Tucker has a gentle disposition. He could stay cool no matter what kind of mischief the kids got into. Tucker also had an encyclopedic knowledge of the golf swing that he loved to share.

Matlock says Tucker was "fantastic" with the kids — a mentor. "He'd ask you after a round what shots you were missing. He knew we couldn't afford $5 lessons. He'd take a few minutes and point out little flaws in your swing," remembers Matlock, a four-time club champion.

"The odd time when we were going to a tournament, he'd slip us a new golf ball. Lloyd was instrumental in giving us encouragement. He was the pappy of the tribe."

Public golf courses such as Rockway were perceived by the country club set as burnt-up goat ranches with second-rate pros. But Rockway and Tucker earned respect as the number one producer of scratch juniors in the country. Rockway's scorecard reads: "Home Course of Champions."

"It was the influence of Lloyd Tucker," says Nick Weslock, a four-time Canadian Amateur champion and one of the world's greatest amateurs never to turn pro. "He really took an interest in the youngsters and he really helped them. More than most pros I've ever seen."

There is no better proof of Tucker's talents and influence than the stable of great juniors who played out of Rockway, many of whom became touring and club professionals, including:
• Gerry Kesselring, PGA Tour player from 1954-1957, four-time Ontario Amateur champion, three-time provincial junior champ;
• Gary Cowan, Senior PGA Tour player in 1991, 1966 and '71 U.S. Amateur champion, '61 Canadian Amateur champ, nine-time Ontario Amateur titleholder and '56 Ontario Junior champ;
• Jerry Knechtel, 1951 and '52 Ontario Junior champ; and
• Murray Irwin Norman.

***

Lloyd Tucker first laid eyes on the Norman kid when the lad was about 13. He was an engaging youth, a whirling dervish of energy with restless blue eyes, who spat out words in a high-pitched torrent, and had an odd habit of repeating himself. "To me it was nothing," Tucker recalls, "but other people thought it was quite funny. Most of the people around put it down to the fact that he didn't go to school," says Tucker, who still teaches in his mid-80s at the Foxwood Golf Club near Kitchener. He liked having the youngster around to enliven the place in spring and fall when most kids were in school.

Tucker said Moe's T-shirts and pants were often wrinkled, ratty and dirty. It often appeared that he just put on whatever he grabbed each morning. "He dressed a little different," Tucker said. "He didn't have the money. His father didn't want him to play. He wanted him to get a job. Golf wasn't the way to make a living."

By the time "The Kid," as he was often described, was in his mid-teens, he was a Rockway member and fixture at the club. He regularly played in a group that would swarm all over the course like locusts. To Moe, the rest of the world was condescending and confusing. Rockway was comfortable and calming. Everyone was there for one thing: golf.

While many Rockway regulars thought he was an odd duck, they enjoyed his company and playful nature — provided that he knew you and you took the time to understand him. "Sometimes a member would try to get a rise out of him," Matlock said, "but Moe would put him in his place very quickly. He was sharp. He could hit you with a witty retort."

Moe loved to hang around the snack bar, wolfing down Cokes and candy bars and chattering endlessly. Like most golf clubs of the day, there always seemed to be a card game in progress in the locker room, which was downstairs. Moe loved numbers and money, and so he loved cards. But he also loved the clubby atmosphere that was created when a bunch of golfers leaned back on chairs, surrounded by blue-grey metal lockers under a low open ceiling.

Moe shied away from strangers, but he'd take on all comers in cards. Many old card sharks who sat down smugly to teach the boy a lesson got up broke and flabbergasted. First-timers at the table with Moe were often psyched out. For one, he had perfected the poker face. Not even a royal flush could thaw his icy features. Moe also held his cards upside down with his left wrist turned down toward the floor, a puzzling trait that distracted many players. (While most people arrange their cards from left to right, Moe organizes from right to left.)

When a card hit the table, Moe responded instantly, flicking his card out with the lightning-quick reflex of a goalie responding to a slapshot. "He didn't have to think about card selection. It was automatic," said Eddie Woroch, Moe's closest buddy in those days.

Pretty soon the word was out about Moe — the kid had a photographic memory. He could recall every card that went down and in what order. The kid was a killer at cribbage, blackjack and poker. Today, Moe says he's a "wizard" at gin rummy.

"Never play cards with him — gin rummy or poker," warned John Czarny, who suffered Moe's wrath many times in the Rockway locker room. "If you do, don't play for money. You'll lose your shirt."

Rich Norman said his big brother would often come home late at night from poker games and "throw a wad of bills on his bed and say, 'Count it.' One time he had 800 bucks!"

***

Today he can recount favourite rounds from tournaments from decades ago and tell you what club he hit on what hole: "No. 1, driver, seven-iron, two putts; No. 2, driver, eight-iron, one putt; No. 3 ...."

Just as remarkably, he can rhyme off the yardage of every hole on courses he hasn't played in 30 years. He can rattle off yardage and par of every hole at Augusta National in perfect order, from the 1st to 18th, even though he hasn't played the course in about 35 years.

In a story in 1958, Kitchener writer Jock Carrol described how Moe was discussing Westmount's fourth hole in a conversation when he said, "The 565-yarder. No, it's 567 yards."

Surprised at his correction, Carrol asked, "Do you know the exact distance of every hole?"

"Oh sure," Moe said, "I memorize a hole. First time I play it."

"All right. What's the sixth at Westmount?"

"One hundred and ninety-two."

"The first at Rockway?"

"Three hundred and sixty-five."

Moe then rolled off the yardage of every hole at Westmount in order. "I'm not sure about the back tees, of course. I don't play them very often."

Moe's memory is amazing. But he has always worked on consciously memorizing things that are important to him or that he believes will help him in the future. Ask about things he doesn't think are significant, or that he perhaps doesn't want to remember, and he can't recall. Or at least that's what he says.

***

If the police ever had to find teenage Moe, he would have been very easy to track down. Occasionally, he'd pop into city pool rooms, but generally he was in one of three places: at Kaufman's, stitching rubber boots; at Rockway; or The Strand bowling alley on King Street. In winter, The Strand stood in for Rockway as his home away from home.

Moe loved to bowl — he recalls sporting a respectable .243 average — but his claim to fame at The Strand was pinsetting.

The Strand was a little different. It was mostly five-pin, but a few lanes were used for 10-pin, where the real serious bowlers held court. The Strand was owned by Norm Kratz, who was "really nice" to work for, Moe recalls. Moe was also a model employee — a paragon of punctuality and deadly serious about his work. Moe was 13 when he started working at The Strand and Kratz paid him two cents a line. He'd usually pinset about 30 games a shift. The Strand would become a pillar of his financial foundation for 14 winters.

In the days before machines, the dangerous and hectic job of pinsetting was done by boys who often resembled the tattered scallywags of a Dickens story. The pinsetters at The Strand sat on top of four-foot high wooden partitions that divided the lanes. They'd jump down, retrieve and rerack the pins in the same motion, and jump back on the partition before the next ball came rocketing down the lane.

One boy would usually oversee two lanes. There was a real art to the job. The pinsetter had to keep an eye on each lane, monitoring each bowler's game and clearing the pins without delay. Or getting hurt. Pins were constantly flying around. And when a strong man bowled, that four-pound ball of wood struck the pins with explosive force, turning them into missiles and making one hell of a racket.

Moe was the prince of pins at The Strand, a blur of arms and hands. A thin rope of a lad, Moe was blessed with exceptional hand-eye coordination. He distracted bowlers with his blazing speed. If there were a pinsetters' Olympics, to test speed, effectiveness and endurance, Moe would be the perennial champion, a hall of famer. "I'd grab the five and make a V in one move, two in each hand, the head pin between the other two. I could do four lanes, the other guys could only do two."

Serious bowlers in the inter-city leagues often asked to have Moe work their lanes. "He was so fast," Woroch said. "They didn't have to wait." They would usually tip Moe a quarter or so.

The six months of southern Ontario winter were high season for bowling leagues. Moe was very busy because he was also working at Kaufman's factory. He hoarded his money in his bedroom all winter for the golf season. "I'd save like a son of a gun. I could just work, eat and save."

He saved so much because he was notoriously thrifty and could account for every nickel. He even worked out extended payment plans. He recalls that one year his Rockway membership was $25, so he paid the club $1 a week for six months. "Six times four is 24, so one week I gave them $2."

During the golf season, Moe made money caddying to augment his factory work. Eventually, he was fired from Kaufman's for calling in sick too many times to play in tournaments. In his late teens, he began working "steady nights" at Dominion Rubber for five years on the assembly line stitching boots so he could play during the day. "That's one reason I have such a strong left hand from stitching for eight hours."

On top of that, Moe scoured ditches for bottles and beat the bushes at Westmount hunting for golf balls, most of which he sold to Tucker. Weslock calls Moe "an ardent ball hawk" who can almost always find a lost ball.

Many people thought Moe was poverty stricken due to his appearance and thrift, and bought him Cokes and candy. But buddies like Czarny and Woroch knew Moe always had enough to get by.

While Moe loved golf, he was not a natural who picked up the club and instantly began hitting ropes. "At 15 and 16, I was terrible," Moe says. "I couldn't break 100."

Indeed, in the Ontario Junior championship at Brantford Golf and Country Club at age 16, he shot 102 while Gerry Kesselring won his second straight title with 74-80. But Tucker and many of his friends from those days say Moe sells himself far short. At 16, his scores dropped into the 80s quite regularly. He was beginning to practice more, hitting his own balls on Rockway's small practice range and debating the finer points of the swing with friends, especially with Tucker.

"By the time Moe was 15 or 16, he never won any junior tournaments, although he should have won the Ontario Junior," Tucker said. "He came along a little later. He didn't progress as fast as others. He did so much research, trying things and dissecting his swing. He was caught up in the mechanics."

Moe's biggest problem was a duck hook. "He had some trouble hitting the ball straight," Tucker said. Like many things in his life, Moe saw this as a black and white problem: the club must be moving off-line, so hold tight and it won't move. "He held on for dear life. He told me 'I'm trying to squeeze the blood out of it.' His hands would hardly cock."

By 17 and 18 he was shooting in the 70s. The more Moe played, the better he got, and the more obsessed he became. That's an overworked word these days, especially when applied to golf, but in the truest sense of the word, Moe was obsessed with mastering the mechanics of his swing. To his friends and family, Moe was unreasonably pre-occupied. It seemed abnormal for anyone to be that consumed by the intricacies of their golf swing.

But golf was becoming Moe's mission. He was excited by improvements in his game. He realized that the key to becoming a great player wasn't playing golf — it was practicing. Hitting balls and working on his swing became Moe's life.

Ask anyone who comes to mind as the hardest working golfer in the history of the game, and the answer is sure to be Ben Hogan.

Mr. Hogan, make room for Moe Norman.

Chapter Five
Blood, Sweat and Blisters

It was so hot at Rockway one August afternoon in 1948, it seemed like you could fire a shotgun across the course and not hit a soul. The brown grass was thin and sparse, covered with dust from patches of grey dirt cracked from the relentless sun. The pollution that disgorged from factory chimneys, combined with the humidity, created a dank soup that made everyone cranky. Playing golf on this day would be like a stroll through a blast furnace.

But out on the driving range, if you could believe it, someone was practicing. The range was about a wedge shot from the pro shop. The sharp thwock of an iron club meeting golf ball and turf was spaced about three seconds apart, steady as a drummer keeping a beat.

The teeing area of the range was atop a hill. Young trees formed a triangle around the range. It was also short. The longest club you could hit was about a four-iron down into the point of the triangle.

Rockway's driving range was a lovely spot to spend some time, looking down over the front nine, Matlock's farm and the rooftops and trees of Kitchener. But to practice in this heat? You'd have to be a masochist, a fanatic or perhaps a few clubs short of a full set.

But there was 19-year-old Moe Norman, his shirt plastered across his back like wet newspaper. He was hitting balls so quickly he must have been afraid someone was going to steal them, which wasn't likely given that he was the only one dedicated enough to be out there. Where the guy found the energy was anyone's guess. Must have been the sugar in all those Cokes he inhaled.

He was just a rake, only about five-foot-eight and 140 pounds, if that. His arms were thin, but the long muscles in his forearms looked like steel cables wrapped tightly in skin. His freckled cheeks were a patchwork of crimson and brown. The back of his neck was fire-engine red, framed by rusty hair glistening with sweat. The peak of his white visor was covered in yellowy rings of dried sweat, like the salt stains on winter boots. A ragged 10-pin canvas bowling bag was tipped over on the grass, spilling its cargo of about 600 balls. Yes, 600 balls. Most were scuffed and sporting cuts that looked like smiles.

Everything about the guy was exaggerated — even the way he stood over the ball. His legs were spread wider than his shoulders, like a gunslinger, while his left shoulder rode high around his left ear and his arms reached way out for the ball.

He followed the same sequence for every shot. He would rake a ball out of the pile with his left hand on the club, look at something out there, a twig, a brown spot, a tree, some kind of target. He would look at the ball, shuffle into his linebacker's stance, look at the target, the ball — thwock! He watched the ball until it started to fall from the sky, and then started the process again. To hit one ball, from tip-up to touchdown, took about three seconds. He was like a machine, fluid and free. The sweat poured off the guy in rivers. There was no place he'd rather be.

In the time it would take someone else to hit a bucket of balls, Moe's huge pile was gone. He would roar down the hill, toss his bowling bag in the middle of the balls, with the mouth open skyward, and chip them into the bag. Then, Moe would tilt forward, stride up the hill, toss the bag on the ground, grab another club and go back to work.

When he was finally too sore to hit another ball, Moe trudged back to the clubhouse, soaking wet, like he'd just stepped out of a shower. While he was sore and exhausted, he felt quiet satisfaction, the pleasant tiredness that comes from working hard at something he loved. His job was golf. He was the king of the driving range hill at Rockway. He was becoming more exhilarated each day as he discovered new ideas and sensations, and discarded old ones.

He was getting closer every day to perfecting "the move."

***

"No one approached golf as seriously as Moe," Tucker said. "The other kids didn't work like Moe did. He'd spend the whole afternoon out there — maybe four hours hitting and picking them up. The heat wouldn't bother him. He'd hit just as many on a hot day as he would on a cool day."

Most people thought Moe just played golf all day at Rockway. And that's how most working-class people viewed golf, just as another form of play. Folks would say, "The kid should be working. He should help to support his family, and not play golf all day. He still lives at home don't you know. Ah, the kid's a fruitcake."

Moe certainly played golf — sometimes 36 and 54 holes a day with buddies such as Kesselring, Matlock and Gus Maue. They could dash through 18 holes in about two hours. "People would let us through," Moe said. "They didn't want par shooters always pressing them."

He also began to play in more amateur tournaments, but the rest of the time he practiced. "Moe worked and worked and worked," Woroch said. "Members would laugh. But he'd just laugh and say 'I'm going to be the best.'"

At 19, Moe had dedicated himself to practicing harder than anyone ever did. He was going to be the best golfer anyone had ever seen. Despite his sister Marie's assertions to the contrary, Moe says "I never dreamed of getting rich. All I tried to do was to become the best striker of the ball. I practiced morning, noon and night."

For anyone else, achieving that goal would have required absolute commitment and a tremendous amount of sacrifice. That wasn't a problem for Moe. He had become so focused on golf, he didn't have a life outside the sport. While other young adults were learning social graces, fumbling their way through dating, learning to make small talk with strangers and dealing with the adult world, Moe was in his own little world.

Hitting balls became a compulsion. If he felt on the verge of mastering a certain move, there was no half measure with Moe. He was unstoppable, almost manic with intensity. And he wouldn't stop hitting balls until darkness, physical exhaustion, or more likely, his hands became too sore.

Moe didn't wear a glove. After a few hours, his hands would start to sting, then blister, pain shooting up his hands with each swing. Soon the skin peeled back, his hands feeling like they were on fire, throbbing, raw and bleeding. But Moe would keep hitting balls. The blood made his hands slippery, so he just wiped them on his pants like a house painter. He was a heck of a sight going home on the streetcar at night.

When Moe just couldn't hold a club any longer, he might have worked through the golf bag two, sometimes three times. In one day! That's maybe 1,500 balls. Moe would retreat to the clubhouse and soothe his bloody hands in cold towels. Sometimes he threw the towels in the garbage, which made Tucker furious. The next day, with his hands covered in Band-Aids, he might cut back and only hit his daily minimum of 600.

Eventually, his hands became rough like sandpaper, black with thick calluses that were so hard, they looked freakish. Eventually, he'd have to cut them with razor blades so that his hands could fit naturally on a club.

He also burned off immense frustration hitting balls. He was the laughing stock, the weird kid, the lowly pinsetter. He was driven with that I'll-show-them intensity that fires up life's underdogs. Becoming a great golfer would show them how wrong they were to call him Moe the Shmo. He was taking pride in himself, and taking out his anger on golf balls. "I was alone. I had no support from my family. They discouraged me from following my dream. My own personal friends laughed at me for playing a sissy game."

Hitting balls alone suited Moe's nature. The range was his private domain, his office. "Oh yes, wonderful. I could study myself." Golf attracts loners and fiercely independent sorts, and young Moe was certainly that. To hit balls didn't require talking with anyone, meeting anyone's expectations — except his own.

Even off the course, Moe listened to his body for clues that might help him hit the ball better. Soon after blasting balls, Moe would go into the Rockway clubhouse and plunge his arms and hands in water that was so hot he could hardly stand it. He said the muscles which hurt the most where the ones he had used the most. "That way I figured which ones had to be softer and have better muscle tone through the ball."

Moe was afraid to tell anyone about his hot-water dipping technique. "They'd laugh. Because they'd think it was childish, 'Crazy, putting your arms in hot water!'

"And then I'd go home at night and think to myself about which muscles were more tired than the others. Which ones still wanted to hit another ball. How did my left eye feel compared to my right eye? Since my right leg was much more tired than my left leg, that means I was keeping my weight back there too long. My body did my talking to me. My body memorized my swing."

Moe developed his swing with the curiosity of a scientist, listening to his body, studying the flight of the ball, concentrating on the lessons learned from his "mental pictures." Moe was a visionary — decades ahead of his time in terms of using mental images to help him envision his swing. Instead of telling himself to move a certain way, Moe pictured the move and then let it happen.

Moe worked from a clean slate. There were no musts, absolutes or do's and don'ts. Moe didn't care what anyone else thought, or what convention dictated. He just listened to his body. That's why his swing was so radically different. "Nobody could teach me this. I learned by feel. Whatever felt good to me. And I had the move and the feeling in my mind. My mental images taught my muscles how to move this way when I was younger, hitting at least 600 to 800 balls a day."

To have so much confidence in doing things his way was remarkable for someone so self-conscious and sensitive to criticism. Moe ignored comments that would have discouraged most people.

Moe's swing is the work of a genius, plain and simple. Between 18 and 19 years of age, he developed the foundations of the game's simplest and most efficient swing, by taking shortcuts, experimenting, altering his equipment and inventing drills that few had ever tried before.

His swing challenges conventional thinking about the swing. It sure looks weird when you first lay your eyes on it, but when you examine how he puts it together, everything makes perfect sense. It's all the more amazing when you consider that every nuance of his swing is geared toward hitting the ball as accurately and consistently as possible. Also consider that it's completely self-taught.

While Lloyd Tucker provided Moe with plenty of guidance on the theories of the swing, he takes little or no credit in shaping Moe's swing. "He figured the swing out on his own. He practiced so much he found out that a lot of his ideas worked. As he got better, he learned a lot from his own research."

"I couldn't afford $2.50 lessons," Moe said. "My allowance was a dime a week." Moe often asked Tucker for advice, but they usually ended up in heated debate. Moe was fortunate that Tucker was Rockway's professional. Just about any other pro would have tried to change his swing radically.

What golfers were being taught about the address in the late 1940s wasn't much different from what's being taught today. That is, the feet should be about shoulder width apart, the knees slightly flexed, arms hanging down from the shoulders and close to the chest, and a slight bend at the waist.

Moe played from a different page. His legs were spread wide and ramrod straight. His arms were stretched out and rigid. His elbows locked. His meaty hands strangled the grip. He seemed bent over the ball. But Moe's stance was very natural. Watch any young buck at a driving range for the first time. He's hell-bent on slugging the ball, and takes a great wide stance because it feels powerful.

While Moe's wide stance looked powerful, he learned that it created the opposite affect. "I lost distance, but I didn't care. With the wide stance you can't twist or explode, but I was never a long hitter. I never tried to be. Because I was small and light. I wanted to become a pure, straight hitter and that's what I became."

Tucker said he tried to get Moe to "narrow up" his stance, because he felt it restricted his turn. Moe wouldn't budge. Tucker said it wasn't just because Moe felt stable over the ball that he preferred the wide stance. "This is what attracted attention to him and he liked attention. When he started hitting balls, people stopped and watched. If he narrowed it up, he was just another golfer and they wouldn't watch."

Moe's grip was also unconventional, although he held the club in the fingers of his left hand with the back of the hand facing the target, much the same as most players were being taught at the time. The biggest difference, however, was in Moe's right hand. Instead of gripping the club in the fingers, it ran diagonally across the palm of his hand, which was turned under the shaft. With his left hand on top and his right hand under the shaft, his arms formed straight lines from his shoulders to the club. The back of both wrists were flat. In a conventional grip, the wrists should be hinged, bent back slightly.

Weslock recalls players scoffing at Moe's grip, muttering how terrible it was. But with his grip, Moe reduced the number of moving parts. His shoulders, arms and hands formed a one-piece triangle. Noting his flat right wrist, he says "Look at the straight line. I play with one lever. Everyone else plays with two. I'm the only pro in the world who swings on a single-axis."

(Initially, Moe played with a Vardon grip, overlapping the baby finger of his right hand over his left hand, but Moe says that when he got down to "real science" in the 1960s he changed to a 10-finger grip.)

Most players were also told to hold the club firmly but lightly. The oft-repeated tip attributed to Sam Snead was to hold the club as if you were holding a bird in your hands — just firmly enough so that it didn't escape, but not so tight you hurt it.

Moe would have killed Tweety. He said, "I'm trying to draw blood with my left hand." He often did, but the key point was that Moe's vice-like grip prevented the club from wavering on the backswing. It straightened his arms, giving him a wide and repeating swing arc. Along with his wide stance, his backswing remained short and controllable. Moe took the club back barely to a three-quarter position.

Moe began gripping down about three inches from the butt end of the grip, even with his driver. Everyone else had their left hand near the end of the grip. But Moe's method shortened the shaft, making the club easier to control. This made him even more accurate. While he sacrificed distance, he was so strong and hitting the ball so solid, he still launched the ball well out.

Since Seamus and Angus played golf on the Scottish linksland, the credo for starting the backswing has been to take the club back "low and slow." Moe took a shortcut. As he addressed the ball, he set the club about 12 inches behind it, and swung from there. You can't get much lower than that. It sure looked weird, but it made perfect sense.

Of Moe's fundamentals, his No. 1 goal was to keep the clubface on line with the target as long as possible, both before and after impact. That was his key to hitting the ball purely and accurately. That's also a key to Lee Trevino's brilliance as a ball-striker. He's acknowledged as the player who keeps the clubface on line the longest, but Trevino says Moe beats him by a country mile.

To achieve this, Moe developed a drill in which he placed a quarter 41 inches behind the ball and another 22 inches ahead of the ball. He'd practice passing the club over each coin, back and forth for hours each week, and often when he hit balls. He wore spots on the front and back of the soleplate of his drivers in the shape of a coin.

He ingrained the feeling that with every swing his hands are square to the target 22 inches after impact. Videotape images show his hands turn to the left far earlier, but the most important thing is what Moe feels. "At impact, every muscle is going forward, not around," he says firmly.

While Moe was honing and refining his swing, he often got an earful of ridicule. "Nobody stands like that, Moe!" amateur critics would say. Occasionally, he'd see kids out on the course, mimicking him, exaggerating his wide stance and having a hell of a good laugh at his expense. But they don't come much more bullheaded than Moe Norman. Despite the put-downs, he stuck with his swing.

"It suited me and felt good. I'm a different type of golfer. Every day it felt better and better. Everyone said it was wrong. All my friends would say 'You'll never be good doing what you're doing.' So I guess I was never any good. Oh well, that's their tough luck.

was never any good. Oh well, that's their tough luck.

"I was never concerned with the look or the beauty of the swing, just the action of the swing. It was the proper swing for me. Maybe not for all golfers, but I did it my way. That's my favourite song."

***

"Different" is a key word in discussing Moe Norman. As a youngster, Moe also played with different equipment. When his friends swung one of his clubs, it felt like they were swinging a telephone pole with an anvil on the end. Moe's anecdote of how he became convinced of the need for heavy clubs and thick grips says volumes about him.

"I went to a carpenter that I knew at the age of about 19 or 20. I said 'Sir, you're a very skillful carpenter. Now don't think I'm trying to get your job or anything, but what's your hammer — heavy or light?'

"He said 'Heavy.'

"'Why?' I asked.

"'Because it doesn't waver as much and you don't bend as many nails if the hammer is heavy. The hammer does more things for me.'

"'Ooh!' I said. 'Gee whiz, a hammer is just doing a little stroke like that, and it never gets raised behind your head. Why not just have a heavier club and raise it to your shoulder.' And that's it. Hammers have a big handle, not little, so I just fell in love with the idea right away."

Moe began experimenting with lead tape, layering great gobs of it on every club. His irons looked like they had grey bulbous growths growing out of their backs. His clubs came in at a corpulent swing weight of E3. (Swing weight is the head weight you feel when you swing a club.) "That's mega-heavy compared to anything else," said Herb Holzscheiter, one of Moe's friends and head pro at Toronto's Weston golf club. To put it in perspective, most amateurs and touring pros play with swing weights that range from D0 to D2, while newer clubs with graphite clubs are as low as C9.

When people asked why he liked heavy clubs, he waxed on about the principle of "mass" like a religious zealot, how it took his hands out of the swing and let his big muscles control the motion. While it was assumed swinging heavy clubs all day would be very tiring, Moe said the weight actually "relaxed" him. But the main reason was "the club can't get off line as much."

Most people were not strong enough to swing his clubs, but Moe was

Weslock, with his Popeye forearms and great strength, said he couldn't swing Moe's clubs. "I couldn't square up the blade at impact."

Moe also began grinding his irons in a friend's garage. The leading edge on most irons is slightly curved, but Moe made his square, removing the bottom groove on each club in the process. He found that a square leading edge made it easier to line up with the target and went through the ground better. Similarly, he bent the heads of his drivers so that they only had a paltry six or seven degree loft. Most pros use nine degree at the minimum. That's one reason Moe's drives fly so low.

After much experimentation, he settled on using super-stiff Double XX shafts in his clubs. A Double XX shaft has a bit less play in it than, say, an iron bar. The shaft made his clubs even heavier.

While most players used standard leather grips — even into the 1970s — Moe found special rubber grips were more to his liking. He'd remove the old grips and wind two or three rolls of cloth-backed tape around the shafts to build them up. Interestingly, he built up the tape where his right hand fit on the club "a shade thicker." Then, he wound black Goodwin rubber grips over top. His grips extended about 16 inches down the shaft, while most everyone else used grips about 10 inches long.

All that tape in the grip end also added weight to the club and acted as a counter-weight to all the lead on the clubhead. Moe said the grips were the last part of the equation. "Then I was just in my glory."

**

Moe won the first tournament of his career with Gerry Kesselring when they captured the 1948 Ontario Junior Better-Ball with a 68 at Summit Golf Club north of Toronto. By the end of that season, Moe knew he had his "move." He was striking the ball crisply every time, controlling the flight of the ball at will. Now it wasn't a question of if the ball went toward the flagstick, but how close it would be. "At 19, I had my move down. It felt so good. I thought, 'Keep this and make it stronger.'"

He no longer had to think about the mechanics of his swing. He would play with what he had. While every other serious golfer was constantly working on his swing technique, trying to correct problems, seeking advice from anyone who might help them fumble across the "secret," Moe hit every ball with the same swing.

"secret," Moe hit every ball with the same swing.

"The main thing I did was stick to one thing. Everyone is searching for the secret that's not there. There's only one secret in the game — and that's hard work."

His blue eyes wild with excitement, he exclaims that all his hard work and alterations to convention allowed him to achieve "the purity of technique. Nothing twists. Ooh, it's the simplest move in golf. It's the best move in golf."

The formative period in his career was over. Now, Moe Norman could just play golf and test himself against all those hot-shot amateurs. Amateur golf in Ontario was about to be turned upside down by a skinny, red-haired kid from Rockway.

Chapter Six
The Red-Haired Amateur

In the annals of golf history, much has been written about the great psych-out artists who crushed their opposition just by the way they swaggered on to the first tee. There's the tale, perhaps apocryphal, of Walter Hagen showing up just minutes before an important morning match in top hat and tails after being out all night. When competitors strode up to shake Jack Nicklaus' hand they got a wintry blast from his eyes that telegraphed killer confidence.

Then, there's Moe Norman's entrance at the Canadian Amateur in 1948 in Hamilton, Ontario. Moe was riding to the tournament with some Rockway buddies when their car broke down near a gas station as they entered the city. In a panic, they asked the attendant how they might get to the Hamilton Golf and Country Club. He pointed to a dump truck parked on the lot. Moe's starting time was fast approaching, so they took the offer. The attendant drove, and with two men sitting in front of the truck and two standing in the back with their clubs, they roared on to the grounds of the regal club.

"Just as we got to the course, they called my name," Moe told Golf Magazine in 1960. "I didn't have time to do anything but run up and hit the ball."

Mr. H. Murray of Montreal, Moe's opponent, was done in from the get-go. "What a nightmare," Murray said. "This boy jumps out of a dump truck, hits the ball as if he's only got a few seconds to live — and knocks me out of the tournament on the 12th hole, 7 and 6."

Moe broke into the world of competitive amateur golf with jarring suddenness, with neither a trace of elegance nor pretention. Moe left chaos and confusion in his wake, and before anyone knew what hit them, he was gone again.   Moe had played in relatively few events in 1948. He had concentrated almost exclusively on fine-tuning his swing, partly because he just couldn't afford entry fees. But after a winter of pinsetting and saving "like a son of a gun," Moe had some money. And after a season of ball-beating, Moe also had his swing "trapped." He was excited about his game and would enter almost every tournament he could in 1949.

On July 13, three days after his 20th birthday, Moe, with his golf bag standing up beside him, hitch-hiked to the St. Thomas Golf and Country Club Invitational Tournament in rural southwestern Ontario. It was the first year for the tournament and the club wanted to make a big splash, inviting the best players from private clubs around Ontario — and offering 35 prizes. (Three years later the tournament moved up to May and was renamed the Early Bird tournament, and it's endured as one of the province's most popular invitationals ever since.) From the onset, the Early Bird attracted Ontario's best amateurs and many fine players from the mid-western U.S. That's in large measure because St. Thomas is a lovely Stanley Thompson course that runs up hill and down dale through swaths of maple and oak.

The favourites in that inaugural tournament were Jack Nash, three-time Ontario Amateur champion, and Nick Weslock, the 1944 provincial amateur champ who was winning everything in sight those days. Moe arrived uninvited on the morning of the 18-hole tournament, and found a few "post-entry" spots available. He paid his $3.50 fee and signed the entry form simply as "Moe." As he darted around the practice putting green before teeing off, many players were amused by the skittish lad. Some younger players had seen him before, but most had not.

The majority of top amateur golfers in those days were from the country club set — professionals, business owners and children of the gentry with their leather golf bags, well-cut togs and social graces. Moe stuck out like the proverbial sore thumb. His ragged canvas golf bag was full of holes and held together at the bottom by carpet tape. Instead of golf shoes, he wore black canvas high-top running shoes. Most everyone had a caddie — Moe carried his own clubs. His clubs were first-class all the way, however. He had a set of Bobby Jones irons and woods given to him by a Westmount member who figured he'd only get $35 for them on a trade-in anyway.

Nash fired a 71 and Weslock a tidy 69. Despite the stares and having never seen the course before, Moe shocked everyone, firing a 67 on the difficult course to win. It was late in coming, but Moe, at age 20, finally had his first individual victory.

He laughs when he recalls what it must have looked like to the crowd gathered on the patio overlooking the 18th green. "Here's a little red-headed kid coming up 18 four-under par. I make my par for 67 and I've been winning ever since." Indeed, he won the tournament again the next year and in 1954.

As the evening awards ceremony drew near, St. Thomas tournament officials were puzzled. Where the heck was Moe Norman? By that time, probably back in Kitchener. Moe had come off the course, signed his card, handed it into the scorer, walked behind the clubhouse and down to the highway to hitch-hike a ride home.

Club officials were angry the winner of their inaugural event didn't have the courtesy to stick around to accept his silver tray and say a few words of thanks, but Weslock wasn't surprised. Moe had caddied many times for Weslock in the past and they were friends. He knew his little buddy was extremely shy. Weslock picked up Moe's prize for him, a circumstance that would repeat itself many, many times over.

Moe was the talk of the post-tournament dinner. The players were in awe of his amazing ball-striking and wondered just who was this odd kid from Kitchener. Weslock characterized most of the tournament amateur players as "snobs but they respected the way Moe could play. Others thought Moe was lucky. Those of us who had seen him play before were already fans. He clearly had a great talent. He attracted peoples' attention really fast."

Just a few weeks later Moe proved that you have to be good to be lucky when he captured the Twin-Cities Tournament in Kitchener and Waterloo at Westmount. It was a big thrill to win as a former Westmount caddie, in his hometown and see his name splashed across The Kitchener Record newspaper. Maybe now, his family, neighbours and the rest of the naysayers would recognize his skill in this "sissy game" and treat him with a little more respect.

But Moe says the biggest thrill of the season was winning the Kawartha Invitational in Peterborough just east of Toronto. That's because he beat Phil Farley, a three-time Ontario Amateur champion, by five shots. More importantly it was a 54-hole tournament, which signalled that he had a game which stood up. He ended the season on a high note, when the team of Moe Norman, Gerry Kesselring, Tony Matlock and Milt Plomski won the provincial inter-club George S. Lyon team championship.

Kesselring, Moe and Matlock were dubbed Rockway's Three

Musketeers. In one weekend in 1950, the trio each went to a separate tournament and all three were winners. Along with Milt and Bill Plomski and Jerry Knechtel, they dominated the provincial amateur circuit in the early '50s, which irked the bluebloods of golf to no end.

"When we pulled into a tournament, the clubhouse shook. 'Here comes the Rockway brigade,'" Moe recalls, his voice rippling with excitement. "'Here comes first low gross, second low gross, first low net, second low net...,'" Moe says, howling with laughter.

As the new decade began, the Three Musketeers were the talk of any tournament. Matlock modestly suggests he was "the low man on the totem pole." Kesselring was one of Canada's top players but Moe had quickly established himself as the rising star. Says Matlock, "Moe's prowess on the golf course was amazing. I stood back and watched him with awe. It was always so good. He was hitting it to perfection, but he went beyond. No matter how well he was striking it, he wanted to hit the ball better."

In the same year Matlock began to notice a chink in Moe's armour. The pair faced off in a match in the 1950 Ontario Amateur at the Toronto Golf Club. "Moe was my easiest match. I think he gave up. I don't think he thought he was good enough yet. If you could slip the ball inside him on the green, sometimes you could demoralize him. He might think something like 'Here's someone who can hit the ball better than me,'" said Matlock, who went to the finals but fell to Weslock.

It appeared to other players that Moe occasionally gave up, and deliberately missed putts. Keith Kirkpatrick was one of London's top amateurs when he finished in a tie with Moe in the Thames Valley Open in London. They went two extra holes and Kirkpatrick prevailed. But it wasn't a satisfying win. "I think he wanted me to win," Kirkpatrick said. "He said to himself, 'Let him win.' But if he wanted to win, he'd kill you."

Nevertheless, Kesselring was undoubtably Rockway's A player. Although nowhere near as shy as Moe, he was also quiet, awkward with people and appeared fragile to many people. Almost six-feet, Kesselring was tall, dark and handsome, you might say, a big-shouldered lad without an ounce of fat on him. His rich brown eyes dazzled many women, but mostly it was his smile — the jaw cocked a tad to the right — that gave him a jaunty look.

"Kessy," as he was known, left a cloud of tobacco smoke behind him on the fairways from his ever-present pipe. He had the peculiar habit of laying his pipe on the ground the same way before every shot, placing it laying his pipe on the ground the same way before every shot, placing it about eight inches from the ball and pointing the stem at the hole. Weslock thought he used this as an aid to help him line up shots, but there were few if any complaints to tournament officials about it.

Although he was only a year older, Kesselring was Moe's idol and inspiration. "Moe idolized Gerry," Tucker said. "It amazed me because Moe had all the shots, but there was something about Gerry he appreciated." Throughout his teenage years, Moe watched Kesselring do everything he couldn't: shmooz in clubhouses, give speeches, but most of all — win. And Kesselring won all of the big events: the Ontario Junior in 1945, '46 and '48; the Canadian Junior in '46 and '47, and the Ontario Amateur four times between 1949 and '53.

"I looked up to him," Moe said of Kesselring. "It was nice to see someone better than you. There's someone to aim for. No one was better. There was no one I could learn from."

Like most of Moe's golf buddies, the pair had no relationship off a golf course. Delving into the past is painful for Kesselring, who has endured a number of personal tragedies, but he saw in Moe a kindred spirit who constantly struggled with his own demons. "A lot of people thought he was offbeat. He'd help anyone he could, give them a few dollars here and there. Golf is a tough game. Everything you do, you do yourself. Everyone has a different personality. Moe is Moe, and I am me. Moe was just a little bit different."

Moe and Kesselring often hurtled through the course in two hours, but Kessy had Moe's number most of the time. "They had some great matches," Tucker says. "Moe would come in all excited, saying he shot 65 and Kessy shot 64. He tried to beat him, but never did."

Kesselring was an excellent long-iron player, but by 1950, Moe could match him shot for shot, except with a putter. Kesselring would spend hours on Rockway's practice green, while Moe spent almost all his time on the range. Moe was fascinated with the air game, but uninterested in the ground game.

It was against Kesselring that many people started to hypothesize that despite his amazing long game and occasional flashes of brilliance, Moe had an inferiority complex. Friends say Moe could have beaten Kesselring many times, but he fell back, lost focus and appeared as if he wasn't trying.

"'Can't beat Kesselring, can't beat Kesselring,'" Weslock recalls Moe saying. Indeed, Kesselring defeated Moe in 1949 and '51 for Rockway's club championship. Moe won the crown in '50 and '53, but his victim was Matlock both times.

Kirkpatrick played in many amateur events with both Moe and Kesselring, and Moe could have easily beaten him a number of times, but didn't. "He'd deliberately miss a putt so he wouldn't beat Gerry. He had a little negative something that said to him 'I can't win.' I could never figure the guy out."

At nearly every tournament with Kesselring, the big fellow was the focus of attention. If Moe beat the great and powerful Kesselring, his fame would grow. More people would want to talk to him, he'd be asked to give speeches, reporters would want to take his picture. And that scared the daylights out of him. Moe just wanted to play golf. Anything more and Moe would be out of his "comfort zone." This helps explain why, despite his ball-striking ability and brilliance as a strategist, Moe cleaned up at weekend invitationals and one-day events but he rarely performed well in the bigger amateur tournaments in his early 20s.

One of his greatest fears was that someone might ask him a question in front of a bunch of people. Moe feared that he would panic, say something stupid and make a fool of himself. On a golf course with a club in his hand, he was fine with people; off the course, he was a mess. "I wouldn't know what to say and I was too nervous and too shy, not knowing what to say, how to handle myself," Moe says. "All I felt when I was younger was put the ball in the hole, shoot 61 and go home and that's it."

For people used to self-assured amateurs and slick professionals, Moe was difficult to understand. Moe was a teeming mass of contradictions: he didn't like people to talk to him but he loved to be the centre of attention. But only when he was holding a golf club. For as Moe's game improved in the early 1950s and he played in front of more galleries, he became quite a showman. Some would say a showoff.

"On a golf course I wasn't shy. The other guys were. If I was in motion or swinging a golf, I was OK. I felt I could do something they couldn't."

Heading into the 1952 Early Bird, Moe was the favourite, having won twice before, even though Kesselring was entered along with a number of U.S. Walker Cup players. Gus Maue, a Rockway buddy, was to caddie for Moe, but Moe duck-hooked his drive into the trees, took about six or seven whacks to escape, made a 10 and ended the round in a huff. Kesselring was among the last groups to finish and won the tournament.

But Moe stole the limelight. "When they came in, Moe was hitting balls from beside the clubhouse out onto the course," Maue said. "He had a good crowd. Someone took a collection for him, and it was quite a bit.

"Kesselring got a silver tray and Moe got the cash."

This kind of thing endeared him to some, ticked off others. Fans, his fellow competitors and club officials at tournaments across Ontario were at once dazzled and mystified by the man. He could hit a golf ball like Ben Hogan, but he sure didn't look or act like Ben Hogan. No one had ever seen a golfer like Moe Norman; golf had never experienced anyone like Moe Norman.

As Moe played in more tournaments in 1952 and '53, word spread about the strange cat from the other side of the tracks who hit a golf ball like a god, looked like Joe Zilch and did almost everything else as if he came from another planet.

Chapter Seven
The Magnificent Ragamuffin

"If you're a golfer you've got to see Moe Norman to believe it! Even then, most people come away a little doubtful...Whereas most people almost turn to stone trying to concentrate on 10 to 20 different things before making a golf stroke, the astonishing Norman rushes up to the ball, shuffles into a stiff, angular stance, crashes his shot away, dead at the hole, and scarcely breaks stride doing it."

Hilles Pickens, editor and publisher of
Canadian Sport Monthly

In 1952 and '53, Moe was the sixth-ranked amateur in Ontario, though Gerry Kesselring and Nick Weslock were still the dominant players. Moe was winning the invitationals and little one-day events left and right, but he had yet to win a major tournament such as the Ontario Open or Amateur. Nevertheless, word was spreading quickly that he was the player to watch. Not just for his golf game, either. To the ink-stained wretches of the day, Moe Norman was as welcome as a cold beer on a hot August night.

Although it was still early in his career, sports writers were gleefully spinning stories that he hitch-hiked hundreds of miles to tournaments with just his golf bag, the shirt on his back and no money. That he slept in bunkers to save money. He was even said to occasionally doff his shoes and play barefoot. Writers had a field day coming up with cute handles for him, including the "Barefoot Boy Wonder," the "Happy Vagabond" and the "Magnificent Ragamuffin."

"With something akin to Huckleberry Finn appeal, Moe and his antics have been a boon to jaded sportswriters and columnists," Pickens wrote.

Moe was blessed with what reporters call colour. And sports writers bored with the grind of writing who-beat-whom stories loved colourful characters. Some golfers were characters because they threw clubs (notably "Terrible" Tommy Bolt) or they cursed, stared down fans for moving a muscle, even blaming spectators for their own mistakes. Moe had the kind of colour that reporters and golf fans loved.

Many pros and top amateurs carried on as if they were high priests, demanding respectful silence that would allow them to summon up their mysterious powers and make the ball find its true reward in the bottom of the cup. To non-golf fans, then as now, golf seemed like a solemn, elitist enterprise.

Only golfers could fathom what psychologist David Morley has called the "aura of reverence" for the game. Morley wrote in "Missing Links: The Mind and Golf," that it was a game of control which has "almost a religious quality, as though everyone involved in the game were participating in a sacred ritual."

The "aura of reverence" stemmed from the universal recognition that golf was an excruciatingly difficult game. The swing itself was considered one of the great mysteries of the cosmos, a series of complex movements that must be executed in perfect sequence with immaculate timing, somehow combining the power of a linebacker with the grace of a ballerina.

The key to attempting this minor miracle with some degree of success was concentration, a conscious effort of herculean proportions to block out all distractions and focus every fibre of your being on propelling the little white ball. To concentrate also meant the golfer took great care and deliberation in analyzing the conditions, selecting the proper club, running through a pre-swing check list the length of his arm, rehearsing the swing and then, finally, pulling the trigger.

In the 1950s, this was the general perception of golf — and Moe blew it to smithereens. "He is diametrically opposite to the generally accepted human form of the tournament golfer," wrote Jim Vipond, sports editor of The Globe and Mail daily in Toronto. "His popularity stemmed entirely from his unorthodox approach to the game."

Typically, Moe strode to the tee, jauntily bouncing the ball off the face of his driver, chattering to someone or no one in particular, stuck his tee in the ground, and without a practice swing or even appearing to line up his shot, bashed the ball straight down the pipe and was chasing after it before anyone had a chance to see him.

Most good players had "classic swings" that were very similar to one another. They looked loose standing over the ball, finishing in an elegant pose with their hands behind their heads. Moe was rigid at address, appearing to take half a swing and ripping through the ball furiously until his arms stretched to the sky.

The most startling difference between Moe and other players was the speed in which he executed a shot. Most golfers took 20 to 30 seconds to hit a shot. Moe took three seconds. If you blinked, you could miss his swing.

On greens, Moe just walked up and popped the ball without appearing to come to a complete stop even on the slipperiest sidewinders. He didn't appear to read the putt. This was a mind-blower for serious golfers, who regarded putting to be as mysterious as sorcery and as delicate as brain surgery.

While other players were putting, he appeared aloof, like he was bored, looking at anything except the putt he had coming up. Sometimes, he'd wave at a 12-inch putt with one hand or backhand a two-footer while talking or looking at something else. And, of course, he often missed. Fans would smack their foreheads in exasperation, but Moe sloughed it off. "Oops, oh well, it's only a game, only a game." It didn't seem to make any sense that Moe would set up wonderful opportunities for birdies and then, apparently, just fritter them away carelessly. "Miss 'em quick, miss 'em quick," became Moe's mantra. "A miss only counts one, only counts one."

Moe roared around the course like a whipped pony. Later, he came to call himself "the 747 of golf." Being known as the world's fastest player made him feel very proud. It's unlikely there has ever been a golfer anywhere in the world who played so fast at such a high level.

Between 1954 and '61, Moe says he hit just one ball out of bounds. That was in the Kawartha Invitational in 1955. A newspaper report said that as one of Moe's drives sailed beyond the boundary stakes, his next shot was in the air while the fans were still straining their necks to watch the first one. Later, as Keith Kirkpatrick was marking his ball, Moe rolled a snaking putt beneath his foot and outstretched arm into the cup.

Moe was asked repeatedly why he didn't take more time or bother to line up his shots. "Why? Did they move the greens from yesterday? Did they move the greens?"

If Moe was paired with another fast player in match play, or given the first tee-time, he could finish in two hours. Trying to watch him was like running in a cross-country race. Spectators dashed from greens to tees in hopes of seeing him drive, making it difficult for his competitors to concentrate on their putts. In an effort to slow him down, tournament officials often stood directly in front of the tee until the fans had a chance to get to the tee. Once, they asked Moe to zigzag as he walked down the fairway.

Sometimes when play bogged down, Moe would register his displeasure by laying down on the fairway or beside the green and pretend to go to sleep.

Moe appeared brash and confident the way he bolted around the course. Looks were deceiving. "It's a way to relieve tension," Woroch said. "He walks and talks fast as a way to get rid of it. He's nervous as hell — a bundle of nerves."

In addition to playing like he was leading a cavalry charge, Moe talked a blue-streak as he played, providing a running commentary of his game. Moe wouldn't even pause for a breath as he hit the ball, chattering away in his sing-songy Moespeak. It was an unorthodox dialogue that described his game, his place in the world, words of encouragement and chastisement.

Bob Hesketh, a sportswriter with the Toronto Telegram, followed Moe in the 1954 Ontario Open and condensed four holes of Moe's commentary as follows: "Ah hooked it nice. Couldn't have put it there better with a hand mashie. What do ya think? Seven-iron? Ah, just hand me a club. What's the difference? Hit it. It's right in the cup if I hit it. Oops! Two-foot putt and I pulled one. It's only a game. What's the difference? It's only a game."

Most golfers wore their scores on their faces, muttering soft curses under their breath, grinding their teeth as if the future of humanity hung in the balance with the outcome of the round. Whether Moe was firing a 69 or a 79, you couldn't tell the difference, though on a few occasions, he has walked off the course after blowing up on a hole. Moe was generally the same laughing, happy fellow with a quick smile, bounding around the course as if he didn't have a care in the world, just happy to be out there. Whatever the outcome, Moe summarized his game usually as "a walk in the park, a walk in the park."

Moe differed from most players by not only acknowledging galleries, but kibitzing with them. If a fan bet him he couldn't hit a certain shot, he'd often take the bet. And then the cash. He often called his shots like a pool player to the gallery, and then hit the shot exactly as he called it.

"OK, here's a big fade around the corner. Ooh man, is that pure. Easy as falling off a log. Hoo boy. Just a half-wedge to the green now, just half a wedge." He looked for kids to talk to, and often pulled one from the gallery to accompany him down the fairway.

With his good cheer and happy-go-lucky appearance, Moe made golf — a game associated with grim determination and unrelenting failure — look like fun instead of root canal. The speed in which he played and his merry demeanour made it look like Moe wasn't even trying. But he hit nearly every ball as pure as the driven snow.

"His seeming lack of concern while reducing a tough layout to a 'soft touch' induces a distinct inclination to burn one's own clubs and take up croquet," Pickens wrote.

What Pickens described was meant as praise, but Moe had the exact opposite — and encouraging — effect on many people. He proved you didn't have to be a tall aristocrat dressed to the nines to play good golf, and that the game didn't have to be a grim affair which took all day. Moe was an inspiration to many people who were also born on the other side of the tracks and who didn't have the prettiest swings. Only two things mattered — where the ball went and whether you had a good time getting it there.

"I made it look so easy," Moe says matter-of-factly. "It never looked like I was lined up. 'Where'd the ball go?' the fans would ask. 'Right there at the flag,' I'd say."

Considering how different Moe appeared to fans, the usual reaction to seeing him hit a golf ball was laughter. It was an incredulous laughter. When many people see a great talent, they often laugh, shake their heads, as if to say 'It's not possible for someone to be that good.' It's not a really a laugh, like you would laugh at a joke, but more of a nervous reaction. The same way people laugh when they see Michael Jordan defy gravity. Or hear Oscar Peterson peel off a lightning-fast run on the piano.

But Moe often thought people were laughing at him. The laughter was in awe, not amusement, but Moe couldn't make the distinction. It bothered him that the fans would clap when one of his competitors hit a good shot, but they'd laugh when he played. And he couldn't understand why.

Galleries were used to pros and country club amateurs in nicely pressed pants and double-knit Munsingwear shirts. Moe's pants were sometimes up over his ankles, his shirts stained and hanging out of his pants. His clothes looked like they needed a good ironing, mending or, better yet — to be burned.

"He was a humorous looking character who hit these beautiful shots," said Rockway pal Ernie Hauser. "People expected a real polished person and a clothes horse, but he looked the exact opposite. People didn't understand him. He dressed funny and acted funny."

Moe was so sensitive and insecure, the laughing hurt him deeply. He had tried to earn respect by becoming the greatest ball-striker, and now that he was hitting the ball better than anyone else, people were still laughing. Moe thought, "people are smart and I'm not," so he concluded that they were right: he must be quite a buffoon.

"These things I've been through," he reflects wearily, "I've been the laughing stock of Canada. Me in golf, Eddie Shack in hockey."

Ed Woroch recalls that in the early days, this caused Moe a lot of anguish, so much so that it made him cry on occasion. "'Why do people laugh when I hit a shot?' he'd ask. It hurt Moe when people laughed. He'd knock in a 30-foot putt and they'd laugh. He made it look too easy."

In the press, Moe was gaining a reputation as a golf clown who could, intentionally or not, always be counted on for a chuckle. At times Moe talked eagerly about being a clown, saying that he wanted to amuse fans, but it may just have been bluster. Sportswriters began using the clown label as an identifying tag, beginning stories with the lead, "Golf clown Moe Norman..." Deep down Moe was hurt by the label, which would dog him for years.

An on-course commentary of Moe recorded by The Telegram's Bob Hesketh is evidence of Moe's grudging acknowledgment of his clown image. "Moe the schmo, that's me. Moe hits a 68, everybody laughs. Moe hits a 79, everybody laughs. Moe isn't a golfer. Moe's a comedian. Hogan, the only man in the world who plays the game right. That's Hogan. Not Moe."

Ironically enough, while he despised the stamp, he exacerbated his image with his on-course antics. This confused Moe's friends, but once Moe put his mouth in motion or got in front of a crowd, he could get so wound up and giddy with excitement, he would just keep going until he went overboard.

Most of Moe's antics were a testament to his exceptional coordination. One was bouncing the ball off his club and catching it in his shirt pocket, but his favourite was just seeing how long he could keep the ball bouncing on the clubface.

Moe said that during a tournament in Belleville, Ontario, a spectator bet that he couldn't do it 100 straight times without dropping the ball, offering $1 for each bounce past 100. Moe would have to pay the same for each ball he fell short. Moe accepted. "His jaw was dropping lower each time I hit the ball," Moe says, laughing. "It was down to his shoetops." Moe intentionally missed at 184. "I had to stop because I was holding up the tournament."

His record for walking and bouncing the ball off his club is 194 yards before it fell off. "It gives the crowd a laugh," he told GOLF Magazine, "but your arm sure gets tired."

About his antics, Moe said: "I just wanted to give the game more colour, put a little excitement into the game." He wanted to entertain the fans, and endear them to him, but Moe also wanted to entertain himself. Moe hit the ball so well, he'd get a little bored even during a big tournament. The antics made a round of golf more fun.

Another of Moe's beloved stunts was hitting the ball off a series of high tees made expressly for him by a Kitchener war veteran. It was a trick he'd been mastering since he was 19. Moe had a collection of four- and six-inchers, but the crowd pleaser was an eight-inch colossus.

Throughout a round, fans would urge him on to bring out "the big tee," but he'd resist. When the fans were pumped up for the big moment, someone would once again say "C'mon Moe, let's see the big tee." He'd look serious, shake his head and say no, causing groans among the gallery. Then he'd raise an eyebrow, smile, whip out the big tee and rifle the ball up the heart of the fairway to great hooting and hollering, while his competitors just shook their heads.

In one tournament, he hit off a double tee — one tee inserted into a hole bored in the top of another. He hit the ball 200 yards up and 100 out. "That," he declared, "is enough of that nonsense."

Moe often dropped the ball on the tee and drove it off the grass. Sometimes he would even step on it just for good measure and crack it perfectly with his driver all the same. At times like this, he blurred the line between showman and showoff, and some of his competitors got steamed at being shown up so brazenly.

Moe could also blast his ball off wooden tee markers, matchboxes, a couple of sticks — anything. One oft-told story that may be true — Moe denies it but it's been mentioned more than a few times — has him setting the ball up on a tripod of wooden matches, striking the ball so cleanly he walked away from a small blaze, saying "That's how you set a course on fire."

But Moe's most infamous trick shot was hitting the ball off a Coke bottle. John Czarny, who lived three blocks away from Moe in Kitchener, recalls with glee that after Moe won a tournament at a nine-hole course in Walkerton, Ontario, his buddy gave an impromptu exhibition that had the crowd in awe. "I put eight Coke bottles on a tee, put a ball on each one. There was a tree in the middle of the fairway. Moe said, 'Set 'em up, set 'em up. Do you want me to draw it, fade it or slice it?' He would hit every shot exactly as I called it. And not one of those bottles fell over."

Hitting off Coke bottles was an astonishing display of confidence and hand-eye co-ordination. He risked injuring himself with flying glass and broken clubs.   Actually, Moe rarely hit the ball off the glass, but off a big tee sticking an inch or two out of the mouth. Still, that the bottles didn't fall over was yet more evidence of how consistently Moe placed the clubface on the ball every time. (Moe hits the ball so purely with a driver, he rarely moves the tee out of the ground. Czarny says Moe's record is 146 drives off the same tee in one exhibition before the tee finally became dislodged.)

Hitting off Coke bottles is one of the most embellished facets of Moe's legend. Other than Czarny, few people have ever seen him perform the feat, especially in a tournament. Like many of Moe's friends, Woroch gets angry at many of the exaggerated stories that circulate about Moe, particularly those that accentuate his eccentricities over his skills as a golfer.

"A lot of the things said about Moe aren't fair," Woroch says. "They stretch things out of proportion. One person says something and by the time the 10th person tells it, it's nowhere near what really happened."

When Woroch hears someone talking about Moe hitting a ball off a Coke bottle, he often confronts the person. "Where did you see Moe hit the ball off a Coke bottle? They'll say, 'Well, I didn't see him. I heard that he did.'"

Not everyone shared in Moe's irreverent approach to the sacred game. Some officials and fans became indignant, thinking that he was making a mockery of the game by zipping around at light speed and engaging in his antics. Every so often, a hothead in the gallery might crack, "Hey Moe, why don't you try for Pete's sake!"

Moe often didn't react, pretending not to hear, or he'd make light of it and laugh. He said people didn't understand that playing fast was his style. "If they didn't like it, too bloody bad," he growled. "I did what I believed. I never cared what people thought. One thing I never let control me was the gallery. No bloody way.

"I just laughed at them. They didn't know what they were talking about. They wanted to hear themselves talk out loud, that's all. The ones who talk like that are the ones who can't break 80."

But Woroch said these outbursts bothered Moe. On rare occasions he might light into the heckler with an onslaught of vulgarities. But he'd often go into a funk about the remark, become completely absorbed by it, well beyond what it was worth. He could complain about it for four or five holes. "Can you believe that guy, can you believe that? Did you hear what he said? What a lunch pailer." Moe often lost his focus completely, ruining his golf game. When angered, he could boil over and stay hot for a long time.

"It took one little comment from the gallery to set him off," Woroch said. "Moe is very sensitive. He would work his butt off, and then people would say 'Moe, why don't you try?'"

Moe had a simple belief that you treat others the way you want to be treated. He concluded that when people invaded his privacy or criticized him, they were unintelligent and selfish. "What right does a person have to say these things?" he'd ask friends like Woroch or Weslock.

Woroch believes Moe achieved notoriety too quickly and he wasn't ready for it. "He was shooting lights-out golf as a kid. He got shoved into the limelight. He wasn't prepared."

Golf fans, reporters and officials were not ready for someone who was such a radical departure from the norm either. This was the 1950s, well before the era of star athletes like Reggie Jackson, Andre Agassi and John Daly, whose eccentricities and rebel images were not admonished but celebrated, at least to a point. This was also the conservative world of golf. It was run by an old boys' network not far removed from the days when golf professionals were prohibited from clubhouses.

As Moe's fame increased, he found that pushing the envelope of what was considered "acceptable conduct" didn't go down so well in many clubhouses and in the offices of golf's governing bodies. They sure envied the way he could powder a golf ball, but he was to learn that they didn't like his attitude, and more damaging, they didn't like him.

Riddled by insecurities and vulnerable to criticism, Moe was to find out that as he won more and bigger tournaments, he would have to deal more often with the country club gentry. He would appreciate that the road he had chosen was paved with a whole lot of laughs, great golfing moments and even a fair number of victories, but also a lot of pain. A lot of pain.

Chapter Eight
Bluebloods, TVs and Bunker Sand

Depending on your perspective, Moe Norman was the best or worst thing to happen to golf in the early 1950s. To many members of golf's establishment — particularly officials of the game's governing bodies — Moe was like an intruder at the garden party, an odd and unpredictable guy who thumbed his nose at the traditions of the grand game.

One long-time course owner who has been associated for about 50 years with the Royal Canadian Golf Association (RCGA) and the Ontario Golf Association (OGA) said Moe was contemptuously treated as an outsider. "A lot of people thought Moe was a button short. But Moe is probably one of the most intelligent people I ever met. The executives of these associations were usually current and former presidents of private country clubs. They were from blueblood. They were embarrassed by someone who didn't come from blueblood."

Another RCGA veteran from Moe's heyday sums up the common perception of Moe by the golf governors: "He was a little child with the greatest talent in the history of golf. It was like dealing with an eight-year-old who had no ability to think."

To be blunt, many of golf's upper crust thought Moe was a golf freak — a moron who could barely sign his name, but man oh man, could the guy hit a golf ball. They had read the stories about the golf clown sleeping in bunkers, living on candy bars and drinking 30 Cokes in a round of golf.

They watched him gulp down hot dogs in a couple of bites, saw him wearing the same mustard-stained shirt for a few days. They couldn't help but notice his grotesquely twisted right eye tooth. They listened as words came hurtling out of his mouth, and shared his rather undiplomatic views — "This course is a goat ranch, a goat ranch!" — when he got wound up and loud.

Moe made many people at golf's highest levels nervous and uncomfortable. They were used to a certain level of sophistication. In the 1950s, before the intoxicating mix of Arnold Palmer and TV spread the sport to the masses, golf was a gentleman's game, dominated by the educated and the comfortable. Most amateurs and administrators had jobs and families; their lives included a lot more than just golf. They were concerned with house prices, mortgages, taxes, problems at home, at school, at work. They were interested in, say, Duke Ellington's new record or Henry Fonda's hit movie, or they were anxious about the Soviet Union stockpiling nuclear weapons and counting Cuba among its allies.

If they asked Moe what he thought, he wouldn't know what or whom they were talking about. Not a clue. It was outside Moe's orbit. His world was golf, and to a lesser degree other sports and a fascination with numbers. If the conversation drifted away from Moe's limited sphere, so would Moe. "I'd get up and walk away. I couldn't understand what they were saying. I didn't think any of that would mean anything in my life. And it still doesn't. That's married stuff.

"All I cared about was golf. That and mathematics were the only two things that I figured mattered to me in my life — hit the ball great, purer than anybody else, and know mathematics off by heart."

This fostered Moe's reputation as a golf oddity, and even generated speculation that he was mentally retarded. Moe heard such talk and it hurt him deeply. But Moe's friends knew that while he was socially disabled, within his world he was quite brilliant. In the early 1950s, Moe and pals such as Woroch, Tony Matlock and George Hillebrecht were just into their 20s, the prime years in a young man's life to be working, spending money on cars and clothes, meeting women and going to bars and parties.

"He never hung out with us other than to play cards," said Hillebrecht, a retired golf professional who spent most of his career at the Peterborough Golf and Country Club in Ontario. "We'd go to bars and he'd never go along with us. The only place we'd see him was at the golf course."

On a course, Moe was exceedingly confident. There was simply no question Moe would hit the shot. It was automatic. His entire life was geared to hitting the ball absolutely purely. When most other golfers were mentally and physically tired of the game, Moe would still be practicing or playing. Even after a gruelling tournament, soon Moe would be back on the driving range. He was at once amazing and perplexing.

The world outside the course gates, however, was dangerous and scary, full of people he didn't know or trust. Friend John Czarny said that when Moe was with strangers, he usually looked morose and "very serious," not saying a word, averting every gaze, his neck bent, eyes riveted on his hands.

Most people can deal with unpleasant social situations, even speaking in public, without feeling like they're inferior. Moe would feel stupid and out of place. That's why he avoided trophy presentations, receptions and the press. His greatest fear was the thought of finding himself in front of strangers, panicking and saying something stupid. "I was afraid that someone would ask me a question that I didn't know and I'd feel like a little kid. If I won, as soon as I signed my card, I couldn't wait to get away so fast before some committee guy would try to get me. When they did, I'd feel like a piece of dirt. I would have dropped the trophy. I couldn't stand the idea of a hundred people looking at me."

Moe's stage fright led to a number of run-ins with officials after tournaments. Shy or not, they wanted the champion at their presentation. Knowing Moe's penchant for a quick exit, some officials confronted him at the scorer's table and insisted he stick around. Many officials didn't buy his explanation that he was too shy. Some thought he was just rude, there for the prize and too selfish to give up another minute of his precious time. He often just walked away from officials, but if pressed, Moe could lose control, yell and curse — anything to beat back his attackers and speed his escape.

"If I had won the Canadian Open, I wouldn't have been at the presentation. I was too shy then. I knew I would have had a fight with an official. He would have grabbed hold of me. I'd have given him a karate chop right in the shoulder. Whap! I know I would. Because they would be trying to tell you how to live — their way. If I'm too shy, I'm too shy. If that's what the man above gave me, I can't get out of it. Are you perfect in everything? I couldn't get up in front of 15,000 people!"

That fear was made worse because few people made the effort to see past his eccentricities and try to make him feel appreciated. Instead, he felt like a misfit. "No one would take him seriously," said Jerry Magee, also a fine amateur in the 1950s and later the head professional at St.

Georges in Toronto. "They'd praise his golfing ability, but as a human being or a person, they'd put him down. It was a shame that they didn't take the time to understand him."

The put-downs were rarely obvious, but Moe suffered the same fate as many people who appear to be cut from a different cloth — people fidget and fumble as you approach, or cut you off in mid-conversation, suddenly excuse themselves to dash off to someone else they "must" talk to. It's subtle, but the message is clear: "You're different!"

Magee said that kind of thing often happened to Moe. "It was like 'Uh-oh, we better get out of here, this guy is going down a different kind of path.' That kind of put-down. People thought he was shy and bashful. Well, he was to a certain extent, but everyone put him down by ignoring him.

"In those days, people didn't know how to handle Moe. A lot of people thought he wasn't too intelligent. He didn't even know who the prime minister was, but it wasn't important to him. It was important to him to know only certain things. People couldn't criticize his golf, so they had to look at his idiosyncracies. Today I know a lot of people who are a little different, but I don't call them crazy."

The curt way people acted around him, the murmuring and side glances, the unease and even the revulsion he sensed in many of the big wheels, it broke his heart. "They made me feel like I was out of place," he adds. "'What am I doing here? I'm just a piece of dirt.' And that's how they treated me. Like a piece of dirt."

These episodes confirmed his feelings of inadequacy and inferiority, and Moe plunged into funks, sullen and depressed. When he was in a blue mood, he was nearly inconsolable, but eventually he'd unload his burdens on friends, perhaps even shed a few tears, and soon he'd be high stepping again. When Moe felt he was being persecuted or ridiculed by golf's royalty, he'd also get fired up, hardening his resolve to do things his way and show the high falutin' so and so's that they'd rue the day they crossed this great ball-striker.

This partially explains why he was so brazen in selling his prizes. Of all Moe's antics, selling his prizes absolutely infuriated the potentates. He rubbed it right in their faces.

You weren't supposed to make a living at amateur golf. Moe was Canada's most colourful golfer and likely the busiest, averaging about 30 events a season and winning about two-thirds of them. He had no time nor any desire to work at anything other than golf in the summer, and his

savings from a winter of pinsetting only went so far. Moe needed money
— not luggage sets, silver trays, radios, TVs, cocktail glasses or another
golf bag. Moe often chose which tournaments to play in depending on
his shopping list.

Besides, selling prizes violates the RCGA's rules of amateur status,
which are intended to protect the integrity of the amateur game from
slumming professionals. Except for baseball, perhaps no game cherishes
its traditions more than golf.

This meant zip to Moe. Besides, amateurs had been doing it for
years, although on the sly. Not Moe. He'd sell his prizes in the parking
lot right after the tournament in broad daylight. As time went on, Moe
began to sell his prizes before tournaments. Now, that's confidence, but
it was well-founded. Except for the big events, Moe was winning almost
every tournament he entered. The question wasn't if Moe would win, it
was by how many. Even in one-day events, he'd win by huge margins.

"When I went to tournaments, I said to myself, 'Do these guys expect
to beat me? When my bad rounds are better than their good rounds?' I
had tournaments won before I even went. A guy would see the prize
before the tournament and I'd sell it to him. I had the money in my
pocket when I teed off. Four hours later, 'Here's your present.' And this
was many times."

Moe offered no apologies. "I needed the money. I didn't know where
my next meal was coming from. The first two years I played in
Peterborough (the 54-hole Kawartha Invitational) I saw a bed only one
night.

"I'd sleep in bunkers. Twice I woke up, snakes across my legs. In
bunkers! That's all I could afford. I only had enough money for the
entry fee. But I loved it. What else could I do? I loved the game so
much and I wanted to be good. This is what I had to do or I couldn't go
to the tournaments."

In the beginning, Moe remembers being unable to purchase even the
most rudimentary equipment. "I couldn't afford golf shoes. I played in
running shoes. Nick (Weslock) gave me my first pair in my early 20s. I
just used clubs people gave me. Of all the winners, I always had the
worst clubs. I'd say to guys, 'Let me play your clubs next week and I'll
kill you worse.'

"I had two pairs of pants to my name. And one for going to church on
Sundays."

Unable to afford a car — not that it mattered since he didn't know how to drive — Moe hitchhiked back and forth from tournaments. "I'd just put my big bag by the road with my name facing the guys driving their cars. Soon as a salesman saw me, he would pick me up and talk golf with me all the way to the club. I'd say 'Pick me up after I'm done on your way back to Kitchener. I'll be waiting here with first prize for you.'"

A Golf Digest story titled "What do you do with 27 Toasters" said he collected a rocking chair in one event four straight years — and ran out of buyers. The next year, before the tournament started, he asked around if anyone wanted to buy a radio. Having made the deal and set the price, he contrived to finish in the place that carried the radio as a prize.

There were other stories that Moe would finish according to the prize he wanted to win and sell, but he firmly denies he ever did. Moe admits he sold prizes, but maintains that many stories exaggerate the extent of his merchandising. "It's all so much crap. I never won a toaster in my life. It makes me so mad. Wristwatches sure. I won 14 wristwatches and seven TV sets. But they (RCGA and OGA) said you're supposed to keep them. We had no place to put them. We had an eight-room house. If I won one more TV, we'd have been the only house in Kitchener with a TV in every room back in the 1950s."

Moe told writer Roy MacGregor: "Hell, all I ever seemed to win were TV sets. One year I had six, so I sold them. They said I couldn't. I said 'What am I supposed to do, watch all six?' They said yes."

Moe's habit of converting prizes into cash like a roadside peddler made the blood of RCGA types boil. He was making a mockery of the game, hitting off outsized tees and zipping around like a gazelle — and now selling trophies to the highest bidder. The insolence! The temerity!

It made it very difficult for those few souls within the RCGA and OGA who were sympathetic to Moe to defend him. Bruce Forbes was one. As president of Brantford golf club, Forbes became involved with the RCGA in the 1950s and rose to become president and executive director. "Moe was a little difficult to handle," Forbes said. "He really flaunted selling his prizes, saying 'To hell with you, I'll do what I want.' A lot of that you have to put to his upbringing. We all have our faults don't we."

While Moe enraged the power brokers of Canadian amateur golf, officials at individual clubs holding events usually loved having Moe in the field. He drew fans, players and press. After many of the small tournaments that attracted mostly local golfers, Moe was often asked to put on exhibitions for the competitors. With drinks in hand, they'd watch spellbound as Moe worked his magic, hitting balls with nervous urgency, displaying skill that seemed other worldly. Most everyone knew Moe was scraping by, so they felt an obligation to help out — and rules of amateur status be damned. Most people thought the rules were unfair and enforced unevenly. Hell, everyone knows that to travel and compete at the highest levels, you need some pocket change.

Sometimes a hat was passed around, but that was strictly against the rules. On many occasions a box was passed among the players and instead of money, they'd place new golf balls inside. Everyone knew the deal. Afterwards, Moe exchanged them with the club pro for cash. "They (fans and golfers) thought it was a way to get around the rules," Woroch said.

Clubs often called Moe to put a foursome together and come out for an exhibition game for the members and prospective members. Moe often received a couple hundred dollars under the table for these, Woroch said. When a big tournament was coming up that required Moe to travel quite a distance, a number of Rockway members often took up a collection, put the money in a wallet and gave it to Mary Norman to give to her son.

As a lifelong friend and former schoolmate, Woroch has heard the legendary stories about Moe, and he contends many are greatly exaggerated and many are dead wrong. Woroch goes so far back with his buddy, he still calls him Murray. He also quit school early — dropping out in Grade 8 — and worked in various factories while playing a lot of golf at Rockway with Moe, Matlock and their gang of friends.

A two-handicapper for most of his life and three-time Rockway club champion, Woroch played in many tournaments with Moe. Retired after a career in the printing business, Woroch is a pleasant man with bifocals and rubbery face etched with lines that convey he's had an enjoyable life. But he gets angry at yarns about how Moe scraped by as a golf hobo, living on junk food and sleeping under the stars — even if it's Moe who tells some of them. Then again, Moe's version of events sometimes goes along with the legend.

Woroch said many of the better players were jealous of Moe, and they took great pleasure in spreading uncomplimentary stories that were usually wildly embellished. "It didn't sit too well with many folks, including the OGA, that they came from private clubs and he came from this public course."

Hitching rides, Woroch and Moe travelled to many tournaments together. "There are so many stories about Moe being poor. All the times I've been with Moe, he always had money. I never ate so much in my life with Moe. He loved to eat spaghetti. You never saw a guy eat so much spaghetti. We ate well, not elaborately. But we didn't starve.

"I can't ever remember Moe sleeping in a bunker. There was always a place for him. He didn't have much money. Someone would often pay his hotel bill."

That someone would often be Nick Weslock.

***

In the 1947 Canadian Open in Toronto, U.S. professional Clayton Heafner was paired with 29-year-old Nick Weslock, the hot-shot Canadian amateur.

Heafner watched as time after time Weslock's wedge shots bit into the greens at Scarboro golf club and spun back to within birdie range, author Jim Barclay recounts in Golf in Canada: A History. In the third round, Weslock fired a 65, the lowest score of the day and Heafner filed a protest that Weslock's wedge must have had illegal grooves. But the RCGA rules committee found that it was quite legal. It was the man — not the club — working the magic. Weslock finished fourth behind winner Bobby Locke of South Africa. No Canadian amateur has ever come so close to winning the country's national championship.

Barclay says that tournament was probably the genesis of Weslock's nickname Nick the Wedge. Jimmy Demaret said Weslock was one of the three best wedge players in the world. He considered turning professional, but by 1951 he was not only two-time Ontario Amateur champ, he was also partner of an auto parts manufacturing company in Burlington. When U.S. touring pro Al Watrous learned how much money Weslock earned from his business activities, he talked him out of turning pro.

Weslock is arguably one of the world's best amateurs to ever play the game. His sparkling career includes four Canadian Amateur championships, four invitations to the Masters, eight Ontario Amateur titles and six Canadian Senior championships. He was low amateur in the Canadian Open an incredible 16 times, a record that will likely never be broken. He also played on 17 Canadian international amateur teams.

Around 1946, Weslock was playing in a tournament at Rockway when

Lloyd Tucker fixed him up with a caddie named Moe Norman. Even though Weslock was one of Canada's top amateurs and 11 years older, the teenager turned out to be a rather forthright little fellow, as Weslock found out on the par-three 16th hole. They stood on the tee, a little breeze blowing in their faces. They had about 145 yards to the pin.

"This is a seven-iron shot," Weslock said.

"No, it's an eight-iron," Moe replied.

"You sure?"

"You hit the seven-iron and you'll carry your bag from here in."

Weslock blinked hard, more than a bit shocked, but the kid was so definitive, and he'd been bang-on clubbing him all the way round. Weslock took the eight and socked it three feet from the hole. "He was right. He was always right. I won the tournament," Weslock said. "I was impressed by his knowledge of the game."

They've been best of friends ever since. There was an instant rapport between them, even though you couldn't imagine two more different people. A barrel-chested man with Popeye arms, Weslock was meticulous about the state of his clubs, which were always gleaming and free of dirt. While most golfers sported white and grey, he favoured a rainbow of colours topped off by flashy checkered caps and immaculately shined shoes.

Weslock was supremely confident in his golf and in himself, and often came off cocky to those who didn't know him. He loved to gab with the press. A very intelligent man, Weslock kept fastidious notes about his golf game, swing thoughts and observations, anything that could help him in a pinch. Except for the brilliance of his golf, Moe was a polar opposite in almost every respect.

As Moe became a top player on the Ontario Amateur circuit, Weslock was a good friend to have. He would give Moe equipment and clothes occasionally, loan him a few dollars here and there, but Weslock was a bigger help as Moe's most trusted advisor.

The dapper Weslock was always after Moe about his "deportment" — the importance of being clean-shaven and well groomed, keeping his clothes neat and clean and matching colours and patterns. Weslock didn't like it either when fans would snicker at Moe's clashing outfits, which made him appear clownish.

Weslock also acted as a buffer between Moe and many players and officials. He'd tell people to give Moe some slack, explaining that Moe was very shy. Weslock was the first golfer of significant social standing to go to bat for Moe. "I always defended him. They didn't appreciate what great talent he had. He had peculiar ways."

Weslock would explain to people that Moe was fine with people he knew, but he feared strangers. "With his gang of guys, he was great. He chatted only with people he knew." Weslock urged officials and other golfers not to crowd Moe or try to engage him in a conversation if they didn't know him. Moe was so excruciatingly shy and anxious, he could react quite oddly if strangers got too close. He left many people puzzled, often hostile. He'd play with a fellow on Wednesday, but on Thursday the same person might walk up and say hello, but Moe could say "I don't know you. Get the hell away from me!" With Moe's incredible memory, he obviously remembered the person.

After a tournament a fan might say "Nice shooting Moe," and try to talk to him, but he wouldn't even look at the fellow. Needless to say, many people thought Moe was rude when in fact, he was extremely nervous — even scared. If he acted like he didn't know someone, Moe figured he'd be less threatened. "He'd walk away and ignore people," Weslock said. "It was a quirk of his."

Like many shy people, his timid nature was often mistaken for arrogance. "He's not a mean person," Czarny said. "If he ignored someone, he didn't do it on purpose. He wouldn't think of doing it. It wouldn't enter his mind."

Moe does, however, have definite ideas about what he considers rude and intrusive behaviour. He can't stand to be approached by a stranger if he's alone, or to be interrupted when he's with friends. As Moe became more of a celebrity in the 1950s, he couldn't handle persistent questioning from reporters, or fawning fans who were naturally attracted to him.

If a fan grabbed his hand in a firm shake and spewed "You're a helluva golfer Moe," he was apt to bark out a blue streak of expletives, tell the guy he had no manners and then tromp off red-faced with anger. Most everyone meant well, but Moe figured that because he was not an intimidating figure, people took liberties and prevailed upon him while they'd leave Kesselring or Weslock alone. It was difficult for people to understand Moe's reactions to unwanted attention 40 years ago. It still is.

He's a different cat who requires different stroking. It's as if Moe has created a cocoon to protect himself. If he knows and likes someone, he'll let that person inside. If someone he doesn't know or dislikes invades the cocoon, Moe feels threatened and scared. He can react very angrily and uncontrollably, hurling obscenities, even racial insults — anything to make the invader go away. It's a counter-attack. While it's very hard for people to realize, Moe is literally scared silly. You can't condone his behaviour. It's wrong. But at least people should try to understand that Moe has not been socialized like most people.

Quite obviously, especially being a public figure, Moe has alienated, offended and confused many people over the years, especially the bluebloods of golf. Weslock, and many of Moe's friends for that matter, have tried to explain that despite Moe's eccentricities, he's a good guy at heart. Nevertheless, it has hurt them through the years to watch their friend go embarrassingly out of control many times. It's cost him opportunities and income.

"It's a hell of a thing," Weslock says. "It's like he's numb. That hurts. It's like throwing gasoline on a fire. I never knew how to break him of it. It hurts Moe. I'd say 'Moe, you have to improve your image. That part of you stinks.' It kills me when he does it. It's just something in the guy."

Moe's extreme sensitivity and inability to socialize explained, to some degree, why Moe would lose matches he should have won easily, or why he played poorly in certain tournaments — especially the Canadian Open. Some opponents took advantage of this weakness with cutting remarks they knew would get under Moe's skin.

"If he didn't like the guy he was playing with, he'd play like a bum," Weslock said. "He just wouldn't perform. If some guy got smart and kidded him, he'd just wanted to get away. That's when he'd goof up and not play his regular game."

In fact, many of his opponents thought it was Moe who was engaging in gamesmanship with his antics, but he was just being himself. Moe was always very courteous on the course, adhering to all rules of etiquette, which he believed were sacrosanct. While the pomp and pretension around golf bothered him, Moe was very serious about the tradition of the game.

If Moe knew he was bothering a fellow competitor, he'd stop what he was doing right away. He was certainly no saint, but Moe adhered to a rigid code of right and wrong developed in the Norman home and in church.

Being paired with Moe would be like playing with a combination of William Tell, Shivas Irons and Red Skelton. Surprisingly, there were few complaints from Moe's fellow competitors. If he liked his fellow competitor, he'd always find something good to say about a shot. Even if it sailed into the woods, a typical Moe reaction was, "Off-line a little, but hit solid, hit solid." He cheered other players' putts. "It's in! It's in!"

Keith Kirkpatrick recalls playing in a threesome with Moe at the Kawartha Invitational. Kirkpatrick had never played the course before and hinted on the second tee that he needed some help in choosing a club. The other player responded: "You're on your own. I'm betting against you."

Moe piped up immediately: "Hit your three wood." With occasional help from Moe the rest of the way, Kirkpatrick won the tournament. "He was the most delightful young kid I ever played with," Kirkpatrick said. "He was great, super. He'd do anything to help you."

While it's against the rules to ask for or offer advice in a tournament, Moe stayed true to the spirit of the game. Accepting trophies, boasting to the press, engaging in gracious chit chat on the clubhouse lawn — that wasn't golf to Moe. He played for the wonderful feeling of a purely hit ball, the steady thrill of hitting a ball exactly where he was looking, the momentary sense of belonging he found among people who shared his passion and treated him with respect.

Yet, he was made to feel that despite his abilities, the chiefs of Canadian golf didn't appreciate him. Nor did they want him on their teams in provincial and international events. They shivered at the thought of putting their team jacket on Moe and letting him loose among international bigwigs.

In 1956, Hilles Pickens wrote, "As early as five years ago Moe Norman was known to be an able and likely candidate for the Ontario (Willingdon Cup) team, but his golf association doubted he'd ever make the grade. You just couldn't tell what he was going to do next." Going into the 1954 season, the bluebloods of Canadian golf were having difficulty figuring out whether to take Moe Norman the man seriously or not. Nevertheless, Moe Norman the golfer was becoming one of the world's best amateurs, and he could no longer be ignored.

Chapter Nine
The Golden Years

After dominating amateur golf in Ontario for years, Gerry Kesselring finally answered the siren song of the PGA and turned professional for the 1954 season. With his idol gone, Moe could freewheel. There was no reason to feel inferior to any golfer in the country. Nick Weslock was in his prime and Moe's main competition, but he was also Moe's best golf buddy.

Moe bolted from Kesselring's shadow in 1954. He was nearly unstoppable, and vaulted into the No. 1 spot in the Ontario Golf Association rankings. At one point Moe won 16 out of 19 tournaments — a unbelievable winning percentage of 84 per cent. In May, Moe won his third Early Bird at St. Thomas with a five-under 66. He was also holding his own with professionals. He was low amateur and runner-up along with top homegrown pros Al Balding, Gordie Brydson and Murray Tucker in the Ontario Open, and low amateur in the $25,000 Labatt Open, which drew many U.S. pros.

Moe was now among the country's top players. Despite great wringing of hands, the RCGA selected him for the Canadian squad in the America's Cup, a team event that included the best amateurs from the United States, Mexico and Canada.

The matches were held in August at the regal London Hunt Club adjacent to the University of Western Ontario in London. Although Canada had proven players such as Weslock, Jack Nash and Phil Farley, the U.S. team was the hands-down favourite. The American roster included Charlie Coe, the 1949 U.S. Amateur champ; Billy Joe Patton, who had caused hearts to flutter at the Masters that spring when he held the second-round lead; Bill Campbell, finalist that year in the British Amateur; and upstart Harvie Ward.

The America's Cup was just one of a number of international amateur team events born in the 1950s, including the Commonwealth matches and the World Amateur Team Championships. Their genesis was the hugely successful Walker Cup, which had pitted Great Britain and Ireland against the United States since 1922. The America's Cup matches were played over two days by six players from each team. On the first day, competitors from each country played foursomes (in which teammates alternated shots). The second day was match play.

It was just the second running of the America's Cup — the first time that Canada played host — and RCGA officials were nervous: about putting on a good show and Moe's unpredictable presence. On the morning of the practice rounds, the RCGA was already in a panic. The tournament hadn't started and already their worst fears were being realized. Moe was nowhere to be found.

In desperation, team captain Jim Anglin called Keith Kirkpatrick, club captain at the private Highland Golf Club in the city's south end, and begged for help to find Moe. Having played the amateur circuit for years with Moe, Kirkpatrick was positive that Moe would be in St. Mary's, just north of London, playing in a one-day tournament. "It was just another little tournament that Moe could win and sell his prize," Kirkpatrick said.

Kirkpatrick roared up to the St. Mary's Golf Club, stomped out in the middle of the course and confronted Moe. "OK Moe, that's enough! You're supposed to be in London. Now!" Moe didn't put up a fight and let Kirkpatrick drive him back to London. Moe would have told most people — especially an RCGA type — to go to hell, but Moe respected Kirkpatrick. Moe's explanation for missing the practice round was simple. "I knew the Hunt Club well enough. I played there lots of times. Jim Anglin knew that. And they were giving away a nice suit (at St. Mary's) as first prize, and I needed a suit."

Once at the Hunt Club, Anglin and other RCGA officials took Moe into a room and tore a strip off him. They also penalized him by sitting him out of the first day's matches. Before the second day's singles matches, they pleaded with Moe to dispense with his antics. Kirkpatrick recalls: "We said, 'Moe, all the photographers and newspaper men are here. These are the best amateurs from the United States and Mexico. C'mon Moe, let's just play golf. OK?'"

Moe was pitted against Carlos Belmont of Mexico and Bill Campbell of Huntingdon, West Virginia. Belmont wasn't considered a factor, but it looked like no contest between Moe and Campbell. The American perfectionist, one of the world's best amateurs and the ace of the U.S. squad, would surely eat up the quirky Canadian. Campbell was especially tough in match play, and ran up an impressive record of 7-0-1 in Walker Cup singles matches.

The contrast between the two was the talk of the tournament. Campbell was tall, trim and athletic with chiselled features and brimming with confidence both on and off the course. Moe was short, a mere 140 pounds soaking wet, and a quivering mass of apprehension off the course. Except for his deteriorating teeth, Moe was actually a good looking young man. He had a sweet, shy smile, bright blue eyes, and a pointed nose that nicely set off his triangular face, weathered from the sun. His hair was short on the sides, longer and tangled on top, although an ever-present white visor conveyed a sense of order.

You couldn't tell Moe was a golfer until you looked at his hands and wrists. Actually, he didn't appear to have wrists. Most peoples' wrists could be described as thin and tapered. Not Moe's. After years of hitting hundreds of balls a day, Moe's wrists were thick and muscular. His burly forearms seemed to extend from his elbows to his hands, which looked two sizes two big for him. His open palm was like one giant callus.

Moe wasn't afraid of Campbell. Moe knew Campbell was aware of his prowess. "He knew he had to play great to beat me," Moe recalls. "I was never off line — dead straight every time."

Nevertheless, the RCGA wasn't so confident. A win would be nice, if unlikely, but the powers-that-be were more concerned that Moe might embarrass them and Canada. They gave Kirkpatrick the job of monitoring Moe for the match like a cop escorting a prisoner. Anglin told him: "Keith, don't take your eyes off Norman for a second."

Kirkpatrick said he took Moe to his hotel the night before, had breakfast with him that morning and made sure he got to the first tee on time. "I was his shepherd. I tried to keep the crowds away from him. Anyone in the gallery might interrupt him and talk to him or distract him." In the early going against Campbell, Moe missed a 12-inch putt, and Kirkpatrick said he warned Moe to concentrate on the greens. "I'd say, 'Moe, sink that putt! Don't bugger it up.'"

Moe wasn't the only one to provide unexpected entertainment. On the 18th hole, Belmont of Mexico hit his second shot on the flat roof of the clubhouse overlooking the green. Undaunted, Belmont played a wedge from the roof to the green and two putted for a five. He eventually lost 7 and 6 to both Campbell and Moe.

Moe was three down after 18 holes, but clawed back to one down when they came to the 34th hole, a 146-yard par-three. "Bill hit first and landed two feet from the stick," Moe says. "He remarked that it looked like it would be a hard hole to win. I hit an eight-iron. It went four feet past the cup and came back to drop. That squared the match."

It wasn't Moe's first hole-in-one, but it was certainly the biggest. When they reached the green, Moe casually tapped Campbell's ball to him with a nonchalant "I'll give you that one." One reporter wrote "the unflappable Campbell was flapped."

They halved the 17th, but Campbell missed a three-footer on the 18th that would have given him the match. Shaken, Campbell hit a weak tee shot on the first extra hole and then hooked his second into a creek and Moe won with a par. It was the biggest victory of Moe's career.

The man the RCGA feared would embarrass them almost led Canada to one of the biggest upsets in international golf at the time. The U.S. edged Canada by a measly point — U.S. 14, Canada 13, Mexico 0 — but Moe's heroics overshadowed the whole affair. Under the headline of "Moe's Ace Steals Show," The Toronto Telegram said "the unpredictable Moe Norman yesterday turned laughter into loud applause. The fact that the Canadians were nosed out by a single point was secondary to the excitement stirred up by Kitchener's native son."

Campbell, who went on to a distinguished career in golf administration, including USGA president, was gracious in defeat and had high praise for Moe. "He is a very, very fine player, both mechanically and instinctively. He is potentially one of the greatest players of our time. His hand action is the finest of any player I've ever seen. Not only that but he's unfailingly good-humoured."

The most widely reported of Moe's comments was not joyful, but defensive. The constant scrutiny and criticism that followed Moe was intensifying his alienation from golf's establishment. Having Kirkpatrick shadow him for the entire match only served to deepen that feeling. "These guys who keep telling me that I should take more time are generally the ones shooting in the 90s. Fellows like Nash and Farley don't try to slow me down. Some of the others don't even play golf, but still want to tell a guy what to do."

When Moe recalls his first major victory, his comments indicate how conscious he was about his perceived place in the golf world, especially how he stacked up against American players. "It felt good to beat a known amateur in the world, one of the best in the States."

A few days later, with most of the top amateurs from Canada and the United States already in London, the Canadian Amateur championship began, again at the Hunt Club. The Canadian Amateur was and remains a coveted title, ranking third in prestige behind the British and U.S. championships. At the time, it earned the victor an invitation to the Masters.

Moe was finally chosen to play on the four-man Ontario team that competed against the other provinces in the Willingdon Cup, played just prior to the amateur championship. Moe proved he deserved to be there, finishing a stroke behind Vancouver's Doug Bajus, the leading individual scorer in the Willingdon Cup.

Fresh from the America's Cup and somewhat a local hero — Kitchener is only an hour away — Moe was the gallery favourite and reached the quarter-finals of the Canadian Amateur against Lyle Crawford of Vancouver. It was billed as the match between Canada's two best young golfers.

Moe's long game was typically flawless, but he three-putted the first, tenth and thirteenth greens. After the America's Cup, Moe seemed to be tiring as he went down the stretch and missed a couple of birdie chances to win. The match was knotted after 18. When he missed a three-footer for par on the 23rd hole, Crawford was the victor. "With this amazing player went much of the local gallery interest, for Norman was easily the most-watched player in the event," Pickens wrote. The drained Crawford was no match in the semi-finals against Harvie Ward, the golden boy from San Francisco, who went on to defeat Campbell 5 and 4 in the final and capture the Canadian Amateur crown.

Moe entered the 1955 season again as the No. 1 ranked player in Ontario and roared into the No. 2 spot behind Bajus in Pickens' national rankings in Canadian Sport Monthly. He gave everyone a wake-up call on June 18 when he pulverized the par-72 Brantford Golf and Country Club, a tough Stanley Thompson layout and one of the most revered courses in Canada. With two eagles, six birdies and a bogey, Moe fired a 63 in the first round of the Brantford Invitational. In the process, he set a course record that beat the old mark by three shots. "I shook the whole city. They couldn't believe their eyes and ears. Little red-haired kid shoots 63," Moe says proudly, as if he's still amazed. Moe "kicked it around" in the second round for 71 to win by a whopping 10 shots. Of his 33 course records, Moe is most proud of his Brantford achievement because it was fired in competition on a course he highly respects.

The victor in almost every tournament he entered, Moe went into July's Ontario Amateur at Westmount with confidence. He had never played well in the Amateur before, but with Kesselring gone, Moe was comfortable and made it into the final of the provincial championship for the first time. He was pitted against Jerry Magee. Magee was an insurance salesman, a fan of Moe's and a Speedy Gonzales himself on the golf course.

Moe felt plenty of pressure and emotion. His love affair with golf had begun as a caddie at Westmount. He was the hometown favourite, although he still felt like an outsider — a lowly public player from the Rockway municipal course. There was added pressure to retain the championship for Kitchener for the fourth straight year. Kesselring had won three consecutive titles beginning in 1951 and Grant Shirk of Westmount had won the year before.

With Moe the key attraction, about 1,500 fans showed up for the final, a huge turnout for an Ontario Amateur. Moe and Magee put on a superb display of golf that had the gallery breathless, not so much from excitement as fatigue. The fans were run ragged, stumbling over the hills and valleys of Westmount in oppressive heat, trying to keep up with the two fastest players in the country.

Moe was one-up after 16 holes, when Magee ran in a 30-footer to even the match. They halved the 18th. Magee ran in a 21-foot birdie putt on the first playoff hole for his 10th one-putt of the day and the championship. Moe wasn't one to fret about losing. It was just another "walk in the park." But he was hurt by much of the criticism that followed his defeat. This was the closest Moe had come to winning his first significant individual title and the consensus was that he blew it through carelessness. Moe recalls the comments with disgust. "They said, 'He doesn't take enough time, he fools around too much, he can't even win at home on a course where he once caddied.'"

With his runner-up finish in the Ontario Amateur, Moe was again chosen to the province's Willingdon Cup squad. The OGA flew the team to the 1955 Canadian Amateur at Calgary Golf and Country Club. It was one of the few times Moe didn't have to worry about travel expenses.

The grand old Willie Park, Jr., course was built in 1925 and, though relatively short at 6,400 yards from the back tees, it was bounded by many trees and played very tight. Moe again showed his mettle in the

Willingdon Cup, firing a pair of 69s to finish behind Crawford for the low individual title. He was losing interest as the pace of play slowed, when someone in the gallery, said "How about your eight-inch tee, Moe?" Pickens wrote that Moe brightened, then turned serious. "Nope, can't use it today. Nick Weslock (Ontario's team captain) made me promise not to during the Willingdon Cup matches." There was a sigh from the gallery, whereupon Moe did a fast double-take and grinned. "How about the six-inch tee, folks? Captain Nick never mentioned anything about it."

Pickens observed: "Amid applause, out came the tee. Off went the drive, long and true. To Norman, even the Willingdon Cup is just another day of golf."

In the playdowns, Moe beat Hobart Manley of Georgia in 20 holes, and then took on No. 1-ranked Bajus in the semi-final. Bajus, a bruising six-foot-four, shot a morning round of 67, but was still two down at lunch. Bajus wilted under Moe's onslaught in the afternoon and bowed out 7 and 6. That set up a rematch with Crawford.

They were like Mutt and Jeff. There was Moe, a 24-year-old phenom of only five-foot-seven against Crawford, a 22-year-old car salesman, a lanky six footer with dark hair and a winning smile. An overflow crowd of 4,000 trooped along the fairways under a cloudless sky with hardly a puff of wind.

Moe stormed out of the gate with three birdies on his first four holes. But he opened the door when he muffed a foot-long putt on No. 7. The match was all square by the 10th and it was a seesaw battle the rest of the way. During the halfway break, Crawford, tournament officials and reporters ate in the clubhouse. Moe disappeared. With memories of the America's Cup, the RCGA folks panicked. They launched a search and finally found him, alone, contentedly dangling his bare feet in the Elbow River, six empty Coke bottles on the grass.

In the afternoon, Moe cruised along and was two-up with three holes to go. But Crawford birdied the 34th to close the gap to one and that's how they stood going to the final green. Moe made a routine par when Crawford knocked in a ticklish eight-foot downhiller for birdie to send the match into extra innings.

They halved the 37th with pars. At the 38th, Moe needed only two putts from 18 feet for the title, but putted while Crawford was marking his ball. He left the first putt four feet short and missed the next one.

On the 39th, a 438-yard par four, Moe drilled a drive and stiffed his approach to about eight feet, leaving himself a lightning-quick sidehiller. Crawford missed the green and chipped to within two feet. Crawford's ball had hardly stopped rolling when Moe stroked his putt. The ball was three feet from the cup and curling home when Moe yelled "It's in! It's in!" And it was.

"Breathless and in a near-state of collapse, Moe, the boy with no advantages, the eccentric about whom officials had expressed doubts was Canadian champion," Pickens wrote. It was chaos as Moe retrieved his ball. Hundreds of arms and hands extended out to him. Reporters shouted questions. Fans tried plucking pieces off his faded orange shirt that he had worn all week. Friends guided him through the mob toward a car for the ride back to the clubhouse.

Moe was the first Canadian to win the country's national title since 1951 and he'd done it in the longest final ever contested. When the big moment arrived for the trophy presentation, he was nowhere to be found. As the ceremony began, he was alone, at peace and safe, at his hiding place by the Elbow River. "Crawford thanked everybody for me," Moe says.

Moe was enormously proud to win the national championship, but the thought of facing all the bigwigs in their blazers and ties in front of all those people and reporters, not knowing where to stand, whose hand to shake, what to say — it was all too much. RCGA officials found him much later and managed to convince him to stand with his trophy beside Crawford for a picture.

Today, when Moe recalls that big win, what he remembers most is not the thrill of being the national champion or the exciting final putt. It's what the victory said about his place in golf. "I showed I wasn't a hometown player. I felt good that I could win 2,000 miles from home."

**

Moe still lived at home when he won the 1955 Canadian Amateur, but he didn't call his parents from Calgary with the fabulous news. He didn't feel that he owed them anything.

Even today, it's nearly impossible to get Moe to talk about his family's attitude toward his career in golf. It's obviously painful for him. When the subject is raised, he visibly tightens. When it's suggested to him that his family must be very proud of his accomplishments, Moe's head whips back as if cuffed by an invisible hand. His eyes widen, then narrow, as anger flashes across his face. "They've never seen me hit a golf ball, not one ball!"

It's easy to imagine how bitter Moe would be, especially after a lifetime of stewing about it, that his family never saw what made him a living legend.

"That's crap!" older brother Ron asserts, with less diplomacy than his other four siblings. They admit that the working-class family was initially puzzled by his fascination with the "sissy" rich man's game in his teenage years, and that Moe had some wild blowups with his father Irwin, who had wanted Moe to get a job.

Over the years, however, Mary, Irwin and Moe's siblings learned to understand that golf was very important to him. They became very proud of him. In Moe's prime amateur years, Rich said Mary often spent a day a week polishing his brother's silver trophies and "there were mashies, gimmick clubs and bludgeon drivers all over the house." He recalls that his famous big brother was always squeezing a tennis ball to build up his hand strength. And he had a couple of golf balls in the pockets of his baggy trousers that he constantly worked in his hands, passing ball over ball with his fingers. "The first thing in the morning, he'd chip a couple of balls off the rug against the back of the couch. One day he broke a stained-glass window and that ended that."

Every week Moe's name would be splashed across the Kitchener Record newspaper and Mary and Irwin would beam with pride. "They loved it," Ron said. "They thought it was great."

As Moe began to compete in major tournaments, his parents and siblings often went to cheer him on, Ron said. "I was very proud of him. I was amazed by the way he could work a ball in any shape or form. His problem was that he didn't take time on the greens because of his nervous tension. He couldn't bear to stand around."

Ron says the last time he saw his brother was around 1956. It was very awkward and, in retrospect, painful. "He talked to me for a bit, but I couldn't get close to him. I never could figure him out. He was the only one in the family like that."

His sister Doreen, a Roman Catholic nun, recalls going with her mother superior and sisters Marie, Shirley and sister-in-law Jean to watch Moe play in Hamilton in 1960. "The superior suggested that we walk over to him. He didn't even acknowledge me. I was hurt that he wouldn't even come over and say hello. Shirley was very upset."

Rich had a similar experience at a tournament. He called Moe's name from behind the ropes, but his brother didn't react. "He knew I was there. He just turned his back. I sat behind him for three or four minutes. I was very embarrassed because all my friends were watching. It made me sad. I expected it though. We know what he's like. Why? We say it's probably because of the car that ran over him."

Moe never acknowledged that his family came around to take great pride in his golf. They crossed him once and that was that. "It's stuck in his mind, the negative attitude his family had when he started," says John Czarny. "It's still a part of his life."

***

Along with his Ontario teammates, Moe took the red-eye flight from Calgary to Toronto after the Canadian Amateur. Moe was so excited, he couldn't sleep. Upon his arrival in Toronto, a bleary-eyed Moe was met by friends from Rockway in two cars, one a convertible. As they arrived in Kitchener, they were joined by a police escort and a cavalcade of decorated taxis. Moe waved to onlookers from the open convertible. The high school dropout, pinsetter and former caddie was the returning hero.

When the convoy reached Rockway, Moe noticed that the ninth fairway was filled with cars. To reach the clubhouse, Marie recalls Moe had to walk through a gauntlet of clubs held aloft by his friends, and he got a few kisses too. Inside the boisterous lounge packed with well-wishers, Kitchener's mayor congratulated Moe and asked him to say a few words. "I couldn't," he says. "I just waved my hands." Moe then made his way through the crowd, receiving backslaps and handshakes. And he kept going right on out the door. The reception and luncheon went on without him.

Doreen says her parents were "just delighted" and went to the reception bursting with excitement, but they never saw Moe. "They were very disappointed. My parents were heartbroken. They were so proud of him."

When Moe ducked out of the reception, he told one person "the one thing I want to do now is get into bed." But only a few hours later, when everyone had gone home and Rockway was quiet again, there was Moe hitting balls on the range. Although exhausted, he was probably too excited to sleep. Among the thoughts swirling around his head were visions of Augusta National. April was a long way off, but as Canadian Amateur Champ, he would be invited to play in the Masters.

He would be ready to fulfil a dream.

Chapter Ten
Augusta

In January, 1956, the Canadian Amateur champion still worked at The Strand bowling alley. Many members of golf's establishment considered this a joke — a 26-year-old national champion scrambling around for bowling pins, for gosh sake. It wasn't dignified work, but this didn't phase Moe one bit. "Some people are too proud," Woroch said. He needed the dough and it made golf possible in the summer, so that was that.

Kitchener was deep in winter's clutch, cold and covered with snow. The residents of Kitchener loved the snow, and they got lots of it. The city was in the "snow belt" of southwestern Ontario. The white blanket would cover the black soot from the factories, making the city look clean and bright. But it was always a short-lived break, as the soot slowly blackened the snow like spots of mould.

Like many golfers from the north, Moe was sick of winter by the beginning of January, itching to get back on green grass. Thoughts of golf helped sustain him during his work at the Strand. Each day though, he grew a little more anxious. Where was that invitation from the Masters? He was a little fearful they might not invite him; Moe knew he was a "different kind of golfer" than they were used to down in Georgia.

Late one morning, the phone rang. It was someone at Rockway. A letter had arrived for Moe from Augusta National Golf club. He roared down to the snow-covered course and tore open the envelope. Inside was a plain white card that read: "The Board of Governors of the Augusta National Golf Club respectfully requests the honour of your presence at the Nineteen Hundred and Fifty-Six Masters Tournament to be held at Augusta, Georgia."

In larger letters below, it read: "Robert Tyre Jones, Jr. President."

"Ooh, I was shaking like a leaf, shaking like a leaf," Moe says. "It was a dream come true to be invited to play in the most prestigious tournament in the world."

Legend has that when the time came, Moe boarded a bus with his golf bag and suitcase and spent two days travelling to Augusta. Great story, eh? Who else but Moe Norman would take a bus down to the Masters, right? But it didn't happen. Another Moe myth.

Some weeks after receiving his Masters invitation, Moe split the snowbound scene and spent the rest of the winter playing golf around the southeastern U.S. with Irv Lightstone and Ken Jacobs, two hot-shot amateurs from Toronto. They got around in a beat-up 1952 Olds courtesy of Lightstone's father.

The trio used Brunswick, Georgia, as home base, paying $30 a month each to stay in a rooming house. Lightstone had met Paul Baumann, a well-known trick shot artist and the professional at the Brunswick Country Club, the previous winter and they hit it off. The trio played for free at Brunswick, and practiced their tails off, especially Moe, who kept up his habit of hitting at least 600 balls daily.

They travelled throughout the southeast to play in top tournaments such as the Azalea Open in Charleston, South Carolina, and the Mary Calder tournament in Savannah, Georgia. They regularly played against the best American amateurs of the day, including U.S. Walker Cup competitors such as Bill Campbell, Don Cherry and Billy Joe Patton, as well as U.S. Amateur champ Harvie Ward, and southern heroes "Dynamite" Billy Goodloe and Hobart Manley.

Moe's legend as Canada's most colourful golfer was spreading among elite amateurs and golf insiders in the United States; for his supersonic pace of play, his incredible ball-striking ability and his off-beat looks. "Moe made an impact on you when you saw him," Lightstone said. "It's not the kind of thing you forget. He looked like a wild cowboy."

Moe gave the game colour all right. In combinations that had never been seen before. His outfits were a cacophony of colourful chaos. He might wear orange pants with a yellow shirt, or a purple shirt with pink pants. He wasn't much on coordinating patterns either, throwing, say, a horizontal striped shirt with checkered pants. "He wore a montage of colours that had no relevancy to each other at all," Lightstone recalls. "Whatever he reached out for in the morning, he put on."

Like Weslock, Lightstone tried to get through to Moe that if he didn't want to be looked upon as a clown, he had to coordinate colours and patterns. Lightstone even drew up a colour chart for Moe. "It showed what went with what," said Lightstone, now the golf professional at Maple Downs in Toronto. "I had colours down the left side. It showed that if you wear a blue shirt, you can wear navy or black. You can't wear orange, or purple or pink." Moe abided by the chart but eventually it fell apart, as did Moe's resolve to coordinate.

The 1956 trip was Moe's second southern sojourn with Lightstone, who was mystified at how Moe financed these journeys on a pinsetter's wages. The mystery ended one afternoon at a drug store food counter in Jacksonville, Florida. "We were broke," Lightstone said. They couldn't call his father again for money. They were scratching their collective heads when Moe piped up, "I think I can get us some money." Lightstone recalled Moe saying, "Call information for West Palm Beach and ask for a fellow named Conn Smythe."

Lightstone was flabbergasted. "Hello Moe. What are you talking about?" Constantine Falkland Cary Smythe was the irascible owner of the Toronto Maple Leafs, the man largely responsible for building Maple Leaf Gardens, one of the great shrines of hockey. He wasn't the kind of guy Moe usually hung out with.

Moe convinced Lightstone to dial the number, and Moe got on the phone. "Hello, Mr. Smythe. It's Murray Norman. I'm down here in Florida with a couple of friends and playing some golf and we're a little short." Soon the lads piled into the car, made the long trip to the Breakers Club and Moe picked up enough money to see them through the rest of their winter tour.

"Connie kind of half-assed financed Moe," Lightstone said. "It was unknown to everyone that Connie was helping Moe. Connie loved a character and Moe was certainly a character."

Known as Major Smythe — he was awarded the Military Cross in the First World War and he was severely injured by shrapnel in the Second World War — and a tough son of a gun, he's remembered for his classic line: "If you can't beat 'em outside in the alley, you won't beat 'em inside on the ice." Smythe liked Moe's fighting spirit: he was colourful, stood up for himself, challenged authority — and he was a winner.

Moe caught Smythe's eye in 1954 at the Labatt Open at Scarboro Golf and Country Club in Toronto. While there were a number of U.S. pros in the field, many fans came to see the mercurial Moe Norman. Moe finished as the low amateur with a respectable 286. After he was presented with a silver tea service, Smythe walked up, introduced himself and engaged Moe in a little chat. Moe was very excited that someone like Smythe would be interested in his career. He says Smythe eventually enquired, "How much would it cost to play golf in Florida during the winter?"

"Oh, two or three thousand dollars."

At a tournament about two weeks later, Smythe caught Moe's attention and motioned to follow him behind a door. When he was sure they were out of sight, he gave Moe a cheque for $3,000. Moe's big blues went wide as dinner plates.

"Do I have to pay you back, Mr. Smythe? It'll probably take about 10 years."

"Oh no, it's a little present. Don't worry about it."

Moe was brazen about selling his prizes, but he kept this hush-hush. Not even Nick Weslock knew about benefactor Smythe. "Oh no, I had to keep that quiet because you're an amateur," says Moe. "Hoo boy, are you kidding? You had to be quiet. Sure."

Smythe financed Moe's winter excursions through Florida in both 1955 and '56. Moe says Smythe came around at the right time. Although he was the king of weekend invitationals in '54, he was becomingly increasingly frustrated with his inability to perform well in the Ontario and Canadian amateur. Moe felt he was losing his sharpness during the winter layoff, and he needed to play at least 10 months a year if he was to break through.

He says today that without Smythe he would have had no future in golf. "Everyone called him a jerk, but he was great to me. He just saw me — a little skinny kid and he liked the way I played. He knew I didn't have anything.

"I wouldn't have kept playing if it wasn't for him. He kept my future in golf going. Nobody in Kitchener would help me."

***

Moe got help from members at Rockway in Kitchener, but they couldn't afford to help fund a trip south. Then there were those fellows from London.

Not long after Moe won his Canadian Amateur title, Keith Kirkpatrick, Moe's escort during the America's Cup, fronted a group of wealthy London businessmen who pledged to sponsor Moe if he turned pro to play the PGA Tour. Despite Moe's eccentricities, they wanted to get the jump on other wheeler-dealers who might have the same idea. "We thought, this is the best golfer we've ever seen," recalls Kirkpatrick, now an insurance broker in Toronto. "He had the physical ability to be the best golfer in the world. I said, 'Let's put this kid on the tour, invest in him and make a buck.' It was business."

Kirkpatrick took Moe out to a nice steakhouse in Kitchener one fall night. "'Gee, I've never been in a place like this before,'" he remembers Moe saying.

"Moe, what do you think about $5,000, a car and expenses to help you out on the tour," Kirkpatrick asked. Moe was very excited, and said he'd get back to him the next week. Kirkpatrick didn't see Moe again until spring. When Kirkpatrick asked Moe what happened, he was told the offer wasn't good enough.

"Moe had absolutely no business acumen. He could do anything with a golf ball, but he couldn't harness it. I thought he was a friend, and I couldn't do it."

Moe says the size of the offer was not the reason for turning it down. "They wanted to change my life, the way I played the game, the way I acted. I could never have stayed in my comfort zone. They wanted me to take more time and stuff like that. I said, 'What do you want to change? My life or the way I play.' They said, 'Both.' I said 'Goodbye.'

"They wanted a different Moe Norman — the way they wanted me to be. So I went on my way and hitch-hiked back home."

While Moe says he never had an official sponsor, it was by choice. If he had to adhere to other people's standards or expectations, he'd have to suppress the qualities — and some of the quirks — that made him such a phenomenal player in the first place. Moe's confidence in his golf game and in the way he did things allowed him to play so well. He was a free spirit. To cage him would deny him the personal joys he got from golf. So while Moe was given the choice to accept a few offers, most weren't on his terms, and he was smart enough to say no.

***

As the Masters drew near, Moe was adamant about getting to Augusta National early so he could learn the course — and to simply play it as often as possible while he had the chance.

Irv Lightstone and Moe pulled into the front gates off Washington

Irv Lightstone and Moe pulled into the front gates off Washington Road on the Thursday before tournament week. Driving down Magnolia Lane toward the clubhouse, Moe's head swung from side to side, his eyes wild, his eyebrows arched up high in amazement. "It's a different world, a whole different world," he remembers thinking.

Moe found it hard to believe that he, the little red-headed kid — the pinsetter — was at Augusta National. He, Moe Norman, was going to play in the Masters...with the world's best...Ben Hogan, Sam Snead, Jimmy Demaret, Byron Nelson...with the legends of the game...Walter Hagen, Tommy Armour, Gene Sarazen, Francis Ouimet.

Moe was also proud to be among the world's top amateurs invited by the club, which treated them with a great deal of respect owing to founder Bobby Jones, the greatest amateur of all time and the only winner of golf's Grand Slam.

Augusta National is like the golf's Land of Oz, for there's no place even remotely similar on this green earth. Augusta National is so storied, brimming with atmosphere and tradition, and so green, it almost seems surreal. Clusters of azaleas explode with pinks and blues, giant sweet-smelling pines sway in the Georgia breeze, golf's glitterati mingle behind the white plantation clubhouse in an ambience of southern gentility.

Yes, the Masters has a warm and nostalgic feeling, but to those from the other side of the economic — or racial — side of the tracks, it's a haughty place. Enjoy the mint juleps, the thick bacon in the clubhouse, the feel of your spikes crunching the immaculate turf, but watch your step.

Moe's feet barely touched the ground all week. "I played 45 holes a day. I was running around there. You don't get this chance every day. I was the first guy off every day."

In Georgia's version of Oz, Moe must have appeared to many people as more munchkin than golfer. Augusta National members, the American kingpins of industry and finance, had played host to some characters, but none the likes of Moe Norman.

Stories about Moe at the Masters have become folklore. One tale has an outraged Clifford Roberts, the stern Masters chairman, nearly having an aneurysm when he spotted Moe carrying his own bag down the first fairway. Roberts is said to have chased after him, thundering that he had to take a caddie. Lightstone and Moe say it never happened. "It's nonsense," Moe says. "Not at the Masters. Are you kidding? Stories. Ahh!" he growls, waving his hand dismissively.

It's acknowledged that Moe certainly surprised Masters officials by carrying his own bag during the first practice round. Afterwards, Masters officials asked him to take a caddie, but Moe explained that he couldn't afford one. So they furnished him with a caddie for free. Rather than intimidate him, however, Moe says the Augusta National membership was nice to him and made him "feel at home."

During Masters week, there's plenty of receptions and functions for players, but Moe steered clear. When he wasn't playing golf, he hit balls. Then he'd fall exhausted into his bed in the clubhouse. All amateur participants in the Masters are invited to stay in a small clubhouse dormitory nicknamed the "Crow's Nest" because it's a converted attic. It had six beds, one bathroom and a kelly green carpet that matched the colour of the members' jackets.

Some of the other amateurs invited to the 1956 Masters included Ward, Campbell, Patton, San Francisco star Ken Venturi and British amateur champ Roger Wethered. Moe maintains they all stayed in hotels while he spent the week by himself in the Crow's Nest. "Those guys had money," Moe adds.

When Thursday arrived, Moe was nervous. Not about his golf game — of that he was supremely confident — but about playing in front of about 30,000 people and perhaps getting on TV. This would be only the second Masters to be televised. "I was just a little kid. It was my first time competing in a world famous event," says Moe, who was 26 at the time.

On the first tee, his heart was racing in his chest, a lump in his throat. He was in the featured pairings on opening day. Per the Masters custom, Moe, the Canadian amateur champion, was paired with Ward, the U.S. amateur champion. On top of that, they were to be followed by Byron Nelson and Cary Middlecoff, the defending Masters champion. He tried to enjoy the thrill of being announced on the first tee of the Masters, but he was scared. "I was shaking like a leaf."

"Please welcome to the tee, from Kitchener, Canada, the 1955 Amateur Champion of Canada" — thwock! — "uh, Murray Norman." The announcer hadn't even said his name and Moe's ball was gone. Dead straight, of course. And so was Moe, striding down the fairway.

Moe made a routine par on No. 1, but bogied No. 2 with a three-putt. "It wasn't bad teeing off, but the first couple of putts. Ooooohhhh," he said, his voice rising. "I couldn't even get the putter back."

Lightstone was following his buddy's every step. He said Moe "pured" the ball all day. "Moe hit the ball like God. Little Harvie Ward drove it longer than Moe, but Moe was in the middle of every fairway and every green." But it was black comedy on the greens. Here was Moe, a nervous Nellie on any green, who never even appeared to read his putts, a first-timer to the Masters, just getting up and popping the ball at Augusta National where the greens are like roller coasters made of marble. Moe had six three-putts, but still managed to shoot 75. He was fourth-best amateur and very much in contention.

Friday's round with Bob Rosburg was another horror show on the greens and he staggered in with a 78. After two rounds, he was eighteen shots back of leader Ken Venturi. In 1956, there was no cut at the Masters, so Moe set off for the range.

Moe caught the eye of legend Sam Snead who, as John Updike once wrote, swaggered around the range "like the sheriff of golf county." Partly out of curiosity — he had also heard stories about Moe — and kind-heartedness, the Virginian star sauntered over. He stood behind Moe for a few minutes, feet splayed apart, arms folded across his chest. When Moe briefly came up for air, he looked back and to his amazement, there was Slammin' Sammy Snead — looking at him!

Snead extended a meaty hand, introduced himself and asked: "What did you do to get here?"

"I'm the amateur champion of Canada."

"That's great. I'd like to give you a little tip if you don't mind."

"Not at all, coming from you."

"You're coming down way too steep on the ball with your long irons. The secret to hitting a long iron is to hit them like fairway woods. Don't hit down or try to force it. Hit it like a nice three wood. Sweep it."

Snead watched Moe for a little while, nodding his approval as Norman hit three-iron ropes to a distant flag. Snead finally bid goodbye. From a distance, Lightstone watched Snead talk to Moe and when the lesson was over, Lightstone left the range.

Determined to master Snead's tip, Moe hit ball after ball after ball. Eventually, the other players started to drift away, going to dinner with friends and family. As the sun went orange as it descended in the sky, Moe was finally alone on the range. Still, he hit ball after ball after ball. His hands were stinging. It was getting dark and more difficult to see the balls.

Lightstone said he had followed Jack Burke for his entire round — about four hours — and was amazed to see that Moe was still practising in the twilight. "Moe, what the hell are you doing?"

"I got it! I got it!" Moe blurted as he went on to explain Snead's tip.

"Moe, look at your hands!" They looked raw, and must have hurt.

Lightstone was flabbergasted at Moe's overzealous reaction to Snead's tip. Moe had been hitting the ball beautifully. He didn't need any help. Snead had a classic swing. Moe's swing likely looked wrong to him so he tried to help. Unfortunately, Moe lost perspective and confidence in his own unique swing. "He hadn't hit the ball too bad that day," Lightstone lamented. "But this quest for excellence he had. Golf was all he had in his life, nothing else.

"There was no balance to what Moe did. In those days, Moe did things that were totally irrational. If Moe were properly managed from that point or the year before, I believe Moe could have been one of the top-five players in the world."

Moe knew he'd overdone it. No wonder, Moe figures he hit 800 balls in four hours. He usually spaced out his practice. His hands ached and throbbed. He went up to the Crow's Nest and soaked his hands in hot water and went to bed.

The next morning, his hands were a mess — blistered, red and raw. They looked like "hamburger," Lightstone said. His left thumb was split open. For the third round, he was paired with veteran Vic Ghezzi, the 1941 PGA champion, but Moe was not his chatty self. He could barely hold a club. At impact, the pain in his hands was excruciating. Lightstone said it was obvious that Moe was having trouble. "On one or two occasions, the club almost flew out of his hands."

Moe hurt mentally too. As he botched hole after hole, fighting the pain and his inability to concentrate, Moe got mad at himself for going overboard by hitting so many balls and ruining his dream trip to the Masters.

After putting out on the ninth hole, he headed not to the 10th tee, but to the locker room. Lightstone stopped him. "Where the hell are you going?"

"I can't go on," Moe said, his face contorted in anguish.

"Moe, this is the Masters. You have to continue."

"Irv, I can't hold the club."

Lightstone looked at Moe's hands. "They were a bucket of crap. I was embarrassed. He could have acquitted himself very well on that course. It was just a tragedy to watch this thing unfold."

Moe told an Augusta member working as a marshall that he was withdrawing. Moe says he didn't get a hostile reaction or a lecture, the fellow just listened and bid him farewell. Lightstone walked over the 10th tee to tell Ghezzi that Moe had withdrawn, explaining in a halting voice that his friend couldn't hold on to a club because of the pain from hitting too many practice balls. Lightstone recalls the late Ghezzi shook his head and said, "This is the Masters. You play on one leg if you have to."

Neither Ghezzi nor Masters officials were pleased. It meant the twosome behind had to join Ghezzi. Roberts didn't like anything out of the ordinary that could gum up the smooth running of the tournament or cause even a ripple of controversy. Lightstone feared this might cause some trouble for Moe down the road. Moe cleaned out his locker and then he and Lightstone drove away in silence, heading home to Canada.

Today, Moe compares receiving a tip from Sam Snead to a young Canadian hockey player getting a tip from Wayne Gretzky. "You're only a kid and you get a tip from the best in the world. Oh, you're excited. Like a dummy, I went and hit a lot of balls."

Canadian golf officials shook their heads with told-you-so-smugness. They were afraid misfit Moe Norman might embarrass them at the world's spring festival of golf, and indeed they believed he had. Moe was angry at himself for fulfilling their expectations. But Moe didn't mope about Augusta. There was this little matter of proving to the stuffed shirts that he was a true champion.

Many members of the golf establishment and press believed Moe fluked his way to his Canadian Amateur title. Hilles Pickens grudgingly ranked him that spring as the No. 1 amateur in the country in Canadian Sport Monthly "in deference" to his national championship, saying Lyle Crawford was still "a mite better."

There was much work to be done.

Chapter Eleven

The Kind of Golf Dreams Are Made of

Moe was a great challenge for sportswriters and broadcasters. It was easy to write about him — a writer doesn't get much better material to work with than Moe. No, the challenge was talking to him. After he won a tournament, reporters would naturally want some quotes for their stories, but Moe would only talk to those scribes he knew and liked. This group comprised only a handful of reporters, including the Telegram's Bob Hesketh, Toronto Star's Milt Dunnell and The Globe and Mail's Jack Marks.

"If he didn't have a relationship with a reporter, Moe would just turn around and walk away," Irv Lightstone said.

It made it difficult to write the story, but even so, most reporters were sympathetic and treated him with respect. A few weren't so charitable, namely the Toronto Star's Gordon Campbell who called him the "Clown Prince of Golf," a label Moe detested.

Some reporters identified with Moe. Like many of them, he was not a member of the country club set. They admired his determination to succeed in an expensive game despite his humble background and excruciating shyness. "He is one of the few golfers who closes up like a clam in the presence of the press," Pickens wrote.

It wasn't just shyness. Moe was very sensitive to the least bit of criticism of his golf game in print — especially comments that he played too fast and carelessly. He could be very gruff and even rude when asked what he thought was a dumb question. "To learn about Norman, the last person to approach is Moe," wrote Jim Vipond, sports editor of the Toronto Globe and Mail in 1955. "He shuns publicity."

Moe also questioned why he should spend time with a reporter. The reporter got paid for the story. He didn't. And the more publicity he got, the more reporters and fans would want to talk to him, which he most certainly didn't want.

As national amateur champion, Moe was now more in demand for interviews, and his confrontations with pesky reporters increased. Like Campbell, those writers who weren't inside Moe's circle became more sarcastic, playing up his eccentricities and clown image.

It was only after being introduced as a "buddy" by Nick Weslock that Pickens was able to get into Moe's inner circle. "After that introduction, nothing was too good! Crashing the portals of Moe's friendship means something," he wrote. As an example, he described a casual game he played at Banff Springs Golf Club with Moe and Weslock in late 1955. On the 15th hole, Pickens sliced his tee shot into the "raging torrent" of the Bow River. "There were the usual muttered comments about having lost a brand new ball. As we marched up the fairway, 160 yards later, someone addressed Norman. Looking about we found no Moe! There, far out in fast, icy water was Canada's top golfer, pants up to his thighs, searching for the ball. Panic overtook us!"

They were frightened Moe might drown. "Don't worry," Weslock consoled, "he's all right. He'll find your ball and probably come up with a pair of salmon, a handful of nuggets — riding a bicycle." Weslock had seen this act many times; he knew Moe's prowess as an "ardent ball hawk." Moe found the ball in the roaring river and leaped nimbly through the rocks and foam, and back to shore safely.

Moe was in his mid 20s, but he was still very much like a kid — once he got an idea in his head, no matter how reckless or potentially grave the consequences, he plunged right in. He didn't bother to analyze or question his actions; he was very much an innocent. That's one reason he liked kids so much. They seemed untainted too. The adult world had yet to take away their openness, their delight in simple pleasures. Moe felt he could trust kids, while reporters and other adults patronized or treated him with contempt.

Kids were straight arrows. Like him. His best pals at Rockway were young teens such as Gary Cowan, Gus Maue and Ernie Hauser. Some people thought it was odd that the national amateur champion ran around with a bunch of kids at a burned-out municipal course.

Hauser was 14 at the time, a three handicap. He played in many tournaments with Moe, and accepted many of Moe's prizes for him. "He related to the younger kids. Quite often people said he was an oddball, but he was excellent with us. Moe is extremely loyal. He had a wonderful way with all the kids no matter how good you were.

"Even when he was already a big star, he was the type of guy that played with kids. He'd come down and watch you, follow you around in juvenile tournaments. He'd say, 'C'mon kid, keep it going.'"

The kids looked upon Moe as a big brother, volunteering to caddie for him in tournaments and shag balls for him. It was pretty easy. They could hold Moe's shag bag open and pivot on one foot and catch his shots. Often, they didn't have to move a muscle — he'd knock shots right in the bag.

Hauser said that when a group of kids played with Moe, they each might play a couple of balls. "And at the end of nine holes, he could tell every kid what he scored on each ball. 'You had a 39 with the Royal, a 40 with the Dot and a 38 with the Spalding.' It was incredible. He has an incredible mind."

Moe's confidence was also incredible. "You'd see him in the parking lot at Rockway before a game pulling clubs out of his bag. I'd say 'Moe, what are you doing?'

"'The wind is blowing down No. 6 so I don't need my five-iron and up 10, so I don't need a four-iron,'" Moe said.

"He knew the clubs he'd hit on every hole so it wouldn't weigh the bag down. I thought, 'No one's that good!'"

Hauser said he probably played 1,000 games with his pal, and Moe shot 62 or 64 "lots of times." Hauser was there when Moe shot the course record of 60 at the Galt Golf Club near Cambridge. "Moe said he'd drive the last green (a par-four) and sink the putt for a two. And he did. You expected Moe to do it. Every time he hit the ball perfect."

Moe was likely playing the best golf of his life in 1956. During the year, he accomplished the following:

- Set nine course records;
- Shot 61 four times;
- Won 17 out of 26 amateur tournaments (a combined 52 under-par);
- Won six TVs (all of which were sold).

Moe said he won so many watches that, one day for a laugh, he strapped 13 to his arms and walked into a pool hall in Kitchener. "Some kid in the hall phoned the cops, figuring I robbed a store," he told the

Kitchener-Waterloo Record. "I knew a lot of the cops at the time so when they came, they saw it was me and just laughed and walked out."

Now that he was winning amateur tournaments with such ease, the obvious question that summer was why he didn't turn pro. Moe told the Telegram's Hesketh that pros were expected to make speeches, but he was too shy and a dud on radio and TV. "If this is a requisite of being a professional golfer, it will forever escape Norman, who speaks his words like he plays his shots — in a tumbling hurry to have them done with."

Moe was also psyching himself to defend his title at the Canadian Amateur in New Brunswick in August. "During the year he developed something like a mania to prove that his 1955 Calgary win was no accident," Pickens wrote.

The Edmundston Golf Club measured about 6,600 yards, but a torrential rainstorm on the second day and shaggy fairways made the course into a bruiser more like 7,200 yards. Players received no roll on their drives, leaving long irons into many of the par-fours and taking some par-fives out of reach in two. In contrast, several greens were very fast.

As the championship was being played in Atlantic Canada, a number of fine American players from the eastern seaboard entered. Twenty-four U.S. players made it into the field of 64, including Doug Sanders, who had just won the Canadian Open as an amateur, John Miles of New York state and former Walker Cup star Jim McHale of Pennsylvania.

Moe got off to a great start, shooting 69-74 in the Willingdon Cup to win low medalist and lead Ontario to victory. Moe cruised through the championship playdowns, until he got to Ohio's Ed Meister in the third round. They went to the final hole deadlocked. The burly Meister got his routine par, but Moe left himself a slippery four-footer, downhill with a sidehill roll. "What a position for the champion to get the lump and freeze himself out of the picture," Pickens wrote. "Anyone could sense it. But while the sensitive, mere mortals were assessing all this, the unruffled Mr. Norman had gotten into his ding-toed stance and plopped the ball, smack into the centre of the cup."

They halved the 19th. On the 20th, Moe nailed a 12-footer for birdie to dispatch Meister. "Moe just shrugged and strolled off the green straight to the practice tee where he hit 200 balls for the edification of the curious who inevitably follow him."

In the quarter finals, Moe clearly enjoyed himself. At the 11th hole, already five down, Victoria's Bob Fleming just waved with resignation when Moe brought out an eight-inch tee to amuse the gallery before winning 3 and 2. In his match with the colourful Sanders, Jerry Magee got up and down on the 18th to advance.

Miles, a strapping six-foot four-inch amateur star, played a masterful morning round against Moe in the semi-final, shooting an even par 73 on the very difficult Edmundston course. "I was even par in the morning round, but I was eight holes down!" Miles said. "Moe carded nine pars and nine birdies."

Moe had fired a 64 at him. That 64 — all holed — was a masterpiece that stands as one of the most remarkable rounds in the history of the Canadian Amateur. It eclipsed the course record set by Sanders two days earlier by four strokes.

"That was probably the best round I ever shot in my life," Moe told reporters. "No one will ever touch that 64. (By the way, no one has.) What really got to him was when I gave him four putts over five feet."

Miles didn't give up. In fact, he improved and played beautifully. But Pickens wrote "he could never pierce that lead enough, and in the end Norman just trampled him down with a steady seige of the kind of golf that dreams are made of."

Moe finished him off 8 and 7 — 13-under par for 29 holes.

When Magee similarly crushed Art Butler of New Hampshire 7 and 6, it set up a rematch with Moe for the first time since their Ontario Amateur tussle a year earlier. It certainly wouldn't be a bitter duel. The pair travelled, roomed and ate breakfast together throughout the championship.

If they ate as fast as they played, they must have had indigestion for they were the two fastest players in the country. In today's parlance, they gripped it and ripped it. Before the match, RCGA president Jim Anglin tried to explain to the gallery that the finalists liked to play fast and they might "catch pieces of the game" by cutting across various points of the course.

The pair rocketed through the first nine holes in 58 minutes, and completed the morning round in two hours, two minutes. It may very well stand as the quickest 18 holes in the history of a national golf championship. They repeatedly left the gallery of about 1,500 fans and RCGA officials exhausted in their wake.

What's more astounding, they also played brilliant golf at that quick pace. Moe was three-under-par after the morning round and one up, while Magee was one-under. "The better Moe played, the faster he played," Magee said. "And he was playing probably the best golf of his life."

One popular Moe story has it that in an attempt to slow them down, the RCGA parked a Jeep in front of the tees so they couldn't drive until the crowd caught up. Magee said it didn't happen. No reports of the match mention Jeeps either.

Moe cruised through the afternoon round with three birdies, an eagle and a bogey to close out Magee at 5 and 4 and win his second consecutive Canadian Amateur Championship. When he saw Pickens, he glared and proclaimed, "Well, now they can't say Calgary was a fluke, can they?"

Indeed not. Moe was 31-under par for the week. Over 64 holes of the semi-final and final he was 22-under, with only one bogey. It was a phenomenal display of speed, stamina and ability.

Obviously not a big fan of the RCGA — among other things he felt they underplayed his previous championship — Moe kept the blue-jackets cooling their heels, delaying the presentation of the Earl Grey trophy while he practiced putting and talked with friends. He stuck around to accept the trophy this time, but didn't say a word. Perhaps that's because his Rockway buddy Gary Cowan, a string bean with a buzzcut, was there. He won the Canadian Junior title, which was held simultaneously.

Asked by reporters whether he would now consider turning pro, Moe said he'd take the plunge as soon as he found a sponsor. The American contingent of players thought Moe could have beaten anyone in the world that week. "That boy is a real star," said Jack Penrose, a competitor and Sanders' benefactor.

Moe had always been less enamoured with the glory of winning than what the victory said about his ability and place in the world of amateur golf. With two consecutive titles under his belt, and the convincing way he had captured his second, Moe proved beyond a doubt that he was the country's best amateur, and arguably the best amateur in the world at that moment.

The feeling of pride and satisfaction after Edmundston must have been wonderful, a memory to cherish for a lifetime. Sadly, it was not. Moe's recollection of the reception accorded his second championship is tinged with bitterness. "I flew back to Toronto with Jerry Magee, the guy I'd beaten," Moe told writer Roy MacGregor in 1975. "No one was there to meet me. No one. But people came out to meet Jerry. His parents were there with the keys to a brand new Oldsmobile."

When asked about the story, Moe repeated it, adding that Magee's parents said "'Here's your present son!'" For coming second. I came first. I could have cried."

MacGregor's story quoted Moe further: "It was raining out, raining hard. I had to go up to Jerry and ask him if I could hitch a ride with him out to Highway 7 so that I could hitchhike back to Kitchener. Jerry took me out in the new car and dumped me off. I was standing there in the rain, standing there with my clubs and this great big trophy, and Jerry drives off in this new Olds. I was the champion. He was the runner-up."

Asked for his recollection of that fateful day, Magee said, "That's not right at all." He remembers driving back from Edmundston with Moe, a male friend and his daughter. Magee got off in Toronto and Moe continued on in the car to Kitchener.

Magee believes it's "a concocted story," not necessarily by MacGregor, and that Moe has just repeated it. Or perhaps Moe's memory of the event has become twisted somehow. It's something like the story of the bus ride to the Masters. Moe would never tell a lie. It's against his nature. It's been said that Moe is a man without guile, and everyone who knows him well agrees. Still, for a person with a photographic memory, it's puzzling why Moe's recollection of certain events differ greatly from what others recall.

"So many people invented stories," Magee said. "I don't know if it's meant to be sympathetic to Moe. It just makes Moe out to be more of an eccentric."

There wasn't much celebration of Moe's second title. Why should there be? Following his 1955 Canadian Amateur victory, Moe was guest of honour at the Kitchener Civic Banquet for outstanding athletes. The mayor invited Charlie Watson, past RCGA president to make the presentation speech and give Moe a new golf bag from the citizens of Kitchener. Moe didn't show up.

In 1956, it was assumed Moe didn't want another major production. There's the contradiction with Moe: he wants his achievements and expertise recognized — by the press, golfers, fans and administrators — but not at the expense of his privacy and sense of security.

Moe has confided to close friends that the poor reception that followed his second amateur title changed him. "Then I really knew what people were like. They expect you to win. You don't win the championship of your country every day. I walked away with it. I thought they'd make a big deal. That really pissed me off," he said incredulously, his voice rising.

Before the season was through, Moe had one more astounding performance to give, and Cowan would play a starring role. Cowan and

Moe weren't exactly buddies, but they liked each other and had a friendly rivalry at Rockway. They were the pride of the club. With Moe the Canadian Amateur champion and Cowan the national junior champ, it was the first time in Canadian golf history that one club had won both individual titles.

It was considered a showdown between the pair when the Ontario Golf Association Fall Tournament was held at their home club. Cowan was on fire, shooting a sizzling 65. Moe shot 61. The headline in The Kitchener Record said it all: "Cowan shoots 65, but still not enough as Norman 61."

As winter approached, there was plenty of excitement about the upcoming America's Cup matches in Mexico. Many people still talked about Moe's hole-in-one that nearly propelled Canada to an upset victory two years earlier. With the momentum from that event and with Moe playing so well, perhaps Canada could pull it off in Mexico.

Meanwhile, Canadian Sport Monthly's September issue came out sporting Moe on the cover. Pickens wrote glowingly of Moe's victory: "He has tremendous strength, no bad habits, gets lots of rest, and with a great yen for spaghetti and meatballs he shows an incessant desire for play and practice. Put all this together and you have Moe Norman — a player who just might be greater than anyone if thrown in with the lions who prowl the pro circuit."

Moe was going to get his chance soon enough to prove Pickens — and many others — right or wrong. Whether he liked it or not.

Chapter Twelve
Moe's Fall

Fall in Ontario is usually lovely for golf. The air is crisp, the changing leaves are teeming with colour and the grass greens up again after the dog days of August. As for Moe, it was the autumn of his amateur career, and the change would not be pretty.

Canadians were excited about the prospect of Moe going down and showing the American golf establishment a thing or two in the U.S. Amateur in Lake Forest, Illinois, in September. Moe's victory in New Brunswick automatically qualified him for the U.S. Amateur, but he couldn't play because of one little detail. He forgot to file his entry on time. Some of Moe's friends wondered if this was an intentional oversight.

It was up to another Canadian to take it to the Americans on their own turf in 1956. Marlene Stewart set off nationalist fireworks when she won the Women's U.S. Amateur at Meridian Hills Country Club in Charlotte, North Carolina, by defeating JoAnne Gunderson (better known now as JoAnne Carner, the popular LPGA Hall of Famer). That stirring triumph followed Stewart's sixth straight Canadian women's amateur title and British championship in 1953. Marlene Stewart Streit, as she became known after her marriage, was the kind of stellar amateur the country club set were used to. She was poised, pleasant, wore the right clothes and said the right things.

"People were looking for heroes," Irv Lightstone said. "Marlene fit the bill. She was a pretty, freckle-faced girl who blended in."

Much was made of her victory, but Moe feels the RCGA underplayed his championships — that they were embarrassed by him. Nick Weslock seconded that view. "They didn't play it up. They accepted it and Moe went into the record books. There was no extra publicity."

"They patronized him because of his talent," Lightstone said, "but they would have preferred to have someone else in there. The governors (of the RCGA) were extremely stiff people, not like the people today. It was a different era. Gerry Kesselring blended in with time, so did Jerry Magee. Moe wasn't of that ilk."

In October, Moe was excited because the America's Cup was approaching and it was being held in Mexico. Moe never dreamed he'd go to such an exotic place. Moe had been fitted with the team slacks, shirts and jacket, inoculated for small pox and given his plane tickets. Moe would also get his chance to take on golden-haired Harvie Ward, who had just won his second consecutive U.S. Amateur championship in Illinois. Many golf insiders shared Moe's assessment of their upcoming match: "It would decide the top amateur in the world."

As the America's Cup approached, unsettling rumours were filtering around that the RCGA was checking with some clubs in Ontario for evidence Moe had been breaching the rules of amateur status. In particular, that he had been accepting appearance money from clubs to play in tournaments and help with travel expenses.

It was common knowledge that Moe had been selling his prizes for years — he all but hung a shingle in parking lots. There was speculation Moe's comments in Edmundston that he was considering turning pro didn't sit well with the RCGA and this gave them some incentive to go after him. It also became known that the Ontario Golf Association had investigated Moe a year earlier, but took no action except to warn him not to give trick-shot exhibitions at tournaments.

At the time, Moe's father Irwin couldn't see what all the fuss was about. "A man would have to be crazy to keep 15 radios, 30 or 40 suitcases, a dozen clocks or razors. Of course, Moe sold them. We're not running a warehouse."

As for Moe's trick-shot exhibitions, Irwin asked, "If you give freely of your time to entertain people and someone sticks a couple of bucks in your pocket, are you going to refuse? He never charged, but sometimes people gave him a few dollars to help cover expenses. Is that a crime?"

To the RCGA it was. Accepting expense money was a big no-no in amateur golf. With the exception of team events, the rules prohibited an amateur from accepting expenses from anyone but a family member or legal guardian. The RCGA's rules, which were almost identical to the USGA's, defined an amateur this way: "An amateur golfer is one who plays the game as a non-remunerative or non-profit making sport."

Moe admitted accepting "loans" of $390, but he repaid most of the money, he had the cancelled cheques to prove it and he planned to repay them all. "I told people who were after me (to play in their events) that I couldn't afford to go to their places," he told the Gazette in Montreal. "Sure I took dough to get to places and back, but I paid them back after I knew it was dangerous. I want to stay playing amateur golf."

He said many other amateurs were accepting expense money for travel. "Sure, just about everybody got something in Sudbury (in Northern Ontario). It's too long a trip for the guys to go on their own." A newspaper report also said the Canadian government had demanded, in writing, that Moe pay taxes on money he had earned passing the hat at clinics, and that he had gone around showing the letter to people.

Jim Anglin, who was president of the RCGA and captain of Canada's America's Cup team, tried to contact Moe by telephone for an explanation. But Moe never speaks on the phone except to close friends and to people he trusts. As an authority figure, Anglin had no chance of contacting Moe by telephone.

As the Mexican trip drew near, the pressure on Anglin was immense. Here, after all, was Canada's national champion for the past two years and the key man if Canada hoped to beat Ward and the Americans. But many in the RCGA were weary of Moe's antics. Despite his popularity with galleries, Moe was viewed as a blight on amateur golf — a maverick with little respect for tradition, the dignity of the game, and worse, for authority. The flap over expense money provided an opportunity to finally boot the troublemaker out.

"Moe was a little difficult. Jim Anglin was a square guy, but you could only go so far," said Bruce Forbes, director of the Ontario Golf Association at the time.

Anglin is now in his 80s and in poor health. Anglin says he can't remember Moe Norman. Unfortunately, former RCGA presidents from that era, Charlie Watson, Bill Hamilton and Robbie Robinson, have all passed away. One U.S. golf official said at the time: "Poor Jimmy, I don't relish a decision like that with a reigning champion."

Anglin couldn't get in touch with Moe while stories circulated he was hiding out in union halls playing cards. Four days before the matches, Anglin refuted the axiom you can't hit what you can't see. He announced in a statement Oct. 19 that Moe was suspended from the team because of "evidence concerning activities ... by Norman of a nature to cast serious doubt upon Moe's status as an amateur golfer." Anglin said the RCGA governors concurred unanimously with his decision.

"I have been trying all day to see Moe and ask him about some of the facts that have been brought to my attention," Anglin told The Toronto Telegram. "I have telephoned repeatedly to his home in Kitchener and wired him offering to go to Kitchener to see him at any time. Moe has not replied in any way."

Doug Bajus of Vancouver took Moe's place. Ward won all his matches and the U.S. romped to victory. Canada was embarrassed to finish third. It was the only time in the nine America's Cup matches ever held that Mexico beat Canada.

"I took him off, not because he took the money, but because he hadn't communicated," Anglin said later. "We had some serious evidence, which we never have disclosed, regarding Moe's amateur status. What else could I do but recommend that he be dropped from the team until the RCGA had a chance to consider the complaints against him."

Therefore, there was never official confirmation that the RCGA was aware Leafs owner Conn Smythe was funding Moe. It's likely that officials were aware because many governors were wealthy businessmen who travelled in the same circles. But no newspaper reports of the day mentioned Smythe, and Moe's saga was big news. By withholding the report, the RCGA also left the lingering impression that Moe was being penalized solely for selling his prizes.

Golf fans across the country were outraged by the suspension. It was common knowledge that other amateurs had been taking expense money for years under a hypocritical veil of secrecy, but many felt Moe was picked on because he was different, unpolished and poor.

"Superficially, Norman's bounce by the RCGA appears to be the act of a haughty, high-handed directorate against a golfer whose every act is symbolic of the masses which were born on the wrong side of the tracks," wrote Telegram columnist Bob Hesketh. "That he should be singled out in all the teeming incidents of conniving that are perpetrated under the embroidery of amateurism is unfortunate. That he should refrain from speaking out on his own behalf is equalling distressing."

Moe still gets angry when he thinks back to this mess. Not surprisingly, he has a different version of the events. He says Anglin never tried to get a hold of him and he learned about the suspension in the newspaper, much to his and the family's embarrassment. "It was the childish way they did it. They didn't even bother to take me aside. The public knew it before I did. I wake up the next morning and there's nine reporters on my lawn. I said, 'Mom what the hell is going on?' They knew it before I did." Moe avoided the media horde by ducking out his back door and jumping backyard fences.

Moe denies ever receiving a letter from Revenue Canada. Yes, he sold his prizes, that was no state secret, and yes, he admitted he took some expense money, but Moe says that's not why the RCGA suspended him. "It's because I was winning everything. I was making a mockery of it. They said I was hurting amateur golf. I was making the rest look like dubs. My bad rounds were better than everyone else's good rounds. When I shot 63 at Brantford, the next guy was 72. I had it won before I even went.

"Others should have been kicked out. Why just me? They had to pick on someone to scare everyone else. You mean to tell me I'm the only one to sell prizes in 50 years in Canada. If you kissed their ass you were treated all right."

Nick Weslock said many amateurs took expense money and regularly sold their prizes, and he asserts it still goes on. "I sold mine too," he said. "What the hell do I want with three or four toasters or radios. Others should have been kicked out too, not just Moe. They singled him out."

Doug Sanders, who won the 1956 Canadian Open as an amateur, confesses he wasn't a lily-white amateur himself. "Back in those days amateurs were out there playing. They didn't have many jobs. You had to get a few dollars so you sold the odd trophy or prize. You didn't feel like you did anything bad, because it was yours. It was against the rules, but sometimes when looking at the rules you've got to decide whether there was any intent to cheat.

"Are you really out there playing for money, or are you just trying to get to the next tournament. You weren't members of a country club where your dad sends you in a limousine, and you signed for everything. Moe and I didn't even know what a credit card looked like. Wouldn't know how to use one if we had it anyway."

And it wasn't exactly confidential information either that Harvie Ward's expenses were being picked up by Ed Lowery, a wealthy San Francisco auto dealer who employed young amateur Ken Venturi as a car salesman. The prevailing opinion was the USGA was hesitant to take action against Ward because he was everything it wanted in a national champion — dashing, good-looking and charming.

In contrast, Moe felt picked on and laughed at. After years of taking on the high and mighty men of the RCGA, he came out the loser.

Distraught, his life shattered, his future clouded, Moe was beaten. "I was flat broke, didn't have two nickels to my name. And I couldn't do the thing I love in life, play golf. I did nothing wrong and yet I got kicked out of doing what I loved. Holy geez, how nice, by your own country. And then they say 'Love thy neighbour.' Hell, it's 'Screw thy neighbour.'"

By late October the Ontario golf season was over. Moe spent November and December working at The Strand and pondering his next move. He had to make a decision: take on the RCGA and face the music over the investigation or turn professional and forget the whole business.

This was scary ground for Moe. For a fellow riddled with anxiety and an inferiority complex, the choices were terrifying. How does a "little kid" take on the lords of the RCGA? He'd always told himself he couldn't give speeches or dress well enough to be a pro, nor could he afford the travelling expenses. He certainly didn't want to be a club pro, giving lessons to hackers and kowtowing to rich members. If he didn't turn pro — what? Spend his life working in factories or as a labourer?

Moe lived according to routine to feel safe and comfortable. He feared change and uncertainty. Yet, this time he couldn't run away, disappear or scream and shout. He was cornered. There were no escape routes.

***

In the spring of 1957, Ward admitted to receiving a loan of $11,000 for expenses from Lowery. He repaid the loan. Although Moe's offence was for far less money, quick action was taken against him while the USGA dithered about Ward. Eventually Ward was suspended for the duration of the season, but returned to amateur competition in 1958 and played for the U.S. Walker Cup team in 1959.

Chapter Thirteen
Misadventures in Limbo

The popular story that still goes around today is that the RCGA stripped Moe of his amateur status. Even Nick Weslock says the RCGA "professionalized" him. But Anglin's action was limited to suspending him from the America's Cup team. The suspension made it quite apparent, however, that Moe was no longer welcome to compete in provincial and national tournaments.

Through the winter, Moe also heard rumblings that unless he turned pro by February, the RCGA was going to force him by declaring him ineligible to compete as an amateur. Moreover, his two national titles might be taken from him. While he hated the idea of giving in to the RCGA, the notion of having to answer questions and argue with the bigwigs was just too terrifying. It was no contest.

In the first week of 1957, Moe announced he was turning professional. Moe informed Anglin about his plans in a letter: "Coming from a family of modest means, I naturally found it necessary at times to find means of paying my expenses in order to play competitive golf. Possibly this has been a mistake, and now that it has been brought to my attention I realized the seriousness of my habit. I am writing my official notice that I would like to surrender my amateur status and become classified as a professional golfer."

It marked a sad end to one of the most brilliant amateur careers of the post-war period. Nevertheless, the RCGA got what it wanted without more ugliness and bad publicity, and Moe avoided a confrontation. It was also Moe's decision to jump into the pro ranks, although it was obvious to all concerned that the RCGA had a hand on his back. Anglin later looked back on the whole affair and said, "My opinion is that he was fairly treated."

Moe found turning pro wasn't so simple. Once again, he had leaped before looking. He had officially declared himself a pro, but he wasn't an official pro. To play in most pro events in Canada or the United States you had to be a card-carrying member of the Canadian Professional Golfers' Association or the U.S. PGA. Getting a card wasn't like applying for American Express either. Moe needed a B1 assistant card, but that required working at a recognized club under a full-time professional with a Class A card. (After five years of apprenticeship and meeting specific criteria, B1s graduated to Class A status.)

That wasn't Moe's idea of a good time. "They won't let me turn pro without me going to work as an assistant for five years," he told Kitchener reporter Jock Carrol. "Five years at 40 or 50 bucks a week? You know what the assistant does? Opens the shop at 7 o'clock. Cleans clubs. Gets to play maybe once a week. On Mondays."

Head professionals weren't lining up at his door looking to engage his services either. No one could imagine Moe in the pro shop suggesting Dr. Smith's wife Winnie take the blue cardigan instead of the red one. Moe was not welcomed with open arms by many members of the professional golf fraternity. They were concerned someone perceived as a dishevelled golf clown might lower their standards in the public's eye.

Some worried Moe's declaration that he was turning professional would give the public the unsavory impression that it was a natural career move for disgraced amateurs. "A lot of people might think because the RCGA bans you, that you automatically become a golf professional," says Al Balding, winner of the 1955 PGA Mayfair Open in Florida.

In those days, most golf professionals fussed over their "deportment" like a boot-camp sergeant. They didn't hang around in open-necked golf shirts like today, but sported polished shoes, crisply ironed shirts and ties. "We had high standards," said Bert Turcotte, a veteran Class A pro for more than 50 years around Toronto. "We had flair, sort of a discipline about our appearance. You were setting an example for the amateur. We'd wear a jacket and tie after a pro-am. What do you do with Moe?"

Without a CPGA or U.S. PGA card, Moe couldn't play in their events. If invited, he could still play in the "open" tournaments around, but there were few of them. Having stripped himself of his amateur status, Canada's most colourful golfer was in limbo. "I'm not a pro. I'm not an amateur. What the hell am I?"

All Moe had was a name and a reputation. He received plenty of support from people who vented outrage at the bluebloods of golf for unfairly treating a golfer born outside the gentry. But sympathy didn't put money in his pockets, or make his future any less cloudy. Besides, even as a pro, there were few events to play in the late 1950s around Ontario and the Northern U.S. that would allow a fellow to make a living purely as a touring pro. Most players worked as club pros, and occasionally ventured out to play tournaments. Only the world's best players could get by on tournament golf alone.

Kitchener reporter Jock Carrol asked Moe what he was going to do. "I dunno. I can't play. I can't sleep. They kick you out of amateur. They kick you out of pro. After all I've done for the game. I added a lot of colour. Pop bottles. Four-inch tees. Eight-inch tees. What's a working man gonna do?

"Don't know what I'll do. It's like all your life is gone. All I've ever done is play golf. I have no training for another job. Maybe I'll go back to working in a brewery."

***

Early in the new year, he headed south and stayed with his friends in Brunswick, Georgia, and around Florida. He practiced daily and played a lot of casual golf, but few tournaments. To finance his southern sojourns, Moe did his share of hustling, or what some called bootleg golf, which was pretty common in the 1950s and '60s. Moe was pretty good at it; he was the master of the poker face, the brazen bluff, the white lie and he wasn't a bad actor.

In any case, Moe didn't exactly strike anyone as a scratch golfer. He certainly didn't look, act or talk like one. He wasn't a dapper gent with a pale left hand and a bronzed right. No, Moe was perfect for setting up pigeons. He wasn't well-known in the southern states so he lined 'em up and shot 'em down.

"There's lots of guys in Florida who want to bet," he told Carrol. "Lots of times I show up in a locker room with my old blue jeans on and shout 'Anyone for $10 a hole?' They look at me and think 'Who is this big-mouth little guy?' So, OK, they give me a game. When they ask what I shoot I say 76-77. Sometimes I hit the first one in the woods to make it look good.

"Nothing wrong with it. They lie to me about their handicap. They're trying to get my money. I remember a guy I played one day. Said he shot in the eighties. So I played him a friendly game, $10 a hole. He finished with a 68. I had to shoot a 67 to beat him. Afterwards, he laughed. Said to me, 'OK now, let's tell each other our real names.' Turned out he was a state champion from out west somewhere."

***

Moe was a pro in name only, but he could still savour another taste of glory as the two-time Canadian Amateur champ. Despite his withdrawal and the stories about his hijinx on the sacred grounds of Augusta National the previous year, he was invited back to the 1957 Masters.

On the course, it was the same story; he played flawlessly from tee to green, but the greens crippled him and he stumbled to an opening round 77. He was paired with Al Mengert on Thursday. Despite stories that Moe ran amuck, committing one faux pas after another at Augusta, Mengert says, "I don't remember much about a guy I play with who shoots 77." Moe needed a miracle Friday, but improved only to a 74 and missed the cut. It was a dubious honour to miss the first cut in the history of the Masters.

Nevertheless, many people — including Balding and Vancouver's Stan Leonard, both of whom played the PGA Tour in the 1950s and '60s — believe Moe is the reason Canadians are no longer invited to play in the Masters. There's the legend that Moe slept on a bench on the course his first night in Augusta to save himself the cost of a hotel room.

"The tournament officials took pity on him and let him sleep in the men's locker room. They were in awe of his ability, but the story about the bench didn't endear him to the people that he was trying to impress," said Leonard, who won three times on the PGA Tour and finished two strokes behind winner Arnold Palmer in the 1958 Masters. Balding was invited to the 1956 and '57 Masters as CPGA champion, a title he won four times. "The CPGA invitation was taken back because of Moe," Balding said.

Moe's withdrawal in 1956 was also said to have left a sore spot with the folks in the green jackets. "People don't pull out of the Masters unless you're dying on the ground. You finish the round," said Dick Grimm, who became RCGA president in 1974. "I think they were very upset. I think it developed into a situation where you didn't see many Canadians invited to Augusta."

But Jerry Magee and past and present officials at Augusta National dispute the stories. For one, the bench story makes no sense because all the amateurs were invited to stay free of charge in the Crow's Nest in the clubhouse. "There would be no reason for that to happen," said Magee, who was invited to the 1957 Masters as a quarter-finalist in the U.S. Amateur. "Amateurs were treated like gold. And the Masters is too well-organized for that to happen."

Kathryn Murphy, the executive secretary to the Masters and historical expert on the tournament, said the CPGA champ was never officially listed on Augusta's list of automatic invitees, but was occasionally a special invitee as a foreign player. "It was never set in stone. It was just something they did back then."

Invitations to both the CPGA and Canadian Amateur champ — and the U.S. Walker Cup team and other foreign players — were discontinued in the 1960s strictly because Augusta National was under pressure to make more room for PGA tour pros in the limited field event, Murphy said.

Neither Hord Hardin nor Charlie Yates, two Augusta National members, have anything bad to say about Moe at the Masters. Granted Hardin, the former Masters chairman, didn't become a member until 1964, but Yates has been a member since 1934. "We were really excited when someone like Moe Norman, particularly from our sister country of Canada, comes. We were glad Moe came," said Yates, club secretary and chairman of the Masters press committee since 1947. "I remember Moe Norman playing but I don't recall anything controversial."

His clearest memory from the 1957 Masters was Doug Ford holing a shot from a bunker on the 18th hole to win.

***

Back home in Kitchener, Moe spent most of his time practicing and playing at Rockway, occasionally hitchhiking to tournaments and giving impromptu exhibitions. He also became sort of a freelance working man's pro, giving lessons and selling equipment at nine-hole courses and driving ranges throughout southern Ontario. This was to Moe's liking — set your own hours, be your own boss, play when you want — but many card-carrying club pros didn't like it; he was underselling some of them on clubs.

As for playing golf, Moe maintained his competitive edge battling, among others, young Gary Cowan for dimes. On July 16, Moe was especially sharp during a round with Cowan at Rockway. It began pretty routinely for Moe. He was one-under after six holes when he eagled the par-five No. 7 and followed with two straight birdies for a 30 on the front nine.

He began the back with a stumble, bogeying No. 10, but got that back with a birdie on No. 11. Two pars followed and then Moe went birdie, eagle, birdie, birdie. Coming down the 18th fairway, Moe was 10-under. A par would give him 60, breaking the course record by one shot. A birdie would vault him to a rarely visited universe — 59.

As he played the last few holes, Moe didn't know he was on a record-setting course. "I was just playing golf. Everything was falling." But on the 18th, Moe was quite aware of where he stood and the nerve endings jangled. Not about setting a course record. That was old hat. "I felt like I could shoot a course record every day," Moe says. "But to shoot in the 50s. Oh! You don't get a chance to do that every day. No one in Canada had ever shot in the 50s on a regulation course before." (An observation that — while possibly true — is difficult to verify.)

Moe split the fairway of the 365-yard final hole, and stiffed a nine-iron to within eight feet. By now word had spread that Moe was within range of a 59 and an excited group assembled on the bank looking down on the small green. Moe could hear someone say, "He needs this for 59" as he walked up to the green, which just increased his nervousness and made him more excited.

On the verge of 59 or 79, Moe only had one way to putt. He barely stopping moving when he cocked his right wrist back, flicked it toward the hole and the ball tracked right into the heart of the cup. He'd done it! Fifty-nine! Everyone threw their hats in the air and mobbed Moe with congratulations. Cowan shot 67 and paid the man 80 cents. Naturally, they immediately repaired to the bar. After a toast was made and many beers were ordered, Moe downed a Coke and left. He only had one way to celebrate a round, even a 59.

A plaque bearing a brass copy of that scorecard hangs on the walls of the clubhouse. At the time, Rockway was 5,962 yards, par 70. The course has since been redesigned and shortened, and the current record is 61, held by Kitchener native David Wettlaufer.

Occasional sub-60 scores had been shot hither and yon in casual rounds before, but Sam Snead is recognized as the first modern-era player to break 60 in a significant tournament. In May of 1959, Snead fired a 59 in the Sam Snead Festival, a PGA Tour event, on the 6,317-yard, par-70 Greenbrier resort course in West Virginia. But it's not in the

Top Photo: Moe, third from left, with brother Ron, and sisters Marie and Doreen.

Middle Photo: Moe, third from left, with his mother Mary, his brother Ron, and sisters Marie and Doreen.

Bottom Photo: Moe's boyhood home in Kitchener, Ontario.

Moe - Front Row, first on left.

Moe at school, age 10.

Moe on left, with his brother Ron.

Centre: Moe, and Peter Finlayson, Tournament winners.

From Left: Jerry Magee, Bill Moreland, Gary Cowan,
Moe Norman, and Junior Champion (Unknown).

Moe, second from left.

Moe receiving cheque for Tournament win, Fred Lyons in centre.

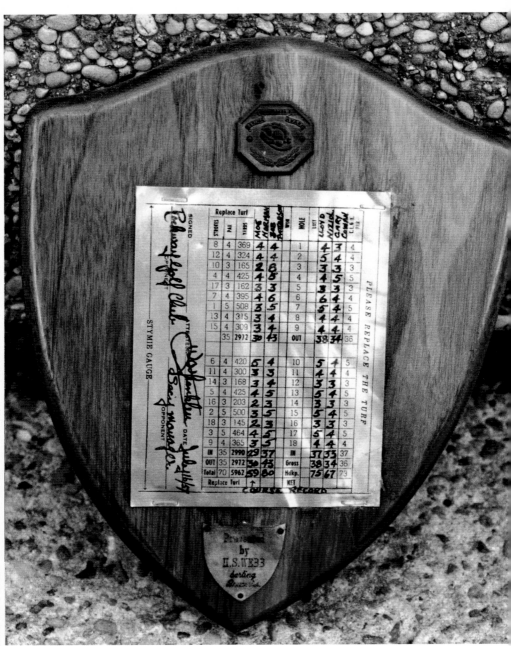

Moe's Course Record 59, July 16 1957.

Moe gives a clinic to Tour stars.
Fred Couples, Ben Crenshaw, Nick Price and Nick Faldo admire the world's best ball striker.

A very happy Moe Norman, on the evening of his induction into Canadian Golf Hall of Fame.

Photo: Jim Walker.

record books because the $10,000 purse was below the $20,000 minimum to be considered an "official" PGA tour event, Desmond Tolhurst wrote in GOLF Magazine.

Homero Blancas was an amateur when he fired a 55 at the 1961 Premier Invitational in Longview, Texas, but the course was only 5,002 yards and the ball ran so far Blancas was driving some par fours. The first official 59 was recorded by Al Geiberger in 1977 at the Memphis Classic. However, many people share Moe's view that the "first 59" was fired by Chip Beck in the 1991 Las Vegas Invitational, because Geiberger was playing lift, clean and place when he broke 60.

With a 59 under his belt, the locals were gunning for "The Kid," as they called him, in the Canadian Open at Westmount. The hometown folks wanted Moe to win, mainly to show golf's muckymucks that the outsider from the other side of the tracks could blow the doors off anyone, including the pampered pros. They were excited because Moe knew every blade of grass at Westmount. He'd knock the dollar-chasers off their games with his big tees and speedy style.

On the morning of the first round, Moe and Ed Woroch went out to Rockway at 5:30 a.m. to practice. Woroch had qualified as an amateur. Knowing Westmount's hilly terrain can result in many wonky lies, Moe and Woroch practiced shots from all kinds of situations — hitting balls above and below their feet, from sidehill, downhill, uphill lies and rough. Although Woroch was a good player, he had never practiced these kinds of shots. Few ever did. Except Moe. "With things like that I can understand how he got so good."

And sure enough, he thrilled the galleries, opening with a 70 and a 68 to sit two strokes back of the lead at six-under 138. North Carolina pro Jim Ferree was left shaking his head after playing with Moe in the second round. On the back nine, Moe walked up and without breaking stride backhanded a one-footer into the hole, sending shivers through the huge gallery following them. Then, on the 17th hole he made a one-handed stab at a nine-inch putt. And missed!

Moe teed off early Friday as one of the early leaders. Any time a Canadian is near the lead of the Open, Canadian reporters go bonkers; besides, Moe was one hell of a story most of the time, but especially so given his recent amateur troubles. Jim Hunt, a reporter for The Toronto Star, wanted to nab Moe for a few quotes. "He came off the course, grabbed his clubs and went down the driveway like hell," Hunt recalls. "I went running after him, 'Hey Moe, you got a minute?'"

"'No, can't wait. I got to go to Rockway. I got a couple of stiffs for a $10 nassau.'"

Hunt laughs at the memory. "What the hell? I don't understand him. Here he is playing in the Canadian Open, he's a couple strokes back and he's concerned about a match with two stiffs. But that was Moe."

And whether it was nerves, bad luck or just poor play, Moe faded in the final rounds with a pair of mediocre 72s to finish well back and earn $150. Typically, Moe wasn't upset by his performance. Even after a poor tournament, Moe's what-me-worry attitude never changed. "It's a part of life," Moe says. "You can't win every day. People make mistakes in their jobs every day."

Moe said the more he played with pros, the more he became convinced his approach was the right way to play. "I see how serious some guys take it and I can't see how they swing the club," Moe says. "Some think it's life and death!"

While Moe didn't like the way most of the PGA pros played — sombrely shuffling around the courses — Moe wanted to play against them. He didn't feel comfortable with the big-names in the clubhouse or locker room, but "on the course, just jolly as hell. But the other guys — so serious," he said, rolling his eyes. "If they hit a bad shot, they were ready to commit suicide. They'd just go bonkers.

"If I hit a bad shot, I just laughed. It's just part of the game. It's a walk in the park, that's all. A walk in the park."

While Moe was confident he could compete against the pros, he couldn't afford the cost of travelling on the tour. His best chance was to enter the British and American Motors Bursary Tournament in August. The tournament was open to Canadian pros 30 years old or younger. The top three finishers evenly split the prize money of $4,500. The money was to be used to finance 10 weeks on the PGA winter tour. The CPGA had an arrangement with the U.S. PGA that if the three bursary winners won enough money to qualify for the rest of the tour, they were welcome to stay. The bursary was an attempt by the CPGA to foster more competitive Canadian touring pros, because in the 1950s the CPGA was mainly an association for club pros.

In the interim, Moe had arranged to apply for membership in the CPGA. It looked like Moe might work this card problem out yet, but many pros, including mentor Lloyd Tucker, were demanding Moe's application be withheld. They complained Moe was stealing sales by drastically underselling equipment. Somewhat surprisingly, Moe came to have an ally within the ranks of the head honchos. George Clifton, president of the Ontario branch of the CPGA, said Moe's card would be processed, provided he filled out the application forms sent to him. Clifton said Moe could sell clubs at whatever price he wanted. "That is his privilege."

When the bursary tournament rolled around at Mississaugua Golf Club, Moe was still in no man's land. Clifton had gone to bat for him before the CPGA executive, but failed because Moe wasn't affiliated with a registered club. Moe saw no point in entering, but bursary sponsor Harry Doughty of British and American Motors, being sympathetic to Moe and seeing the publicity he would create for the event, said if Moe showed up, he could play. Moe hurried down from Kitchener and the grand poobahs of golf soon found themselves in the midst of another controversy. In an act of desperation on the day before the tournament, Moe signed on as an assistant to Bill Mark, the pro at Don Mills Fairways, a Toronto driving range. There was still a problem: Mark had a U.S. PGA card, not a CPGA card.

The CPGA rejected Moe's bid for a card. Bloodied but unbowed, Moe entered the field of about 80 players, hoping that if he won, the public would pressure the CPGA to give in. "Sure, that's why I came here," Moe told The Toronto Telegram. "And that's why I signed with Don Mills. Anything to get a card. And if I win here, how can they turn me down? The people like me."

Doughty agreed: "If he wins, I don't know how they can turn him down."

The script that unfolded was beyond the CPGA's worst nightmare. The Telegram said "the magnificent ragamuffin" had the only gallery worth mentioning for the 36-hole tournament and it all came down to a dramatic and emotional finale. Bob Dean and Moe were tied for third coming to the last hole, but Moe birdied to sneak in and grab the third and final bursary award.

The CPGA was in an awkward spot. Moe's victory was exciting and very popular. Fans began to talk excitedly about how "Moe would tear up the PGA." But the CPGA held firm, ruling that Moe was ineligible for the $1,800 and his chance to play on the PGA winter tour.

"I birdied the last hole to make it," Moe recalls bitterly. "Dean's in the locker room crying like a baby. Half hour later, I'm hitchhiking back to Kitchener and I'm crying like a baby. California here I come, I thought. Then they tell me, "We made a mistake. We shouldn't have let you in here.'"

Once again, Moe's world of golf had imploded.

"The year before, I'm kicked out of amateur. Now I win $1,500 fair and square — I'm not a pro. What the hell am I," he says, his voice rising in anger at the memory. "I haven't done a thing wrong. Now what do I do?"

Chapter Fourteen
Operation Moe Norman

Moe was an unhappy young man through the fall of 1957. Public pressure had failed to change the minds of the CPGA brass. Although he shared partly in the blame for his woes, he believed that he was being denied his God-given right to play golf.

But Moe had more than just the public on his side. While he rankled quite a few folks who thought he was a rebellious trouble-maker, many people also perceived him as a troubled young man who meant no harm, but struggled with authority because of his severe shyness and inability to empathize with others. Moe had travelled many hard roads and everywhere he saw conspiracy, prejudice and people who wanted to hurt him. "The world hasn't treated him in a confidence-inducing manner," said The Globe's Jim Vipond. Moe just wanted to stick his tee in the ground, hit the ball and afford to do it again tomorrow; to him it was as much his right as breathing. The cards, the rules, the associations were suffocating him.

George Clifton, Ontario president of the CPGA, again lobbied for Moe that fall. He told Moe in October that something might be worked out for him in the new year to allow him to get a PGA card. It gave him encouragement as he set off for his annual winter trip to Florida.

***

While Bob Dean and the rest of the PGA pros meandered through California and Arizona on the winter tour, Moe was in Florida, doing a little hustling here and there, playing with old buddies and new friends who picked him up hitchhiking and giving the occasional exhibition.

These exhibitions weren't formal affairs. What usually happened was Moe would start hitting balls and people would gather around like bees to honey. You couldn't help but notice him, often resplendent in clashing colours or a hodgepodge of checks and stripes that could cross your eyes.

That gunslinger set-up, that fluid compact swing and extended follow-through was mesmerizing. And the non-stop commentary in a quick, high-pitched sing-songy voice to no one in particular. "Ooh, is that pure. Whoo." Who is this guy?

People were intrigued by the exactness of his pre-shot routine, the haste in which he beat ball after ball and, of course, the astonishing straightness of each shot.

The students of the game wanted to watch his swing, but they couldn't help but watch the ball. Dead straight. Every time. The same swing, the same breath-taking result. Every time. Even with one-irons and drivers, the balls fell in tight circles, often bouncing against each other. And this from someone who looked like he had just rolled out of bed and picked out his wardrobe from the lost-and-found rack at the neighbourhood five and dime.

When he was swinging in front of a semi-circle of oohing and ahhing fans, Moe was in his element. No shyness here. He was performing, swinging freely, revelling in his own ability. The more people reacted, the faster he worked through those balls and the farther he socked them. When he began to run out of balls, people would buy buckets for him to prolong the show.

"OK, watch this. Here's a hook, here's a hook. Runs like a rabbit. Oh, you want a big slice now? There you go. Ugh, that's ugly. OK, here's the hardest shot in golf — dead straight." And, of course, he'd do it.

Soon, he'd be hitting off big tees, matchboxes, sticks, purses, and he'd have the folks in his back pocket. They'd start asking him questions, and if he liked the question, he'd answer quickly, dispensing only a few words at a time. "I hit with effortless power," he'd tell the crowd, "Everyone else swings with powerless effort." He spoke concisely, even lyrically, with unusual clarity and directness that made perfect sense. "Let your body enjoy the shot. The most important word in golf is let."

Moe had spent four winters in Florida. Usually someone knew Moe — or knew of him — and word of his lack of finances would filter through the crowd, and pretty soon a hat would go around for a collection. And once the last ball was hit, his pocket jingling with change and bulging with bills, golf bag slung over his shoulder, down the road he'd go to hitchhike to his next stop like the mysterious stranger in a western movie.

***

Back in Ontario it was time to get serious, make some real money and get his butt on the PGA Tour where he belonged. Shortly after returning in April, Moe signed on as assistant to Class A pro Bert Turcotte at de Havilland Golf Centre in Toronto. The golf centre wasn't registered with the CPGA, but Turcotte was. He was a forthright, respected man in the business.

Turcotte approached the CPGA and said he'd hire Moe, keep an eye on him and refine him a bit if the board would grant him a card. Pressure was mounting on the CPGA from the public and many pros who thought Moe was an exceptional talent who needed a break. Still, the board remained reluctant.

"They were stupid and I told them so," Turcotte said. "He was the greatest drawing card in Canadian golf. He was abused as an amateur. What he needed was help. They were kicking him. He's not a bad person. He's not an animal. I don't know anyone or anything that he ever hurt. He does things to hurt himself. You can't fault ignorance. There were a lot of things he had to learn."

It took a few raucous meetings, but finally the board approved the plan and Moe got his card. It was hard to imagine someone of Moe's ability and quirky personality "teaching duffers" as the Toronto Telegram elegantly put it, but "the obvious pot at the end of this rainbow is a PGA card and a pass to the money game."

For $50 a week, Moe was to teach, put on clinics and represent de Havilland in tournaments. There were mutual advantages for both parties. Moe had his card, some financial stability and, importantly, he was comfortable. He felt good among the average people who came to bang balls at the golf centre. He felt a connection with the common folks, and they with him.

Turcotte was also smart enough to take advantage of Moe's reputation as a showman. Moe was one heck of a drawing card to the $300,000 de Havilland Golf Centre. It was the largest and splashiest golf centre in North America when it opened in 1957, featuring a double-decker driving range with 240 tees, an 18-hole par-three course, a nine-hole regulation length course and 36-holes of mini-putt golf. The entire centre was lit up at night by floodlights purchased from 20th Century Fox. The game was just starting to spread among the masses and Turcotte was keen to take advantage of what he called "commercial" golf.

It seemed like the perfect fit — Canada's most colourful player performing at a golf theatre lit by movie lights. Turcotte said Moe wasn't compelled to do exhibitions, but Moe and many others say that's exactly what Turcotte wanted. And Moe performed eagerly, especially for kids. He liked to give them tips, provide encouragement and just goof around. Moe, after all, was like a perpetual kid trapped in an austere adult world. De Havilland was perfect for Moe. He would have been hidden away at a fancy private country club and uncomfortable with the upper crust.

"It was good for Moe and it was good for me," Turcotte said. "He always had quite a following. He was a good attraction for the operation." When Turcotte signed Moe in the spring of 1958, there was plenty of publicity and about 1,000 people a day streamed into the centre daily to see the magnificent shotmaker perform his magic, hit some balls themselves and maybe play a little golf.

To Turcotte's surprise, Moe turned out to be a pretty good salesman and made decent money on his seven per cent commission on equipment sales. "He could keep up with the best pro," Turcotte said. If Moe believed a certain club or piece of equipment could help someone's game, he had a persuasive way of pitching it because Moe was never one to pussyfoot around. "His confidence level was always high if something pertained to golf."

Moe was one of six assistants giving lessons at de Havilland for $6 a pop. Like the other assistants, Moe booked his own appointments and was expected to show up on time. Many people doubted Moe could follow such a routine, but Turcotte said Moe was a conscientious teacher and a model of punctuality. "He never let me down. He was honest and dependable." He gave about 65 to 70 lessons a week and worried a great deal about upsetting his students' progress whenever he had to cancel or postpone a slate of lessons.

Dependable, yes, a great teacher for novices, no. Moe's students were pretty distracted by his idiosyncrasies, faster-than-a-speeding-bullet speaking style and unpolished manner. Some people went through an entire lesson and didn't hear a word — they were too busy trying to figure out the instructor. Moe also had little patience or ability to explain the mundane fundamentals such as grip and posture. "He didn't think that stuff was too important," Turcotte said. "He wanted people just to take it to the top and 'Hit it! Hit it!' In a lot of ways he was right, but some people wanted their money back. He was a little too advanced for most students of the game."

Reporter Jim Hunt was an avid golfer, although he admits never a very good one, and went out to take a lesson from the great Moe Norman. They went out on the range, Hunt said, and he hit a couple of balls. "Moe took the club out of my hand and said 'This is what you should do.' But he never gave the club back to me. For the rest of the lesson, he just hit golf balls."

Advanced students learned a great deal from Moe. He had a regular clientele who benefitted from his ability to create mental images that they could understand easily and put into action. "Swing to the target, swing to the target," he'd say over and over. "Keep your knees soft and mobile, soft and mobile." He simplified instruction. He wouldn't say maintain the cock in your right wrist as long as possible while shifting your weight left in the downswing. He'd say: "Lead and lag. The more delay, the straighter you hit it. Lead and lag."

Moe's future wasn't in teaching, however. Turcotte had established, in consultation with the CPGA, what became known as "Operation Moe Norman." Toronto Star columnist Milt Dunnell neatly summarized it: "To apply the polish and the poise of the pro, without destroying the saleable colour of the clowning amateur.... Moe will be good for the professional game provided he can find the dividing line between showmanship and showoffmanship."

Turcotte impressed upon Moe that one reason the pros are so serious on the course is that they're playing for money, and that clowning around might destroy the concentration of their partners. "There is a certain amount of responsibility connected with being a playing professional and we are not going to permit any person to lower the dignity of our game," CPGA President Lou Cumming told Dunnell. "On the other hand, Moe could be one of the most colourful golfers since Walter Hagen."

Turcotte said he took Moe out to fancy restaurants and showed him dining decorum: how to get a table, order food and when to use specific cutlery and dishes during the meal. Moe was introduced to the cuisine beyond spaghetti: steak, chicken and seafood.

Turcotte tried to teach Moe how to make small talk, move through a crowd in a room, accept a prize graciously, deliver a speech after a tournament, the importance of heaping praise on the tournament organizers, the members and commenting on the great shape of the course.

One lesson didn't go so well. "When Moe first began teaching, they would usually come into the clubhouse after the lesson and generally the man or woman would ask Moe if he wanted a drink. Moe drank about a case of Coke a day back then, so he'd say 'sure.' This happened so often, I finally said, 'Moe, you're getting to look like a scrounger. When the lesson is over, why don't you take someone over and ask them if they'd like a Coke?'"

"He took it overboard. When people would come in, and they weren't even there for a lesson, he'd ask them if they'd like a Coke. Maybe it was my fault for not explaining it very well."

Turcotte was more concerned, however, that he might make Moe too serious on the golf course. Dunnell wrote: "A subdued Moe would be out of character — and probably out of the running for championship baubles. A serious Moe would be a bad golfer." A serious Moe might also have temper tantrums like many pros, stare down and alienate fans. A gregarious Moe was good for the game.

Moe made his first entry into a tournament as a bona fide pro in the 54-hole Ontario Open at Cataraqui in Kingston, at the eastern edge of Lake Ontario. Moe opened with a 68 in the cold gale force winds, and followed with 69 and 74, cruising to a three-stroke victory over none other than Gerry Kesselring. It was a great beginning because it appeared to prove a few things: that he could beat nemesis Kesselring, that Turcotte and Clifton were right in lobbying for his CPGA card, that he belonged in the pro ranks and that he had a great future. He also pocketed $1,000.

Scott Young of The Globe and Mail thought the new Moe was much the same as the old Moe. "Moe was bouncing a ball six feet in the air off the face of his putter and catching it in the left breast pocket of his golf shirt."

In one morning round, Moe was paired with a Jake Kleist of Syracuse, New York. On the first hole, Kleist's drive rolled into a deep grassy bunker, his second landed in rough behind the green and his third came out like a bullet and would have gone down the fairway except it hit the flag about three feet up and dropped a foot away from the cup. Easy par.

"Moe burst out laughing," Young wrote. "He walked in circles laughing. Moe lay down on the grass and rolled around laughing. He got up, pointing his putter at Kleist, still laughing."

Most newspaper reports focused on "the new Moe." The Telegram's headline read "A Serious Clown Wins Open." Moe threatened to punch a drunken fan in the nose for fooling around as he prepared to hit a tee shot. He also stepped back from a six-foot putt on the last hole when a fan yelled, "We got five bucks on you Moe!" He stepped back from a putt three times when a movie camera started up each time he addressed the ball. Moe even took aim on three-inch putts.

Reporters asked why the change? "There's big money at stake now," he said. "Big money. Everybody thinks I'm a clown. I want to be a clown. I always score well that way. I want to stay a clown. But when I'm shooting, I'd like the same silence as the other golfers get. I talk and fool around between shots. That's the time. The right time. I like it — then. But when I'm making a shot, not then, not then. I'm no different from other golfers."

Moe's comments concerned Turcotte. He was worried that he'd curbed those parts of Moe's character that made him so popular, and possibly turned him the other way — into one of those boring, scowling pros. "I tried to polish him but only to a point. The main thing was he had to be a credit to his profession. I didn't want to change his character, or mould him into an educated golf pro. I just wanted him to be himself."

Despite those concerns, Moe's victory in the Ontario Open sent hopes soaring among his supporters and fans of Canadian golf. Canadian Sport Monthly said Moe's win was "the forerunner of what could be one of the most colourful and crowd appealing professional careers that the golfing world has ever known."

Soon after the victory, Bill Hamilton, the head pro at Toronto's Oakdale club, called Turcotte to crow that he'd just signed young George Knudson, the 1955 Canadian Junior champ, as an assistant. A smooth swinging, bespectacled youngster, Knudson was regarded as the next big thing and Hamilton challenged Turcotte to pit Moe against his new young swinger. In the battle of the hotshots, Moe buried Knudson with a 65, and edged him in the next match 68 to 69.

Even so, Knudson was now the new darling of Canadian golf; many sports writers and golf insiders were proclaiming that he was Canada's best hope for the PGA Tour. Knudson had a swing that was the envy of many pros. It was marvellously fluid and appeared textbook perfect, fostering comparisons to Hogan. Unlike Moe, he could shmooze among the country club types, and the contrast endeared him to the bigwigs who never knew what Moe was going to do next. "Everyone was making a fuss over Knudson, I think it was a heartbreaker for Moe," Turcotte said. "He went into a bit of a shell."

That was apparent in the next meeting between the two in the British and American Motors Bursary Tournament in August. If he could finish in the top three, this was Moe's ticket to the PGA winter tour. Moe, Knudson and Irv Lightstone were the leaders going into the final round. There wasn't much chatter among them as they stood on the first tee of Toronto's Don Valley Golf Club, Lightstone recalls. Knudson and Moe respected each other and usually talked, but this morning the lanky youngster wouldn't even look at Moe. When it was finally time to tee off, Knudson surprised them both and unsheathed his driver. Don Valley's first hole is a short but sharp dogleg left with a creek running in front of the green and out-of-bounds guarding the left side.

Knudson then turned around and, looking Moe square in the eyes, declared: "Just watch me. Watch the way golf should really be played." He belted a cracker drive over the creek and the trees onto the fringe of the green. It was dangerous, reckless, but there was never any question as soon as the ball left the clubface that he'd pulled off an absolutely perfect shot.

Moe was clearly flummoxed. "His face went into a frown and his eyebrows went way up," Lightstone said. "Moe wasn't expecting that comment. I think George was inferring, 'Moe, I'm going to blow you out the window.'" Moe bunted a nine-iron off the tee and made a routine par while Knudson snagged a birdie.

Knudson shattered Moe with a brilliant display of shot-making, whipping him by six or seven shots. Lightstone said it didn't strike him that Knudson had sunk to using gamesmanship, but rather "it was a challenge. George was pumped that he was going to tear the course apart and he could do it. They were the two best ball-strikers in the country and it was a challenge."

If Moe was going to survive on the PGA Tour, he'd face many such challenges. It was the gentlemanly game of golf, but at the game's top level — with big money at stake — the competition was hard-nosed and intimidating. Moe wasn't so much an easy target for gamesmanship, Lightstone said, but a victim of "the things Moe comes up with in his own head. Moe would create the effect. First, he couldn't beat Kesselring and then, he couldn't beat Knudson."

Nonetheless, Moe finished in the top three of the bursary tournament, won the $1,500 in expense money and an invitation to play on the PGA winter tour. It wasn't the greatest sendoff, but after his brilliant amateur career, the trauma of being forced to turn pro and the arduous chore of trying to get his professional's card, Moe was finally going to test himself against the world's best.

Chapter Fifteen
The PGA Tour

It was quite natural for many people to assume that Moe was dirt poor. His clothes were usually old, faded and a little tattered. It didn't appear he could afford to see a dentist to fix his increasingly wobbly teeth. Yet those inside Moe's circle knew he had money and that he was so tight-fisted he made Scrooge look like a philanthropist. Moe could out-fumble anyone in reaching for his wallet when it came time to buy a few Cokes after nine holes. Moe was also a saver possessed of iron-willed discipline. "He wasn't nearly as poverty stricken as he pretended," Turcotte said.

Despite warnings from his friends that he might get mugged, Moe kept almost all of his money in his front pocket. He paid for everything in cash. And so it was to the utter disbelief of Moe's friends that Turcotte convinced him, in 1957, to invest about $3,000 in six-year-old TransCanada Pipelines Ltd. TransCanada's sales ballooned into the billions by the 1970s, and Moe's stock would have been worth several hundred thousand dollars. But Moe sold in 1958 and saw only a modest profit, according to Turcotte.

Woroch recalls hanging out with Moe at The Strand bowling alley one wintery night when Moe leaned over and said, "Eddie, lend me two bucks will ya?"

"Moe, why should I lend you two bucks?"

"Cause I don't want to break a hundred dollar bill."

Woroch explains: "Moe saved hundred dollar bills. He kept them in his pocket. His thinking was if he broke a bill, he wouldn't replace it."

Moe's inspiration to save throughout 1958 was to buy wheels so that he could travel around the southern U.S. on the PGA winter tour. He called Bruce Forbes, who owned a car dealership in Brantford. Forbes was the director of the Ontario Golf Association, but Moe had no complaint with Forbes. They liked and respected each other.

Moe's instructions were simple: get him a car with a big trunk. One night after Moe finished giving lessons at de Havilland under the lights, Forbes rolled into the parking lot with a one-year-old brown Coupe de Ville Cadillac. Moe looked it over for a few seconds and said to Forbes, "If you say it's good, it's good." Sold.

Moe didn't take the car on a test drive. He didn't know how to drive. Forbes said it was the first time he'd ever sold a Cadillac to someone who didn't know how to drive it. The car was $2,600 — big money for a car in 1958. Forbes said, "How do you want to pay for this?"

"What do you mean?" Moe asked, screwing up his face, obviously puzzled.

"Do you want to finance it or I can take you down to the bank?"

"No. I got the money right here."

He reached into his pocket and "brought out a wad of bills that would choke a cow," Forbes said. Moe peeled off 26 $100 bills onto the hood of the Cadillac. Every year for the next 20, he would trade in his old Caddie for a newer but slightly used one.

Woroch says Moe always wanted a Cadillac. Not to show off, but because "they have room and a nice ride." This was important because Moe spent so much time in his car driving long distances to tournaments. He'd also seen Snead and Hogan in their Cadillacs at the Masters, and figured that he was just as good a ball-striker. Now that he was a touring pro just like them, he should travel in comfort and style too. And, sure, he didn't mind people looking on with a touch of envy. He'd suffered some hard times. He'd earned it.

Until Moe passed his driving lessons, Woroch's younger brother Richard chauffeured him around. When he finally got his licence, many people thought Moe was a bit of a show-off — a driving range pro traipsing around in a Cadillac. "I never cared what people thought," Moe says.

Woroch recalls that shortly after Moe bought his first Coup de Ville, a fellow parked beside him at a tournament and asked, "Moe, why did you buy a Cadillac?"

Sensing some sarcasm, Moe said: "Is this your car?"

"Yes," the man said.

"You paying your car off?"

"Yes."

"My car is paid off. I could afford my car. You can't."

Moe's car became his home. The room at his boarding house was just a place to sleep. Moe's trunk was his travelling pro shop, storage locker, safe deposit box, basement and closet. Moe's trunk became famous over the years. Whenever it was open, people would try to steal a look inside. They'd see two or three cardboard boxes brimming with practice balls, bowling-ball bags stuffed with balls, pairs and pairs of shoes, dozens of clubs, rolls of lead tape. He needed a Cadillac for the heavy duty suspension. The backseat was a twisted heap of unfolded shirts and pants, while magazines, newspapers clippings and papers poked out of pockets behind the front seats.

Ted Maude travelled with Moe as a fellow Canadian touring player. He told author Curt Sampson about packing the Cadillac one day to head south when he asked Moe if he had any money. "Money? Hah! Money?" He pulled wads of cash out of his sock, from behind the spare tire, from the glove compartment. "Here's money," Moe said. "Here's money."

***

Moe's arrival on the PGA Tour in January of 1959 was eagerly awaited. He was already a legend among insiders and touring professionals who had heard all the stories about pop bottles and holes played backwards. He was the greatest character to come on tour since Walter Hagen, and there were great hopes that he'd enjoy the same degree of success. Golf World magazine hyped his arrival by placing him on its cover proudly showing off his arsenal of high tees. The story said: "Now that Moe has joined the tour, Doug Ford is the second fastest player in golf."

"U.S. golf writers hailed the arrival of a colourful newcomer to the grim business of playing the game for a living," wrote Milt Dunnell of The Toronto Star.

PGA officials were less than thrilled, warning they wouldn't put up with his legendary antics for one second. "The first time he tees off from a pop bottle in tournament competition, he's done," declared Harry Raynor, tournament director of the Los Angeles Open, Moe's first event among the big boys. "The PGA isn't about to put up with young Norman's shenanigans."

Sure enough, Moe's first tournament was one to remember and the gallery grew steadily during the first round of the Los Angeles Open at the Rancho Municipal course. Despite the constant pleas of spectators to bring out a big tee, the remodelled Moe hit off regular tees. Finally, he relented, teed it high and bashed the ball straight down the pipe as the fans hooted and hollered. "The big tees they didn't mind," Moe said of PGA officials.

Moe knocked his ball in a green-side bunker on one hole and the fans moaned. "Don't worry," he consoled. "This is the easiest shot in the bag. I can knock the ball out with one hand." A fan bet him $10 he couldn't. Moe accepted, took his Sandy Andy wedge in his right hand and blasted the ball to within two feet, sank the putt, collected his loot and almost skipped to the next tee.

Despite having a bad case of nerves playing in his first event on the tour, it had gone remarkably well. The fans liked him and he was enjoying himself. It had finally happened. Here he was — strolling down a fairway on the PGA Tour. Hoo boy.

On the 15th tee, feeling good, almost giddy, he could resist no longer. He unzipped the side pocket of his golf bag and retrieved a Coke bottle. Like a cop on surveillance who has finally caught the suspect in action, a PGA official nearly jumped out of his jacket, marched over to Moe and thundered: "None of that here!"

"Oh they stopped me right away as soon as I brought out the first Coke bottle in Los Angeles," Moe says. "They said 'This is business now. This is the bread and butter of pro golfers. Don't do childish things.'"

He shrugged and gave the bottle back to his caddie. Moe says he wasn't angry or embarrassed. He only brought out the Coke bottles to entertain the crowds. He could see the PGA's point. "If the glass blew up, they could get sued. I couldn't do something out of the ordinary on the tour because it would hurt the concentration of other players. Before, in my amateur days, it didn't matter because we weren't playing for big money, just for glory." Since that day in 1959, Moe says he has never hit another ball off a Coke bottle or played another hole backwards.

Even though Moe finished the L.A. Open well back of winner Ken Venturi, he was excited by his first U.S. PGA tournament, thrilled to be playing against legendary veterans Ben Hogan, Sam Snead and Jimmy Demaret, and the exciting new breed led by Venturi, Arnold Palmer and Gary Player. "It was great, wonderful. It was a different outlook entirely. For the first time in my life, I knew I was up against the best. Right away, it puts energy up your spine."

Moe looked forward to the Tijuana Open, the Bing Crosby National at Cypress Point and Pebble Beach (two of Moe's favourite courses), the

Thunderbird Invitational in Palm Springs, and the Opens of San Diego, Tucson, Phoenix and Panama. It wasn't all sweetness and light, however. Some players weren't thrilled to have Moe on the tour. At a time when the players were trying to gain more respect and put together a classy tour, Moe dressed poorly and lacked certain social graces. He was an odd duck who made some people nervous.

"There were those who didn't understand him, but they just never took the time to try to understand where he was coming from, or his mannerisms," Doug Sanders said. "I always enjoyed seeing Moe out there. He was always saying, 'How ya doin'? How ya' doin'? You started your day off with a couple of laughs and a smile. It was refreshing."

"I always enjoyed my time with him," said Player, playing his cards close to his vest. "It was always interesting playing with him."

He also got an important thumbs-up from Sam Snead, in large part because Moe kept everyone light and loose around the range. "I liked Moe," Snead said. "He was always a very congenial guy. Of course, he jabbered a lot. He was always jolly and had a ball no matter what people thought. Moe was his own man and he did what pleased Moe Norman and I thought that was great. Moe would do funny things on the course, and the guys would look at him and say 'He's having a ball.' I respected Moe and I thought he was a hell of a guy."

Doug Ford said Moe would amaze players with his work ethic on the range, because he was always hitting balls. Players even asked to look at his powerful hands. "I wouldn't let him shake hands with me," Ford said. "I'd have a bruised hand for a week."

Bob Goalby said Moe seemed relaxed with what he called the second-echelon players — guys like himself, Sanders, Don January, Gene Littler, Miller Barber, Art Wall and Ford. "He was uncomfortable around a Palmer or anybody from the upper echelon of golf, or people with money," Goalby said. "He'd back off and almost get lost. He didn't push himself forward. He was a little quiet. I'd say the tour was not his bag. It's kind of a stuffy sport. Moe was a little out of place."

Moe felt patronized by many of the rich American pros. "No one really took Moe seriously," Venturi said. "Moe was always such a free spirit it was hard for people to take him seriously. I think Moe was one of the sweetest, kindest, gentlest guys I ever met. He wouldn't hurt anybody. You couldn't get close to Moe. He was so shy."

While he could fool around with the American PGA players on the range or inside the ropes of a tournament, once the golf was over Moe was an outsider. He didn't fit in. He didn't ask to join them for drinks or dinner and he was seldom invited. He ate alone almost every night and roomed by himself. "He didn't try to socialize with us," Sanders said. "He was a loner."

In clubhouses and locker rooms, Moe was riddled with anxiety, especially among the star players. "I'd be eating a hot dog and they'd leave half a steak and a two-dollar tip."

Moe felt like a poor cousin compared to the dandies decked out in perfectly coordinated shirts and trousers. He watched them drop $150 for a new pair of shoes, while he taped his shoes to hide his toes and keep the soles from flapping. "I was the worst dresser out there," Moe says, blaming his tattered wardrobe on the fact that he didn't have a sponsor. "I had one pair of pants with a hole in the back. I felt out of place."

Once out on the course, however, he felt right at home. Moe became a gallery favourite in every tournament. The chunky, frenetic marvel from Canada in the turtlenecks galloped across courses like he had a plane to catch — even on the hottest days. He'd storm down a fairway, grab a club from his caddie and take a rip without appearing to break stride. Often a fan would ask, "Don't you ever look at the green before you shoot?

"Good grief," Moe would reply, "has it moved?"

Fans loved the quirky little man who kept up a stream of non-stop commentary and sometimes even broke into song. Moe would bounce balls on the face of his clubs as he walked and would generally carry on with the merry air of someone playing in his own Saturday foursome.

Many players loved to watch his incredible ball-striking. He was a short hitter by tour standards, but it didn't matter. His partners would blow it by him, and then Moe would knock a three-wood or two-iron stiff and they couldn't get inside him with a four- or five-iron. No one could hit full shots so accurately or consistently. Only Hogan was in the same league.

Everyone had a little movement in their shots. But Moe's bread-and-butter shot was dead straight, never wavering an inch left or right for the entire journey. "He had an odd looking swing, sort of short, sort of quick, but it didn't make a darn bit of difference," said Goalby, a third-year pro from Illinois in 1959. "He could hit a ball as straight as any human being who ever lived."

Venturi is credited for coming up with the nickname "Pipeline Moe", but he says the story has been embellished. "In those days, the sprinkler line went right down the middle of the fairways and I said he was the only guy who could knock down the sprinkler line. The story got twisted and they changed it to pipeline."

His shots even sounded different, with a distinctive click produced only by a ball struck purely on the sweetspot. Most players trapped the ball between the turf and the club, taking beaver-pelt divots with their short irons. Moe swept all his clubs and took bacon strip divots. "He could hit an iron off a putting green and never take a divot," Venturi remarked.

And no one hit a ball on such a trajectory. Moe's shots rode through the air like ferris wheels — perfectly end-over-end. Pure backspin. Not a hint of sidespin. His shots appeared to ride a steel cable set on a low angle in the sky. When the spin ran out, the ball dropped straight down as if it had toppled over the edge of a cliff. Every one of Moe's shots, even a long-iron or wood, fell softly — like the proverbial butterfly with sore feet. A favourite saying on tour was "Moe's the only guy who can stop it on a highway."

Moe wasn't just straight. He could move the ball in the air at will. Whatever degree of bend, height or spin Moe needed, he could get it: low running draws, high sweeping slices, knock-down irons, soft four-woods from deep rough, Moe had all the shots. Venturi said most players saw only one shot in a given situation, but "Moe always had multiple choice. He'd see probably three ways to play it. Moe had more varied shots than anyone I've ever seen.

"Hogan was a static shotmaker, but I think Moe could do more things. I think I'm a pretty good shotmaker, but I could never do some of the shots he could. Never. Like hitting a driver out of a divot. It's hard enough hitting a driver from a tee."

Whether he was playing in front of five people or 5,000, Moe's long game was always bang on. "I played better than them tee to green, but I couldn't putt the ball in the hole!"

On the greens, Moe had neither confidence in himself nor his technique. With a putter in his hand, he was a completely different golfer. Instead of gripping firmly and stroking with determination, he held the putter limply and putted tentatively. Although he was now taking more time over his putts, he still struggled. "I couldn't get in my comfort zone," Moe said. "You'd stumble over your own emotions. Your thoughts would get in the way."

It also appeared that Moe putted quickly so he could escape from view as soon as possible, the same way he handled almost every situation that made him feel uncomfortable. Writer Lorne Rubenstein put it nicely: "The green is a stage upon which a private person might feel ill at ease." Moe was proof of the credo "you drive for show and putt for dough" because he finished well back in nearly every tournament, missing cuts and picking up paltry cheques of $100 or less.

Moe had an exceptional putting round when he fired a pair of 31s for a 62 in the 1959 San Diego Open. He also made his share of putts at The Greater New Orleans Open that year. He was three strokes back of leader Gene Littler going into the final day after rounds of 70-72-70. Moe played in the last group Sunday and was leading at one point, but managed only a 72. He finished fourth and won $1,100. Bill Collins fired a 70 to collect the $2,900 first-place cheque. Moe blamed his mediocre finish on another spate of three-putts and the pressure of "trying to bring a win back for Canada."

Goalby was one of his playing partners in the final round at New Orleans and Moe left him flabbergasted. "He teed it up on a matchbox and on a stick — he teed it up at least six inches. He had a chance to win the tournament and was doing that kind of stuff. But he could hit the ball the same way whether it was on a little tee, a double tee or a matchbox — right down the middle."

Moe won only $260 in his other tournaments for a total of $1,360 in 10 events during the 1959 winter tour. He headed back to Toronto for another season at de Havilland. He finished third in the bursary tournament that fall, and played the winter tour again in 1960. Moe's second tour of duty was much the same. He pocketed $1,529.46 to break even on his expenses. And that was that; he never played the PGA Tour again.

In attempting to explain Moe's lack of success on the tour, Venturi suggests that Moe was so gifted it worked against him. "He'd go off on these tangents. He'd never get where he could get geared in for four hours and grind it out and use his talent. He'd drift in and out. He'd be playing and then he'd have to do something different, saying 'I'm going to play these different kinds of shots now.' He had so much talent, he got a bit bored unless he was doing something with it."

Moe's lightning speed of play also hurt him. He was a devastating match-play competitor because he could keep moving. But PGA tournaments were medal play and the players were a methodical bunch. When play would inevitably bog down, waiting around made Moe either antsy or bored, and he'd lose his focus. "If Moe could have gone off first in every tournament, he would have won a lot," Venturi said.

Moe said poor putting cost him the victories and cheques he needed to remain on the tour. He couldn't get a sponsor and after the 1960 season he was 31 and ineligible for the bursary. "I couldn't afford it. I couldn't fulfil my goal."

But Ford and Goalby said Moe had money — he just wouldn't spend it. Although the 1959 New Orleans Open was the 10th and final stop for the Canadian bursary boys, Moe's good finish qualified him to play the next week. Ford saw him after the tournament and said, "I'll see you next week in Pensecola."

"Oh no, you won't," Moe said. "I've only got $1,500."

That's the same amount he had won in the bursary to help with his expenses, so he'd broken even. Ford said Moe didn't want to risk his own money to keep playing. "He never took advantage of his greatness in the United States. I always thought Moe was the best player ever to come out of Canada, but he had a quirk — he loved the dollar," said Ford, winner of the 1955 PGA and '57 Masters.

Goalby said Moe wouldn't spend the money it took to play golf at its top level. "He didn't want to take his money out of his pocket. And I think that hurt Moe. He didn't want to stay at the good places, eat at the good places, or pay the right caddie. In other words, he didn't have the right edge."

The issue of sponsorship wasn't the point, according to Goalby. "Hell, none of us had sponsors. I had $1,400 when I went out. It cost only $150 a week and Moe got by on less than $100. He had enough to play. He didn't know you had to spend money to make money. Moe was not in a position to win because he didn't have the lifestyle."

Moe had come a long way from hitting balls in schoolyards in working-class Westward and selling prizes as an amateur in southern Ontario, but his roots betrayed him on the tour. He never had much money, and once he got his mitts on some, how could he be expected to risk it? For the poor and uneducated, money puts food in your mouth and a roof over your head; it's not a tool to make more money.

Another reason Moe left the tour was loneliness. Most PGA players thought Moe was a loner, but the opposite was true. With friends, he's a very sociable guy. "He needs people," Lightstone said. "He goes from place to place seeing people he feels comfortable with. And he'll talk up a blue streak. The tour wasn't the right fit for Moe. He had all this free time. Golf was the only thing for him. I think the tour wore him down."

His Kitchener buddy Gus Maue believes he knows the main reason why Moe never went back. In 1960, Maue was renting a house at the Riviera Golf Club in Florida. He was very excited to read in the newspaper that Moe had played well again in New Orleans. "I said, 'He's going to win in Pensacola.'

"Two hours later, Moe shows up with six Cokes and says 'Want to play cribbage?'"

"Moe, you should be in Pensacola."

"I'll never play that tour again."

"Why not?"

"I'm not going to tell you."

Gus went over to Riviera's driving range to see touring pro Bert Weaver, who had been in New Orleans, and asked what happened. Weaver said Moe hit off a big tee and attracted a huge gallery, and was carrying his own bag. But he was dressed down by a top player and some PGA officials. They said he had to dress better, hit the ball off a proper tee and take a caddie.

Moe was humiliated. "The dressing down he received completely destroyed him," Maue said. Perhaps another person would have shrugged it off, thinking that he had just run into some loudmouths. Or try to change to fit in. But Moe saw the world in black and white. Moe felt he was rejected and unwanted, so that was that. Moe's entire life was spent running away from pain. He was hurt badly and there was no going back, especially if it meant risking a confrontation.

Deep down, Moe also thought he just wasn't good enough on the tour, the same way he thought he could never beat Gerry Kesselring. The former barefoot boy-wonder eventually loaded up his Cadillac and headed north, back to the double-decker driving range under the bright Hollywood lights, his dreams of riches and fame just a dark memory.

Chapter Sixteen
A Teaching Pro

After strolling down the fairways of PGA Tour stops such as Pebble Beach, it was a long and depressing drive back to Canada in the spring of 1960. Moe returned to the fold of Bert Turcotte, who had since moved to a new double-decker range in northwest Toronto called Pleasure Park.

It was not a happy time for Moe. He had been proud to say he was a PGA Tour golfer, but that was history now. His dream of getting rich playing the tour was dead. Abandoning the tour also had a positive side, however. Working out of Pleasure Park gave Moe a home, a place to go every day. This was always important; there was security in knowing that he'd see the same people and friends — and feel comfortable.

He entertained folks with his ball-striking exhibitions, which were advertised in newspapers and on radio, and gave up to 70 lessons a week. "I'm a teaching pro, not a playing pro," he told a reporter. "I don't get much chance to play now. Now I teach, teach, teach all the time. I'm not complaining, but it's hard to play good tournament golf when you're a pro at a club."

For serious students who proved their dedication by practicing for hours, Moe was like a guru (though this particular mentor wore a black turtleneck, wine-coloured pants and always had a Coke in his hand). Many golf people thought Moe was a natural talent, incapable of understanding the complicated workings of the swing. But he was the equal of many fine teachers. "Moe's a terrific teacher because he's plain and simple," said Lee Trevino, who has shared many driving-range moments with Moe. "He doesn't tear the house down to repair a leaky roof. He'd correct one thing that corrects another thing and another thing."

Nick Weslock received instruction from Moe in the early 1960s, when Weslock captured three of his four Canadian Amateur titles. Moe could watch him swing just once and "spot a fault right away," Weslock said. "Moe is so perceptive." He could also drive Weslock crazy when they played together, especially if Weslock was struggling. "Nick, I can't believe what you're doing. I can't believe it!" But Moe wouldn't tell Weslock what he saw for five or six holes, which was torture for Weslock. "C'mon Moe, tell me what I'm doing! Mo-oe!" When Moe finally did reveal his diagnosis, he was absolutely right — every time.

Moe was especially enamoured with the kids at Pleasure Park. He talked slower, repeated his words less and spent more time and effort explaining the swing. He was a mentor to many kids, including Lorne Rubenstein and Mark Evershed. He became enthusiastic about his new career as a teacher when he took Ken Tucker under his wing as a protege. The nephew of a Pleasure Park pro, Tucker was a plucky young teen and dynamite hockey player. Tucker remembers that when he was about 14, Moe returned from Florida one spring, took him out to his Cadillac and opened the trunk. "There were seven sets of clubs in there. He said 'Take your pick.' They were heavy with thick grips, just like his."

Moe was like an uncle to his little buddy and set out to teach Tucker to swing the club exactly like him: the same grip, wide stance, out-stretched arms — the works. "People said I looked like a little Moe Norman. Short, stocky and with a brushcut, and I'd be pounding balls until my hands bled."

Some of Moe's drills seemed funny to Tucker and he'd start to laugh, but Moe was dead serious. He'd look at him sternly: "'You can't laugh. You've got to practice. Discipline. Discipline.' He didn't know how strong he was. Sometimes he'd grab me by the arm and it would deaden it. I'd have to sit down until I got the feeling back."

Moe worked with Ken almost daily, and his protege practiced dutifully, but he never played. It was part of Moe's theory that you practiced first, until perfect, and then played. "That spring he told me just to hit balls and do drills. Don't play on a course. The next spring the first time I stepped on a golf course I shot 89. Then as the year went on, I was shooting in the 70s every time out."

Under Moe's tutelage, Tucker became a scratch player competitive on the amateur circuit, but it was his hockey skills that won him a scholarship to Michigan Tech. Tucker posted sub-par rounds on the school's golf course and made the golf team as a walk-on. But the coaches hated his unorthodox swing. They eventually convinced him to change to the model swing of the day epitomized by smooth-swingers like Gene Littler and Don January. "They were looking for the perfect swing," Tucker said. "They said, 'You could get better if you narrow your stance and hold the club this way.' I went from scratch golf to a five-handicap in one season. I almost lost my golf game," says Tucker, who today is a single-digit player.

Once Tucker lost the swing Moe taught him, he could never go back because only one person could teach it — Moe. And Tucker couldn't go back to Moe. He was heart-broken that his little buddy didn't follow his footsteps into golf. Using Tucker as an example, Moe also wanted to show the golf world his method of swinging was better and worked with all players. When Tucker went to a U.S. college, another of his dreams died. Their relationship has never been the same. "I think he felt I abandoned him," Tucker said.

***

In the early 1960s, Moe's days as a competitive player appeared over. It was sad. Even though he was barely in his 30s, he was already out to pasture, just another marvel who failed to live up to everyone's predictions of greatness.

That didn't mean he disappeared from view, however. Moe could always find a way to draw attention to himself even though it was the last thing he wanted. In 1962, Moe and Turcotte showed up on Showtime, a Canadian TV program with host Robert Goulet. The writers came up with a corny sketch in which Turcotte would show Goulet he could teach any beginner how to hit great shots just by whispering a few key instructions into his ear. The gag, of course, was that the beginner was Moe, weird swing and all. Before the program, Moe asked if the canvas backing he was to fire against was strong enough. The producer said, "You could hit a cannon against it and the ball wouldn't go through."

When the show began — broadcast live, of course — Turcotte went through his routine and whispered something to Moe who proceeded to rifle the ball through the canvas. The ball ricocheted around the set, sending technicians and performers ducking in all directions. "He made a hell of a racket and it made me look like a hell of a whisperer," Turcotte recalls gleefully.

One of the few times Moe resurfaced in a tournament was in the 1962

Ontario Open where he finished runner-up and eight shots back of Weslock. Moe ventured onto the short-lived Caribbean Tour, which began in the fall of 1962 sponsored by the Joseph E. Seagram's Company, a Canadian distillery. Run by the U.S. PGA, the satellite tour involved five tournaments with five competitive rounds each.

The "Pan-American Tour," as it was also known, lined the pockets of the smooth-swinging George Knudson, Canada's top player on the PGA Tour. He won the Maracaibo and Puerto Rico Opens in 1962, the Panama Open in '63 and the Caracas Open in '64. Only the Jamaican Open escaped him.

Moe won some money on the circuit, but no tournaments. And he's quick to play down the image of fun in the sun. "It was work. We were afraid to drink the water or eat the food. It was just terrible. That's why it's not on any more. Too many guys got sick. A lot of the guys didn't want to go."

***

Turcotte was always looking for ways to make a buck for Moe and himself, and create some publicity for Pleasure Park. Moe had such a reputation as a guzzler of Coke, he even approached the company about a sponsorship and advertising deal, but it fizzled out. Early in 1963, Turcotte came up with a publicity stunt for Pleasure Park and Moe that had some people shaking their heads in awe and others in embarrassment. Turcotte advertised a "special driving show" featuring the "amazing Moe Norman." Turcotte called it an "ability test," but most people thought it was a marathon because Moe predicted he would hit more than 1,000 balls in one afternoon in record time.

Under sunny skies on the big Saturday, thousands of people and a herd of reporters and TV crews streamed in to watch Moe hit from a specially built wooden stage. Almost immediately, spectators and journalists were introduced to "a special distraction" brought in for the event — 17-year-old Marianne Shaw, a red-haired beauty. "Chances are Miss Shaw doesn't know a chip shot from a chipmunk, but a guy could take one look at her in white shorts and pine for another whack at youth," wrote Dick Beddoes in The Globe and Mail.

Moe began at 2 p.m. In the first hour, he hit 390 balls, all over 225 yards. After his frenzied start, he slowed to about six balls a minute. A radio station broadcast from Pleasure Park, providing updates on Moe's tally. "Moe Norman has hit more than 800 golf balls. Can you believe that? You have to wonder how many more balls this incredible man can hit. His hands must be getting awfully sore."

Moe hit nothing but drivers. Each was fitted with a women's shaft to lighten the club and soften the shock of impact. He threw in a few of his famous tricks, including hitting an upside-down left-handed club and nailing shots from a variety of tall tees. Moe took only five minutes to rest in each hour, to eat, gulp down bottles of Coke and wind electrical tape to cover his booming blisters. Late in the afternoon, a man in the crowd yelled, "Hey Moe, what are you? Some kind of nut?"

The crowd instantly went silent, as if all sound had been shut off by a switch. Heads turned in the direction of the man, then back to Moe. He stood with his arms limply by his waist, his head cocked to one side, the squinting of his eyes causing deep furrows in his forehead, his cheeks fire-engine red, puffed in sharp round points, his mouth frozen open in that trademark grimace-grin. He had a look that indicated no pain and no pleasure — just startling intensity. Moe's eyes locked onto the man like two laser beams.

"All nuts," he retorted, "should hit so straight." The crowd roared with laughter.

By 6 p.m. 3,000 people had been through the gates. Moe was still at it in the evening even though it was only May 21 and the temperature had dipped considerably. Moe was obviously tiring. Some people were worried that Moe might hurt himself. Turcotte said he kept checking with his star attraction. "Moe, are you OK? Can you hit more?"

Moe nodded his head up and down briskly, "Sure, sure."

Finally, at 8:51 p.m., he couldn't hit another ball. In six hours and 51 minutes, Moe had hit 1,540 drives. "That's more drives than most golfers hit in five years," Turcotte crowed to reporters. It was much more than a marathon, Turcotte said. "Any jerk can swing a club that many times." But every one of those 1,540 balls went beyond the 225-yard marker; what's more, each one fell within a 30-yard wide landing zone, the equivalent of a fairly narrow fairway. "It was a gimmick for promotion, but it was an authentic test of ability because it took talent to do it. I defy anyone to hit that many balls — all in bounds."

Turcotte believed it was the first such test of its kind, and would go into the Guinness Book of World Records. He also hoped it would a set a target that would start a trend as players tried to beat Moe's incredible mark.

At first, Moe laughed at the memory. "You wanted to feel a hot pair of hands, hoo boy." Then, he turned serious: "It was a stupid thing to do. It could have hurt me. My friends warned me not to do it. I couldn't make a fist with my left hand for four days. It's the worst injury I've ever experienced from playing golf." Turcotte denied a rumour that he forced Moe to perform. In retrospect, it was dangerous. Moe could have injured himself and ended his career, which would have been a tragedy. His entire life was hitting golf balls.

Moe's feat was soon forgotten — a little-known part of the legend. It never made it into the Guinness record book and no trend of ability tests developed, although it's hard to imagine anyone ever matching him. Like many things in Moe's life, the Pleasure Park test was both amazing and lamentable. Certainly it provided more evidence of Moe's immense skill and talent, but it was also tainted by the slimy feeling that he was being reduced to a circus act — complete with a leggy lass — to put money in the till. A golf clown.

**

Moe made a big comeback to competitive golf in 1963. He took more time away from Pleasure Park, played in more events and sharpened his tournament play. It made a huge difference. He won three Canadian events, capturing the Saskatchewan Open and his second Ontario Open, edging Cowan by three shots.

His most exciting tournament was the 36-hole Ontario PGA at St. George's in Toronto. After the first round, Moe was tied at 70 with his rival Knudson. The second round was eagerly awaited because it would be a major test of Moe's faith in himself. By now, Moe's fatal flaw was self-evident. Moe had the game to be among the Nicklauses, Palmers and Knudsons, but he refused to believe it and was awed by their fame. In the company of the superstars, he was unable to play his normally brilliant game. Although his tinted glasses and chain smoking didn't give him the clean image associated with touring pros, Knudson was Canada's most celebrated touring pro. By 1963, he'd won twice on the PGA Tour. He was also gaining a reputation as one of the game's great ball-strikers — his swing was a classic move that blended balance, tempo and power. Perhaps this explains at least part of the reason Moe had such a hard time playing against Knudson.

Although golf insiders still believed Moe's swing was more accurate, many people automatically assumed Knudson was the better player because of his higher visibility. Moreover, Knudson had proved that he could get the ball in the hole under the pressure of a PGA Tour event. Moe had not.

During Moe's two seasons on tour, he felt awkward with Knudson. They were never close, but as they got older, they shared many laughs and engaged in many rambling discussions about technique. "There was tremendous respect between Moe and George," Irv Lightstone said. They had plenty in common: each found socializing very difficult and hitting a golf ball very easy.

Moe was standing in front of Knudson in a dinner line one time and overhead him talking. "He said I didn't know how good I was, and that I had one of the best moves in golf. I started to cry and there were 200 people there," Moe says. "He is the most sensitive man I know," Knudson told Lorne Rubenstein.

They also had a common problem — they were both poor-to-average putters. Jack Nicklaus once remarked that Knudson had a million-dollar swing and through the years of retelling, the line was erroneously expanded to quote him as saying Knudson also had a 10-cent putting stroke. But it makes the point. Contemporaries such as Trevino said Knudson could have won many more tournaments if he had worked as hard on his putting as his long game.

Moe and Knudson were bored and baffled by putting. They could control a ball in the air at will, but the unpredictability of the ground didn't allow for that kind of control. The putting stroke seemed more of an art than a science, and this frustrated the two consummate technicians. As a result, Moe says they never practiced putting. "We didn't believe it was a part of golf. We figured if we hit the ball close enough, we didn't have to putt."

Later in their careers during casual games together, they often played for $20 a shot. But they didn't keep score the conventional way. They played for fairways, greens and pins hit. "If the other guy hit the fairway and you missed, you paid $20. We didn't even putt. George hit six pins in one round. I hit four."

Going into the second round of the 1963 Ontario PGA, the pair were in a logjam of players tied for first. Many people expected Moe to fade against Knudson, but Moe was in a group behind and this made a big difference. Knudson fired a sturdy 69 but Moe birdied the last two holes to edge him with a 68 for the title.

Would he have folded if he had played with Knudson? No one could say obviously, but it was an affirmation that Moe could beat Sir George in his prime.

***

After winning his second Canadian Amateur in 1956, Moe was asked why he didn't play well in 72-hole stroke events such as the Canadian Open. "I don't have anything to play for in these tournaments. If I turned pro and the bucks were on the line, it would be a different story."

Aside from his brief flirtation with the leaderboard in 1957, Moe usually played indifferently in the Open. Playing for the bucks hadn't made a difference. Like many Canadian golfers, such as Stan Leonard, George Knudson and Dave Barr, Moe found it difficult dealing with the immense pressure of trying to win the country's national championship. What's worse, it's the tournament they'd most like to win. The last homegrown to win was Pat Fletcher in 1954, but he beat a weaker field than most Opens — only four PGA Tour regulars competed.

In 1963, the Canadian Open was at Scarboro, site of many of Moe's best moments. He played solidly, firing three consecutive even-par 71s. Going into Sunday's final round, Moe was in second place, only three shots back of Doug Ford, one of his pals from the PGA Tour and another fairway flyer. They played a practice round together at Scarboro in two hours and five minutes, leaving the gallery exhausted. "By the time we got to the last hole, you could hear them heaving and panting on both sides of the fairway," Moe told Golf Digest.

Reporters and fans were very excited about Moe's chances in the final round. If he prevailed, it would be a huge victory — far bigger than Fletcher's. What a storybook ending it would make: the eccentric Moe Norman, the ragamuffin in scuffed shoes and faded shirts, who had slept in bunkers, sold his prizes to eat and played the game with other-worldly brilliance, winning the country's most prestigious tournament. And wouldn't it be something to win the Royal Canadian Golf Association's biggest event.

Moe's friends and supporters squirmed with nervous excitement as their embattled buddy prepared to contend for the biggest win of his career. "We thought he could do it," Lightstone said. "I thought he was the best player in the field. It would be nothing for Moe to shoot 64 or 65 anytime he wanted to at Scarboro."

A victory would prove to the world he wasn't a golf clown, but a competitive pro golfer who deserved respect. A victory would catapult him back on the PGA Tour. And perhaps more importantly, it would show Moe there was no reason to ever feel inferior to another golfer.

On top of a bad case of butterflies, Moe faced the added strain of playing before a home crowd in Toronto. When he teed off, it seemed like all 8,000 fans were around the tee to watch him, Ford, and crusty Herman Keiser, the 48-year-old winner of the 1946 Masters. It was a brutal draw. Moe and Ford were speedmeisters and Keiser was a dead-slow, methodical man who cared little that his funereal pace aggravated the hell out of his playing partners.

Moe held up well early, but struggled on the 439-yard fifth hole and emerged with a double-bogey six. Keiser's torpid pace of play forced Moe to stand around on every shot. "He got so mad at Keiser," said Globe reporter Jack Marks who followed the group. "He lost his patience. He was boiling inside."

Moe was hitting the ball great, splitting every fairway and knocking down pins, but he was shakier than usual putting. "I was nervous on the greens. I couldn't get the putter back, couldn't get the putter back. I was trying to manufacture it in the hole instead of stroking it into the hole."

As the round continued, Moe also became upset by highly partisan fans. They were yelling encouragement to Moe, but applauding Ford's and Keiser's miscues — an unpardonable breach of etiquette to Moe. Even so, he was still in contention early in the back nine. Then his mind betrayed him with thoughts of what winning the Canadian Open would mean.

"You can't believe how different the world becomes when something like that happens to you. Things that have never come to you before. You drop the puck at a Leaf hockey game, kick the first football at the (Toronto) Argo game, throw the first pitch at a baseball game, attend celebrity dinners with Bobby Hull — he represents hockey, you represent golf. All that comes to your mind. Now everyone is going to want you. Now you'll be the talk of the country for years and years. They're going to want you in Vancouver, in Halifax, all these places you won't even find but they'll want you for their main dinner. 'Here's the Canadian Open champ.' All these things on your mind.

"That's just human nature. The biggest win of your life."

Moe putted with even more haste than usual; he astonished the gallery by sinking a putt between Ford's legs as he bent down to retrieve his ball. Moe hit the ball close to the pins, but stickhandled his way to bogies and disappointing pars. "It was murder to watch," Marks said. "He was putting quicker than he normally did. Everyone in the crowd could tell."

Nevertheless, Ford said Moe trailed him by only a shot or two when they came to the 15th tee. Keiser hooked his drive into the wilderness and Ford yanked his deep into the left rough. The crowd clapped and a well-meaning, but indiscreet fan, hollered: "OK, Moe, show 'em how the shot should be hit!"

Moe was aghast. He dropped his driver and rolled his eyes in exasperation and embarrassment. "The only time I ever saw Moe get upset was at that Canadian Open," Ford said. "He really told that gallery off. Even so, he hit a beautiful drive. He never missed. Moe was a straight arrow. As we walked down the fairway, he couldn't apologize enough for the gallery's behaviour. He kept going on and on about it. I said 'Moe, that doesn't bother me. I've been around too long.' The gallery really upset him. It hurt his concentration and deflated him."

When the day was done, Moe had hit 17 greens in regulation, but suffered six three-putt greens. Ford secured the victory and $9,000 first prize with a one-under 70. Moe hobbled in with a 75, finished eight shots back and received $625. "I don't know whether, in his heart, Moe wanted to win," Lightstone said. "I don't think he could have handled what came after — the speeches, the endorsements. He would have been back on tour."

Instead, he would be back at Pleasure Park, comfortable but unchallenged — a stallion among ponies, out to pasture, an enigma who frustrated himself, fans and supporters. The question continued unanswered: how could this much talent remain unfulfilled?

Chapter Seventeen
Cleaning Clocks and Tying Shoelaces

Back in the 1960s, before tour purses went through the roof, a hot-shot golfer could make some pretty good dough hustling or playing for big-time gamblers. Lee Trevino was routinely retained by wealthy gamblers to take on someone else's hired gun, such as Fred Hawkins or Raymond Floyd. Like prize fighters, the lads would duke it out on the course for a fee, travel expenses and a percentage of the take.

The most notorious hustler in golf was the late Titanic Thompson. He wasn't a great golfer but fleeced many pigeons with his cunning schemes. Martin "The Fat Man" Stanovich was another legend of gambling golf games, but he was an excellent player who, the story goes, once relieved Dean Martin of $40,000.

"Marty was the best gambling golfer that ever lived in the United States," proclaims Chico Miartuz, a minor legend himself who has been teaching for 40 years at Bayshore Golf Club in Miami Beach. Miartuz, an itinerant tour player in the late 1950s, played many stakes games partnered with The Fat Man. His powerful legs and solid round belly explained his nickname. "Titanic Thompson couldn't clean Stanovich's shoes as a golfer," Miartuz said. "Stanovich was a remarkable golfer. Marty took on the pros and they all had to give him two-and-a-half shots. And he beat them all."

Rumour has it The Fat Man once bested Sam Snead, but Miartuz says he watched Stanovich beat Ed Furgol, the reigning U.S. Open champ, in October of 1954. "I can't recall anyone who ever beat him," Miartuz said of Stanovich, who died a few years ago.

One of Stanovich's pals was Jeff Alpert. In January of 1964, Alpert was a freshman on the University of Miami golf team and pretty cocksure of his abilities. The future All-American also liked a little action and he had a suitably snazzy nickname, "Hollywood." He usually played for a nickel or a dime a hole — $5 or $10 — and he emerged with jingling pockets most of the time.

Hollywood Alpert recalls one particular morning at the Bayshore club, a very tough, 7,000-yard public course. "I was in the locker room and this guy comes in and says, 'You want to play a little golf game, want to play a little golf game?' He looked a little dishevelled, like he had just woke up."

The next morning, Hollywood, The Fat Man and Pipeline Moe teed it up. Stanovich had heard about Pipeline, but Hollywood hadn't. Besides, there was no way this stocky oddball with the rapid-fire speech was a player. They'd just humour the loudmouth and send him on his way packing a lighter wallet.

Hollywood was set up. "Moe made his living down there by hustling," Jack Marks said. "He'd figure out who the best players were at the different clubs and ask them for a game. They'd look at Moe and say, 'This guy's not a golfer.' And in those days Moe could shoot any number he wanted. It was nothing for Moe to set course records at courses he'd never seen before."

Alpert picks up the story: "I was probably two or three down early on, but I thought he's gonna make a bogey or a double sooner or later. I thought maybe he's just lucky. But that swing! Every hole, he stuck it in there two or three feet from the hole. He constantly, absolutely staked it. I didn't know what was unfolding.

"It wasn't even close. He made 11 birdies and seven pars and shot a 61. Nobody shoots 61! I'm positive it was a course record. I was 69 and Marty was 70 or so. He waxed everybody's ears. I paid him $70 and Marty paid about $300. I thought 'Who is this guy?'"

Determined to win his money back, Alpert agreed to play Moe at another club, Miami Shores, with a different friend. "The Fat Man packed it in. He had enough of Moe. I didn't have enough smarts. Nothing changed in the second game. He hit close every single time. He shot a 64. Coming down the stretch, he said 'You can press now, you can press now.' Everybody was very quiet. We took our licks. I shot a 67 and paid him $30.

"We told him: 'Do us a favour. You know where we live. When you drive by, just beep the horn and keep on going.'"

The course record at the old Bayshore course is 61 — it's since been remodelled — but it's credited to someone else. Alpert said hustlers were interested only in money, not in broadcasting they'd set new course records and drawing attention to themselves. Especially Moe.

***

In the early 1960s, Moe did most of his practicing and playing at Tomoka Oaks near Daytona Beach. It was the unofficial winter home for Canadian pros. Moe and many young northern pros played on the Florida PGA Section winter tour, a forerunner of the many mini-tours that thrive in the state and across the U.S. today.

It was in Florida that Moe met up with fellow Canadians Orm and Verna Membery. Along with their son Ed, they owned and managed Golf Haven, a 6,400-yard public course in the town of Gilford north of Toronto near Lake Simcoe. The Memberys were like a second family to Moe. He hadn't spoken to his brothers and sisters for years; it was still fixed in his mind that they thought golf was a sissy sport.

The Memberys and Moe talked about the possibility of signing up together, and the thought buoyed Moe's spirits. He felt chained to Pleasure Park, performing for the crowds and giving lessons, which didn't leave much time for practicing. Moe also felt that at age 34, his competitive golf game was slipping away.

The 1964 season was disappointing for Moe. In the $200,000 Carling World Championship at renowned Oakland Hills in Michigan, Moe was psyched out by all the big-name pros and the tough reputation of the Donald Ross layout. "What a course, what a field. I can't play here." He couldn't and shot an 82.

There was one bright spot in 1964.

Moe made it to the finals of the Millar Trophy, the match-play championship for Canadian pros. His opponent was Jerry Magee, his victim in the 1956 Canadian Amateur. It was his fifth straight match during a week of scorching heat at Pine Valley Golf Club, which is now the revered National Golf Club of Canada. Moe lost 11 pounds that week, forcing him to hitch his pants up after every shot. It took only two hours and 32 minutes before Moe dispatched Magee 3 and 2.

The turning point in Moe's playing career arrived the next year when the Membery's finally did what no other club owners had been willing to do — they took a chance on Moe as their "playing professional" at Golf

Haven. Moe says they paid him $110 a week, but Ed Membery said that figure was exaggerated. He said the family paid Moe "a small annual retainer," but took care of his books, taxes, mail and organized his affairs, such as making sure his licence was renewed and health insurance was in order. "Moe needed that kind of assistance," Membery said.

Moe's part of the deal was to represent the club in tournaments. The side of his golf bag said Golf Haven in big, bold letters. Besides creating some publicity for Golf Haven, Orm Membery told The Toronto Telegram his motive was to get Moe back on the road playing tournament golf. "The guy is one of the best. How can he ever beat that complex about name players when he only has one or two chances a year to play with them, to find out that they are no better than he is. We have tried to convince Moe he belongs as a person and as a golfer."

Working out of Golf Haven was wonderful for Moe. He was finally a full-time playing pro. "It took pressure off," Moe says. "Now, there was time to practice." It was also his first taste of freedom since 1956 — to roam around visiting friends and play in as many tournaments as he wanted.

The 1965 season was a rebuilding year for Moe. He won only one event, the Manitoba Open, but his scoring average was around 69. Moe's greatest strides were made not on the golf course, but at a table in the Golf Haven clubhouse with Verna Membery. She was the first woman Moe felt comfortable with. He could confide in her, share his thoughts and feelings. He took to calling her Mom. "I had never met a woman like that. Not even close. I didn't understand women."

"She was like a mother to him," Ed Membery said of his late mother. "He put a lot of trust and faith in her."

Verna even succeeded in teaching Moe some social graces and courtesies, how to make life easier with other people. She also taught Moe not to wear striped shirts with striped pants, and how to coordinate colours. There had been a number of attempts to make-over Moe, but it wasn't until Verna Membery and the sense of closeness that he felt from her family that anyone succeeded.

"Moe's whole attitude to life and golf changed during those years," said Ed Membery, who now owns a course near Barrie, Ontario.

Picking up more cheques in tournaments, Moe was finally making an income that was commensurate with his phenomenal ability. "Now I started to get better. I'd never had money before. I kept it all in my pocket — $20,000, that's not much." The Memberys were afraid for Moe, and Verna finally convinced him to put much of it in a safety deposit box. He still wouldn't go for an interest-paying bank account. The Memberys also got Moe a room in Aurora, north of Toronto.

***

Moe was in his mid 30s, a time when many golfers are at the prime of their career. They're hardened by tournament experience, more mature and at their physical peak. Moe was now a burly 200-pounder — he terrorized managers of buffet tables with the vast quantities he could inhale — but he was as solid as a tank.

Moe was serious about getting in shape for golf. He made a habit of filling his golf bag with about 400 balls and carrying it for 18 holes — even during tournaments — to build up his legs. "I've got all this weight on me — got to keep my legs strong." At Brantford golf club, he was often spotted running up and down the hill of the par-three third hole with his bag, full of balls, strapped to his back as he sweated and grunted. This exercise also built up his shoulders and torso. With the added weight, his unique brand of strength training and the routine of hitting 600 balls a day for nearly 20 years, "Moe was mega-strong," Herb Holzscheiter said.

Feeling better about himself, Moe set out in his Cadillac in the summer of 1966 and played across Canada and the northern United States. Anywhere there was a cheque to be won, Moe would usually be there.

At the time, the Canadian pro tour was a loosely organized series of provincial open championships overseen by the CPGA. Veteran Al Balding and good young Canadian touring pros such as Wilf Homenuik, Jerry Magee and George Knudson mostly played the PGA Tour, but they occasionally returned home to play the Canadian Tour, as did a number of young American players looking to make some money and sharpen their games.

The fields were inconsistent because of the great distance between tournaments and the relatively small purses. For example, travelling from the Manitoba Open near Winnipeg to the Saskatchewan Open in Regina was a 360-mile journey. The trip from Winnipeg to Calgary was 470 miles.

The summer of 1966 was phenomenal for Moe. He won five big tournaments and finished second in five events. Moe captured the opens of Manitoba, Quebec and Alberta. When he liked a city, the course, fans and people associated with the tournaments, he was comfortable and capable of killer golf. And he loved playing in Calgary. He had won his first Canadian Amateur title in 1955 at the Calgary Golf and Country Club.

Calgary's Willow Park, a 6,600-yard course that demands plenty of finesse, was owned by E.B. Keith, a millionaire builder and friend of Moe's. Moe was in his comfort zone. During that summer, Moe also won the Willow Park Classic Pro-Am and $5,000, the biggest pay-day of his life.

Moe's greatest triumph of the season was also a moral one. The CPGA had caused Moe untold grief when he tried to turn pro, by refusing to give him a card. Moe won the 54-hole CPGA Championship, also at Willow Park, by firing a 67 for a nine-under par 204, a record score for the title.

His CPGA title wrapped up a stunning Canadian summer season in which he won $13,300 in prize money. It's also believed that Moe was a whopping 110-under par for the Canadian Tour season. Moe won the scoring-average title for the second straight year with a record 69.8. The runner-up, Bob Breen, was at 72.4.

Having thoroughly dominated Canadian golf, it was even more obvious that Moe should be regularly plying his trade on the PGA Tour. After his great season, Moe said he now had saved more than $40,000 and he even owned real estate around Lake Simcoe. But he wasn't going to risk his own money on the U.S. PGA Tour. "Sure I'd love to go," he said, "but find me a sponsor. If somebody wants to share the investment, I'll be there."

Homenuik said: "Give Moe a manager who'll travel with him, handle everything but the play and Moe will make $60,000 his first year." It was a sentiment repeated often.

Moe was the man to beat in most Canadian events. He knew it and so did everyone else. But alas, when he was paired with Knudson and other big-name players, he fell apart. Earlier that summer, Moe faced off against Knudson in the Millar Championship, which was being contested for the first time as a stroke-play event, an unwise change that spelled the event's demise in 1968.

Moe played masterful golf throughout the event but, when he was paired with Canada's prevailing golf star in the final round, Moe disintegrated and finished a distant seven shots behind Knudson. "I used to beat him all the time," Moe lamented. "Now I can't tie his shoe laces." Moe's sensitivity made him "the perfect mark for any act of gamesmanship," Knudson said. That was a shame because he also considered Moe to be "one of golf's outstanding sportsmen."

Knudson liked Moe, but he liked winning championships better. "He knew how to upset Moe," Marks said. "Actually, Moe would upset himself. He wanted to talk to George on the tee. He wanted to be right on his shoulder. It was a strange respect he had for George. But George wouldn't talk to him. This really threw Moe."

Moe's victory in the CPGA qualified him to play in the Canadian Open in Vancouver at Shaughnessy. It also paid his expenses to three events on the Caribbean tour. But Moe didn't go to Vancouver. Instead, he skipped the $100,000 Open to play in a $2,500 event in Rochester, New York. He told organizers he was too tired and couldn't afford to travel to Vancouver. Most people said it was a lame excuse — that Moe just didn't want to be challenged by the big-name pros. But Moe also knew he rarely played well in the Open and it was a long way to Vancouver, so why bother? As happened many times, the politics of the situation completely escaped him.

Moe once again was in the CPGA's bad books. "It's a bloody poor show," barked CPGA president Jock McKinnon. A number of pros and McKinnon demanded Moe be temporarily suspended from the CPGA and that his expenses be withdrawn from the Caribbean tour. Moe, however, got off with a tongue-lashing.

Despite angering the big chiefs of the CPGA, Moe was part of the Canadian delegation that went to Royal Birkdale in England in early September to play in the Carling World Championship. The Memberys and Moe's friends were very nervous about this trip. Memories of Moe's disastrous journey to the 1956 Masters were still fresh.

"Suspicion is that the British spectators who revere tradition and staid behaviour on golf courses may not be ready for Moe, nor Moe for them," wrote The Toronto Star's Ken McKee. "Everyone is also aware of his tragic flaw, an inability to play to his potential in company with the superstars of the game. That's problem enough. A cold reception from the customers could finish him."

But if Moe could play his regular game, it was also possible that he would convince himself he could hold his own against the best, and that he should get back on the PGA Tour. It was also looked upon as his last chance to convince someone to sponsor him on tour.

It was Moe's first time playing in England and his initial taste of links-style golf. Although neither Palmer nor Nicklaus were entered, there were a number of top Americans in the field, such as Billy Casper, the new

U.S. Open champ, George Archer and Bert Yancey, winner of three PGA events that year. As well, there were top international players, including Australians Bruce Devlin, Ken Nagle, the 1960 British Open champ, and Peter Thomson, winner of five British Open championships.

Moe got off to a mediocre start with a 75. When he teed off in the second round with Archer and Texan Wes Ellis, there was a sizeable gallery around the first tee waiting for the big stars. "These spectators looked on in stunned horror as Moe struck his ball almost before Ellis's landed. One bloke declared, not quietly, 'He'll never learn to play the game that way,'" McKee reported.

Moe heard the remark and others like it throughout the round. He saw the pointing fingers, the hands over muttering mouths. He heard the snippets of sarcasm and titters of laughter. Moe staggered to five-over par after the front nine, partly because of the snail's pace of play and his unfamiliarity with the bump-and-run style of play, which required hitting shots short of the green and letting them run up to the hole.

It looked like everyone's fears would be realized when a hard rain began to fall, slowing play up even further. Archer's wife Donna insisted George put on a jacket, delaying play. Moe chided Archer: "Hit the ball, then put it on." Archer continued to fumble through his bag for the jacket and by the time he hit the ball Moe was standing up the green. This derailed Moe. He missed three birdie chances in four holes, but settled down and finished strongly, making birdies on three of his last five holes for an even-par 73, a decent score considering the weather. Moe made the cut comfortably with a two-day total of 148, while Knudson struggled with the conditions and links style of play, and went home early.

The British, a savvy lot of golf fans who take the game quite seriously, took a fancy to Moe and he commanded quite a following in the third round. McKee said they gasped as Moe broke off from bouncing his ball on his clubhead, and bashed his drives down the middle of the fairway with nary a look. Spectators didn't know what to think as he stroked putts seemingly without taking the trouble to stop walking.

"What about that follow-through?" one fellow remarked. "Who does he think he is, (ballerina) Margo Fonteyn doing the Dying Swan?"

"It reminds me of (cricketer) Colin Milburn slamming one of his sixes," said another.

"More like a woodchopper if you ask me," his pal chimed in.

Moe's caddie, Sam Niblock of Belfast, was a new and loyal fan. "I wouldn't change him for anyone else in the field. I suppose he's got the ugliest style of anyone I've caddied for. But it's the score that counts."

Moe was disappointed to finish the day with a 75. He added a lovely two-under 71 to finish 13 shots back of winner Devlin. Nonetheless, he was the top Canadian finisher and pocketed a cheque of $1,200. Many of Moe's fans were heartened just to see that he didn't blow up against the all-star competition. The Toronto Star trumpeted his achievement with the headline: "Moe proves he can play in the big time." It was a reminder that Moe, if he could get past his own psychological traps, was among the world's top golfers and that he should be playing with them regularly. "This is, without a doubt, one of his finest moments in international competition," McKee gushed. "It is, however, the long-term repercussions of his play that will be most rewarding."

Chapter Eighteen
Dr. Jekyll and Mr. Hyde

Moe doesn't take long to do anything — whether it's hitting a golf ball or crushing the hopes of his friends. Just when things seem to be going so well, he'll do something no one can understand. True to form, it didn't take Moe very long to burst the bubble of optimism that had formed after his successful debut among Britain's demanding golf fans.

Moe had already confounded everyone by skipping the Canadian Open after his CPGA victory qualified him. That victory also earned him an opportunity to represent the country on the two-man team that was to contest the 1966 Canada Cup in November in Tokyo. (The tournament name was changed to the World Cup a few years later.)

Ironically, RCGA officials were now asking him to get on their international team. Moe's appointment to the Canada Cup team was an acknowledgement that, despite earlier run-ins, the RCGA greatly respected his abilities. And what greater honour could be bestowed upon a golfer than to be asked to represent his country in an international competition.

Moe received his invitation in mid-September, shortly after returning from Britain. The RCGA waited for an answer but got none. What's more, no one caught sight of Moe for weeks. Finally, the RCGA called Ed Membery at Golf Haven and got the news: Moe wasn't going.

"Having already made arrangements for the Pan-American tour, Moe was greatly upset to learn of the invitation," Membery said. "Moe didn't know what to do and was puzzled over not having been advised earlier, especially by the CPGA. I think he was thoroughly confused about what to do, and consequently, he dropped out of both events. It seems that Moe has kept strictly out of sight, not wanting to see anyone until he figures out for sure what he should do."

Although he had made arrangements with Seagrams Ltd., the sponsors of the Pan-American tour, he could easily have been released from that commitment for something like the Canada Cup. Instead, Al Balding went in Moe's place. CPGA president Jock McKinnon, who was already steamed at Moe for skipping the Canadian Open, was furious. Telegram reporter George Laughlin wrote: "Moe's extremely sensitive nature, which influences many of his decisions, may have unfortunately placed him in a position that could greatly damage his golf future."

A week after news broke of Moe's rejection of his Canada Cup invitation, the CPGA held a special reception to hand out awards for the year's top players. Moe had won the A.T. Hunt Trophy for low-scoring average for the third time in his career. He didn't show up to receive it.

The next week, Moe finished tied with five other players in an 18-hole $1,000 pro invitational near Toronto. A playoff was called. Moe didn't show up for that either. The Toronto Telegram headline read: "Where, oh where has Moe Norman gone — THIS TIME?"

During the third round of the Caracas Open in November, a dog bit him on the leg and Moe required a tetanus shot. Many CPGA types thought that after all the times Moe had bitten the hand that fed him, the favour had finally been returned.

***

Nineteen sixty-six was a smashing success on the golf course but as Moe had found 10 years earlier, with every victory came more attention from fans, photographers and reporters, more strangers invading his cocoon, more bigwigs telling him what to do and how to live. Moe just couldn't handle it. As one writer put it, the consensus was that Moe had progressed from "golf's enfant terrible to a fast-playing phenomenon who is now widely regarded as a wasted world asset."

"From a social standpoint," Herb Holzscheiter said, "Moe felt he didn't fit in a lot of times. His defence was to do stupid things. You'd say 'What is Moe doing?' He's flipping his lid. But he didn't know any other way to fight back. He just wanted to play and be left alone. People were coming at him from all sides. He just couldn't handle being in the limelight. That held him back. He could have won a lot more golf tournaments if he had handled himself better with people."

This partially explains why Moe could shoot 61s in casual rounds, but rarely in competition. Those kinds of performances attracted attention.

"Moe loves to win and he could win any time he wanted," said Irv Lightstone, who also played on the Canadian Tour. "But Moe's head worked in strange ways. I don't think Moe was unhappy finishing second or third. I think Moe looked for escape hatches."

***

The Sixties were good to Moe financially. He was wiping up in the small pro events and pro-ams, setting course records and consistently finishing in the top-five of the provincial opens. In 1967, he won only one big Canadian tournament, his third straight Manitoba Open, captured the scoring title with a 68.6 average and more than $16,000. In 1968, he won the Saskatchewan Open and the season-ending Canadian Pro Tour Championship and its $3,000 first-place cheque. He won his fifth scoring title, averaging 69.7 per game. He won about $11,000 that season, making it the sixth straight year he won more than $10,000 playing golf in Canada.

The circuit of provincial open tournaments had acquired the title of Canadian Pro Tour — but many people called it the Moe Norman Tour. "If you could beat Moe, you had a chance to win the tournament," said Holzscheiter, who worked as a consultant with the tour in the early 1970s.

Holzscheiter says Moe was the undisputed leading money winner in Canadian golf tournaments in the Sixties. He used to carry as much as $30,000 in his front pocket at tournaments. On his way to the British Columbia Open one year, Moe was stopped on the highway for speeding. Moe asked the officer the cost of the fine. The cop said $61. Moe started to laugh. The officer said, "You're the first guy in 16 years I ever met who got a ticket and started laughing."

"What am I supposed to do? Cry?"

Moe reached into his pocket and pulled out his fat wad of bills. "Here, this should put a dent in it."

"What's your name again?" the officer asked as Moe's passengers burst out laughing.

He paid the fine right there and went on his way.

Moe was doing well, but how? He wasn't earning huge dollars. Aside from gas and trading in his Cadillac annually, Moe didn't have much in the way of expenses. He was given equipment. He ate simply, subsisting most of the day on hot dogs, Coke and junk food until a giant meal at dinner. Moe's rent for his room north of Toronto was a pittance.

He slept in cheap hotels on the road, and on a few occasions, in his car.

Moe was pretty cheap, but he didn't scrimp on clothes. No, Moe had gone full circle from his early days when he looked like a colour-blind waif from the caddie shack. Now Moe veritably strode the fairways like a peacock in expensive, high-quality threads. Moe's clothes weren't always spotless or perfectly pressed, but he took enormous pride in looking good, resplendent in $70 pants, $50 Munsingwear and Lacoste shirts and turtlenecks, $100 alligator shoes — significant outlays almost 30 years ago.

And Moe's look was certainly consistent. It could be 90 degrees Fahrenheit, irritatingly humid under a scorching sun. But Moe would be wearing dark pants, all wrapped up tight in a dark turtleneck — usually navy, black or red. On cool days he'd wear an alpaca wool sweater with vertical stripes of assorted bright colours that prompted his buddies to ask, "Gee Moe, where do you keep the batteries and the switch?"

Many pros wore their polyester pants short — what would be called flood pants today — so they wouldn't get wet from the dew, but Moe's were often above his ankles. Nevertheless, Moe was looking better than at any time of his career, making decent money, enjoying many friendships, playing well — but enjoying competitive golf less.

Moe was far more serious about his game than in years past. He still chattered incessantly and bounced a ball off the end of a club — that was nerves — but he was no longer the entertainer, calling shots off the tee or hitting from high tees. The clown prince of golf was gone. Besides, he knew that shtick bothered his fellow competitors.

He was playing for his daily bread now, and he didn't want distractions. This was serious business. Even though he called himself the fastest player in the world, he'd get mad when fans would bolt for positions just before he was about to hit. Many fans tried to talk to him during tournaments, as in the old days. This greatly angered Moe. He didn't see the fans trying to engage Knudson or other big-name pros in conversation during tournaments, so why prevail upon him?

Some fans could be outright rude too. "You know how sports fans can be," says Bob Beauchemin, who played on the Canadian Tour before becoming tour commissioner in the 1980s. "Some people tend to think they own you just because you're an athlete, and they'll think nothing of talking to you at the wrong times. Most athletes could deal with this diplomatically, but not Moe. It could get really nasty. It wasn't really Moe's fault. He just couldn't handle it."

Some fans made fun of Moe and tried to humiliate him, Gary Slatter said. Some mimicked his rapid speech and repeated phrases over and over in front of Moe and other spectators. "Some fans egged him on. They knew they could get him upset. People could be cruel."

Moe used to slough off comments from the gallery, even laugh, but now he'd get mad and lecture the fans or worse. Instead of the likeable, happy-go-lucky elfin character of his amateur days, Moe appeared to be a crusty curmudgeon always on the brink of blowing his stack. He was fed up with being the buffoon of the golf world. Moe played many times with Winnipeg's Dan Halldorson, winner of two PGA Tour events. "Moe was always offended. He'd tee off and people would start to laugh. They couldn't believe how much talent he had. Moe had a lot of problems because of this. There were confrontations. Moe was very defensive," said Halldorson, winner of two World Cup team titles with Jim Nelford and Dave Barr.

Golf fans were more sophisticated in the 1960s. They were used to watching the methodical Nicklaus and smooth swingers like Don January on TV. Moe played an agonizingly difficult game with a weird looking swing — and so fast, so effortless — that people couldn't comprehend. Some inconsiderate spectators laughed at him. Moe had heard the laughter for 15 years and it still irritated him to no end.

Holzscheiter was a close friend and confidante, but he witnessed Moe in many unpleasant moments. It was hard for him to take because Moe was one of his dearest friends. Sometimes Moe got in spats with players because of "foolish things" that he did in tournaments. If play was too slow for his liking, he might lay down on the grass and pretend to go to sleep. Or he'd tromp off in the middle of a round and return 10 minutes later with a Coke. "Guys would be on him. 'Moe we're waiting!' Moe would say, 'Well, we're waiting on every shot!'"

Most of Moe's confrontations, however, were with fans, many of whom didn't understand his style of playing. "The odd guy in the gallery might say 'Hey Moe, why don't you try?' Right away this would tick Moe off. He would give that guy an earful, call him everything under the sun, and meanwhile there would be people with kids there. You just wanted to crawl into a hole and wish you weren't around.

"You'd try to calm him down and say 'Moe, good Lord, you can't do this!' If he was off-target, you couldn't do anything about it. His face would go beet red. He'd still be going on about it four holes later."

Some fans were naturally curious about how he played and asked questions. "Gee Moe, how can you hit your shots so perfectly when you don't even line them up?" Moe would put them down for asking a question that he thought was stupid. Holzscheiter adds that Moe's indifference was not due to a lack of warning. "I and a 100 other guys would tell him, 'Moe you can't treat people like that. They're interested in you. You make it look so easy. They're not out to get you. They just want to know more about you.' But he couldn't see it.

"If I asked him a question for someone, he'd answer it. He knew I wouldn't hurt him. He could trust me. But he didn't know about strangers."

Even when people just tried to be nice and say, "Hi, how you doin?" Moe would often mutter "That's my business, that's my business." He'd glower at the ground and march away. "He used to like galleries even when they called him a nut or a freak," Jack Marks wrote. "He would jive back with 'This nut just made $3,000 and you paid to watch. Who's the freak?'"

Those days were over. At the Manitoba and Saskatchewan Opens in 1968, Moe got into nasty confrontations with some fans. It was reported that he used obscene language. Moe admitted later that he did. "The fans were saying things like 'I hope he hits it in the water,'" Moe told a reporter. "Sure, I said some things."

The day after Moe won the 1968 Canadian Tour championship, the CPGA convened a hearing to investigate his conduct. Going into the meeting, a number of pros were pressuring the CPGA to suspend Moe from the organization and possibly from the tour for the next season. Instead, Moe was fined $300 for "verbal improprieties" and 10 per cent of his winnings the previous day. It was the largest fine ever imposed since the CPGA was inaugurated in 1911 and the first in the two years of Canadian Tour competition.

"A lot of us like him and we've tried to help him overcome these problems, but we're not going to allow the players on tour to give the tour a bad name," said Bill Hamilton, the CPGA's executive director.

Moe's difficulties cost him more than just fines — they denied him opportunities to make money off the course. "Organizations and clubs shied away from having him for pro-ams or clinics — partly because of his social graces — but they also feared that he'd tell a CEO to go screw himself," said Gary Menaul, a former Canadian Tour player.

Many players dissociated themselves from Moe too. They had livings to make and it was important fans and sponsors respected the players of the Canadian Tour. "Those guys who understood him, stuck with him and tried to help him," Holzscheiter said. "Even though he screwed up, he didn't do it intentionally. We tried to get him to adjust to the rest of society a little better. He's just a sensitive guy.

"He was in his element on the golf course. But there's more to life than hitting the ball. Golf was 99 per cent of his world and one per cent was other sports. Those things wouldn't fight back and hurt him."

***

To the public, Moe often came off as a nasty man with a bad temper, a foul mouth, little patience and no professionalism. You couldn't really blame the fans. They were used to polished sports celebrities who enjoyed the attendant fame and attention. For some, signing autographs and dealing with fans was drudgery, but they did it with tight smiles, always conscious of maintaining their public image.

Moe didn't sign autographs for adults. Only for kids. He once saw a man throw a piece of paper with his autograph on it into the garbage, and swore he'd never give an autograph to another adult fan. He could certainly be moody and inconsistent. One tournament he'd be chatting up the galleries, handing out souvenir golf balls to kids and hamming it up. The next day he'd be sullen and grumpy. One day he'd talk engagingly with someone, the next day he'd act like he never met the person before. And when he unleashed a volley of invective at people, of course they'd be alienated.

How could they be expected to understand Moe?

Despite his often churlish demeanour, for every one person that ran him down, there were four others who would defend him. They knew he was an odd duck who needed special handling. Unless you were inside Moe's circle, you didn't see his other side. For those people he knew and trusted, there was no better friend than Moe. His friends use words like sweet, kind, funny, loyal and loving to describe him. But this was impossible for outsiders to see, especially authority figures in the RCGA and CPGA, the big wheels he feared and mistrusted. They weren't out to get him or run him down, but that's how he saw it. "If you know Moe, he's a caring, giving human being," said Tom Stewart of Florida's Adios club.

Many of Moe's chums on the Canadian Tour loved him like an uncle, and they tried to shield him from harm's way. That's a common feeling among most people who get to know him. If fellow players saw a fan heading up to Moe, particularly one who looked like he'd a few drinks, they'd often try to intercept or head off the intruder. "The guys tried to protect Moe," Beauchemin said. "We kept an eye out to keep him away from situations where people might take advantage of him or there could be a confrontation. If someone tried to engage Moe and we thought it could get nasty, we'd try to get in the way. It wasn't Moe's fault, people just didn't understand the guy."

Moe's friends and supporters said that if you needed help, he'd do whatever he could for you — from fixing a faulty backswing to lending money. "He has a heart of gold," said Lars Melander, a weekly newspaper publisher who played on the Canadian Tour in the 1970s. "Several times he spotted some of the young guys a couple of hundred for entry fees."

Moe was better off than most of the young Canadian pros who were scrounging their way from tournament to tournament. If he thought a guy needed money, he wouldn't hesitate to lend him some — often without being asked, just saying "Pay me when you can."

Unfortunately, not everyone was as trustworthy. "Moe believed everyone was honest," Nick Weslock said. "He loaned a lot of money to young pros, but few ever paid him back. He's probably out about $30,000 over his lifetime. They really took advantage of him."

Moe also lent sums upwards of $5,000 to people other than golf pros, but he never bothered with paperwork. A number of these borrowers were not of the highest moral standing and he got burned time and time again. Acting on Moe's behalf, Ed Membery said he had to threaten a few people with legal action to get them to repay, but Moe still lost thousands in bad loans.

Moe only lent money to pros who were serious about their games and dedicated to practicing like he was. "If you were running around at night, drinking and chasing women, he wouldn't help you," Menaul said.

Ken Venning was sharing a house with Moe in Daytona Beach one winter when he ran short of money. Venning needed $800 to enter the second half of the winter tour, but he was busted. Moe dropped a wad of hundred dollar bills on the kitchen counter and said, 'Take what you need. You're playing too good.'

"I ended up winning money in the next two events and paid him back," Venning said.

Slatter was on the practice green at the 1972 Canadian Open when Moe asked him if he was going to play in Winnipeg the next week. Slatter said he couldn't afford to go. "Moe took a wad of money and threw it on the putting green and walked away. Arnold Palmer was practicing beside me. He went over and started pushing the money around with his putter like he was counting it. He saw it was all hundred dollar bills. He picked it up and it was about $3,000 or $4,000. Arnie laughed and gave it to me. Moe wanted me to use the money, but I gave it back to him the next day. He never asked for it. I think Moe cared more about how other people were doing than himself."

In his relationships with people, Moe is like Dr. Jekyll and Mr. Hyde — a completely different personality depending on whether you are a stranger or friend. With friends, Moe loves to laugh and tell jokes, emphasizing his punch lines like an eager-to-please actor. When he gets really wound up, he'll giggle as he tries to talk, barely able to catch his breath.

If he played golf with someone he didn't like, he might not say a word the entire round. Paired with a friend, however, he could have a ball. "You had too much spaghetti sauce on that putt. Boink, boink. Too much meat sauce. Ha Ha."

Even now in his 60s, Moe is still very much a rough-and-tumble boy. Moe will often fake like he's going to give you a shoulder block or punch you in the stomach. A favourite ploy is to wave a cup full of Coke like he's going to splash you. An old trick was to hold a cup over your head and pretend that he was about to soak you. He stopped this little gem after he accidently spilled some Coke on the head of Ed Woroch's wife, Cheryl. "He turned as white as a ghost," Woroch recalls.

Moe often didn't know the limits of horseplay or his own enormous strength. Holzscheiter says Moe would often sneak up behind some poor unsuspecting soul, wrap his arms around the fellow's chest in a bear hug and pick him up off the ground. Moe would squeeze the air out the unsuspecting victim, who would kick and howl in agony until Moe plunked him down, red-faced and winded. "He'd almost break your ribs. He'd go overboard but he didn't realize it. You'd have black and blue marks for a week."

Melander said he never met anyone as strong as Moe. "Every once in a while, he'd grab you by the wrist and there was no way on God's green earth that you could get away."

With friends, Moe can dish out a good-natured tease and he can also take it. Some guys even mimicked the way he talked. Everyone would laugh — including Moe — and he'd chase the perpetrator over hill and dale while everyone hooted, Holzscheiter said. "If he caught you, he'd say, 'You're fooling with me, hoo hoo, you're talkin' like me, hoo hoo.'

He knew we were having fun with him. He enjoyed that. It was a form of flattery."

During tournaments he often searched out kids in the crowd, and entertained them by bouncing a ball on his club. The kids would be mesmerized. Today, Moe keeps three golf balls in his pocket at all times. If he passes by some kids playing at the side of a road, he'll often roll down the window and toss them the balls. "It's something to pick up and have fun with. They're fun for them. Kids can grab on to them because they're small and light."

When asked what is it about kids that he likes so much, Moe smiles and squints. "They're jolly. No fear has set in."

Chapter Nineteen
Adjusting and Adapting

It was an abnormally cold October day, especially to be playing golf. Most players in the second round of the 1968 Ontario PGA Championship were swaddled in snug turtlenecks and layers of sweaters. Fingers were numb. Moe was walking down a fairway with playing partner Ken Girard when it started to snow. Moe walked up to his ball, picked it up, placed it in his bag and headed in the direction of the clubhouse. Startled, Girard hollered: "Moe! Where the hell are you going?"

"To Florida."

By the third week of October or when the thermometer hits 50 Fahrenheit, whichever comes first, Moe's homing signal kicks in. He hops in the car and drives south, usually alone, taking the same route, staying in the same hotels, eating in the same restaurants, and stopping in on the same friends such as teacher Paul Bertholy in Pinehurst, North Carolina. His first trip to Florida was in 1954 and he hasn't missed one yet.

"Some guys think I'm crazy," Moe told reporter Jack Marks. "But in October I say, 'goodbye, see you in April.' While they're shovelling snow, I'm shovelling sand. It's nice to be crazy."

Since the early 1960s, Moe's winter home has been Daytona Beach, site of Tomoka Oaks Golf Club where the Canadian pros got special deals on memberships. Even though Royal Oak Golf Club in Titusville became the official winter home of the CPGA in 1978, Moe, the lover of things familiar, has continued to rent a room in Daytona Beach and make the 45-minute drive there and back along US Highway 1 on the coast. Moe makes his return trip to Canada in early April after the Masters, when the snow is finally gone in southern Ontario and the grass is starting to green up.

Among Floridians, Moe is one of Canada's most famous snowbirds. By the late 1960s, he was already a minor legend of the state's grill rooms. Stories circulated about his prowess as a hustler — ironically, his fame cut off that little sideline — his impromptu exhibitions, his course records throughout the state and his success on the Florida PGA Section winter tour. Moe, Ken Venning, Herb Holzscheiter, Ken Duggan and most of the young Canadian pros played on the circuit. The purses were relatively small for these two-day, 36-hole tournaments, most of which were held in northern and central Florida. The total prize money often started at about $2,000.

When stories are swapped about Moe's days on the Florida mini-tour, one oft-told tale concerns a run-in with a starter. The story goes that Moe strode to the first tee of one tournament that opened with a hole that bent sharply right around a thick grove of trees. Moe hammered his drive over the tops of the trees and it disappeared.

"That's out of bounds," the starter declared.

"That's perfect!" Moe shot back.

"No, that's out of bounds."

Moe quickly teed up another ball and fired it dead right into the woods.

"Now that's out of bounds," Moe proclaimed and tore down the fairway.

When Moe got to his first ball, it was perfectly placed on the extreme right side of the fairway. By cutting the corner, he had knocked more than 40 yards off his second shot.

Moe felt comfortable against the wide assortment of players who competed; from northern club pros to young bucks honing their game to old pros trying to find it again. Some of Moe's competitors included young playing pros who went on to better careers as teachers, including Wally Armstrong, Jim McLean and John Redman.

Redman, now Paul Azinger's coach, recalls getting a shock after he hit his opening drive in the Indian River Open at New Smyrna Beach Golf and Country Club. "I was kind of admiring my shot a little bit and the next thing I heard was another ball go right behind me. It was Moe. He'd already hit. Before I could pick up my tee, his ball was in the air."

Moe won 11 tournaments on the Florida mini-tour. He captured the 1968 Mayfair and Indian River Opens back-to-back and pocketed $3,000 in five events. In 1971, he fired two 66s to win the Cypress Gardens tourney and in a pro-am for the Jacksonville Beach Open hit the flagstick three times in one round. "Moe found it a lot easier to play down there," Holzscheiter said. "He didn't have to worry about people bugging him.

On the Canadian Tour, there was the press and public and he didn't like that stuff. Down in Florida, if you won, they gave you the cheque, five minutes later it was all over and you'd be out of there."

Ken Duggan recalls running into Moe at breakfast at the New Smyrna Beach tournament one year and asked him why he wasn't playing. "I hit the flagstick on the first three holes," Moe said. "Can't do better than that. Why go on?"

Duggan said: "I'm hitting it in bunkers, he's hitting the pin on the fly and he won't play. I was mystified."

Holzscheiter says he's had "zillions of chats" with Moe and gotten to know him pretty well, but he got an exciting insight into Moe's personality in Florida. One night in Daytona, Moe was anxious to visit a club repair expert in West Palm Beach, about a 200-mile journey south on US Highway 1. Not wanting to drive alone all night, he convinced Holzscheiter to come along. They left around midnight and talked all night as Moe drove, pointing out courses in the dark along the way. Moe got the club fixed, and they headed back around noon.

"We were up all night and dead tired," Holzscheiter recalls. "Moe's driving and I fall asleep in the passenger side. All of a sudden the car is starting to bounce and jump. I wake up and the car is starting to go across the median into the oncoming lanes. My instant reaction is to grab the wheel, yank it back and say, 'Moe! What are you doing?'

"He looks at me and says, `Sleeping. Just like you.'

"Any other guy would have filled his drawers. We were two seconds from getting killed. If you delve into that response, it goes along with his personality — if it happens, it happens. He'd accept it."

***

Upon his return to Canada in the spring of 1971, Moe announced that he was reducing his summer schedule. He would turn 42 in July and planned to play in a few events close to home, but would skip most of the far-flung provincial opens. "No incentive," he explained. "I've won them all." The prospect of a tour sans Moe sent a shiver through Imperial Tobacco, which manufactured Peter Jackson cigarettes. It had just become the first sponsor of the Canadian Tour. Renamed the Peter Jackson Tour, the circuit comprised seven events with a total purse of $78,000. It was great news for Canadian golf and the many American players who came north to play for some of the action.

Moe began the opening tournament, the $16,000 Ontario Open, by hitting a hook off the first tee. It was probably the worst drive anyone had ever seen him hit in 20 years. Soon enough, he had a change of heart about his travel schedule and decided once again to head out west.

Two months later, Moe had won the Alberta Open — his favourite tournament naturally enough — and lost the Manitoba Open in a bizarre six-hole playoff. On the second extra hole, he lagged a 40-footer to within inches of the hole, and opponent John Elliott of Florida said "Pick it up." And Moe did! He was immediately disqualified because it was a stroke-play event.

The gallery protested angrily and Elliott begged him to continue, but Moe said he was finished. Under pressure from the gallery and Imperial Tobacco, the tournament committee buckled and ruled that they could continue. "The R&A and USGA walls cracked a little," Golf World magazine said. Moe replaced his ball, tapped in and they played on. Golf World mentioned Elliott was married to "pro-ette" Sandra Post, Canada's star player on the LPGA at the time.

Moe was the leading money winner on the 1971 Peter Jackson Tour by a mile, raking in nearly $7,000 while No. 2 Elliott took home $3,700. Moe averaged 69.9 strokes for 20 rounds. Said the Telegram, "From coast to coast he drew the biggest galleries and gave them the best show."

And surprise of surprises, Moe made acceptance speeches. Darn good ones too. Although they made him extremely nervous, Moe came to realize giving speeches was part of a pro's repertoire. "The pros really admired Moe when he started to give speeches," Gary Slatter said. Moe had lots of practice that summer. In the seven events, he never finished worse than third. Generally, he gave the same speech every time, inserting new names where necessary, but he said all the right things — acknowledging the superintendent for keeping the course in great shape, thanking the volunteers.

His stellar play earned him a berth on Canada's two-man team going to the World Cup in November in Palm Beach Gardens, Florida. This time he accepted. Teammate Wilf Homenuik played well, but Moe was erratic and Canada finished eighth behind winners Lee Trevino and Jack Nicklaus at the PGA National Golf Club. Venning was on hand to give his buddy some support, and it was there that he saw the respect Moe commanded among the world's top players.

Moe was hitting balls on the range when Gary Player came over and asked if he had a few minutes to talk. "Soon Nicklaus wandered over and then Trevino came over," Venning said. "They were watching Moe hit balls and asking him how he hits the ball to a peak so that it falls straight down. He didn't feel threatened at all. They were all talking, and then they watched each other hit balls.

"It was a four-hour clinic of the golf gods. I just sat on Moe's bag with my mouth open. Wow! There was a huge gallery of people around. The respect he received was incredible. For golf's elite to seek him out, that's what was supposed to happen to Moe."

**

An hour after Moe left in his car to head south for the World Cup, his father Irwin died. Marie said the family tried to contact him through the police but he was already across the border. "Six months later Moe came back and we were sitting with Mary and family and he said, 'Where's dad?'

"Well, didn't you hear?" Marie said.

**

His hair flecked with grey, the boyish cheeks puffed out and his belly protruding over his belt, Moe wasn't a model cheerleader, but he certainly was a spirited and encouraging one. In the early 1970s, Moe appeared more excited about the chances of the youngsters on tour than his own. If his playing partner had it going in a tournament, Moe would tell him over and over, "It's your day, it's your day." To Gary Slatter and Dan Halldorson, it was as if Moe believed you were destined to win or play well that day, and he would try to spur you on.

It was rarely Moe's day, however. He lost his enthusiasm for competitive golf. He'd won just about every tournament in Canada with the glaring exception of the Canadian Open. Many times he appeared to have no motivation at all. "He was a reluctant winner," Slatter said.

Run-ins with fans, the grind of the day-long drives to tournaments, it was all wearing on him. He was still hitting the ball like the Pipeline Moe of old, but his scores became secondary to entertaining himself with creative shot-making. He carved the sky with balls, trying to pull off miracle shots through narrow openings or to heavily guarded pins that would only accept a perfect shot. If it splashed in water or rolled into a bunker, Moe would shrug. "It's just a walk in the park, that's all, a walk in the park."

Moe didn't win any big provincial opens in 1972 or '73, and therefore he didn't qualify for the Canadian Open. Although many people still thought Moe could win the Open if he set his mind to it, he refused to enter the Open qualifying tournament. With his record, Moe thought he should get an automatic place in the tournament but it didn't happen. "Why should the best golfer in Canada have to qualify?" Moe said.

Moe rationalized his poor scoring, saying he was getting set to retire from playing competitive golf. He was now a real estate baron and didn't have to worry about playing golf to eat anymore. "Just don't care - just don't care about anything except the lots," he told Dunnell. He professed to have $200,000 in assets, about $50,000 invested in the Membery's golf course and real estate enterprises in which work was starting on a shopping plaza and new homes were to be added to a subdivision.

The Kitchener-Record newspaper and Moe's family talked proudly how the freckle-faced kid from Gruhn Street had made it big. Many newspaper stories referred to him as the "millionaire land developer." Not Jack Marks's stories. He knew it was hokum. "It was a figment of his imagination."

The Memberys put up with hearing Moe talk about non-existent investments. To those who asked, they'd set the record straight, but they didn't contradict him publicly. There was no point embarrassing him. Ed Membery said his father Orm owned land adjacent to Golf Haven that was being developed into housing. Orm advised Moe he could probably make a nice return down the line if he bought some lots. Orm offered the lots to Moe at a reduced price. "My father tried to do Moe a favour, but Moe never took advantage of it. I don't know if Moe dreamed he was part of it or what. He wouldn't tell a lie, but I think some things get exaggerated."

When asked about these business investments, Moe shakes his head and looks at the floor. "No, no." A few seconds pass. "You can't go by what you hear."

**

Each January, the PGA Merchandise Show is the must-attend extravaganza for members of the golf business. For four days, anyone selling anything remotely connected with golf sets up a booth in the Orange County Convention Centre in Orlando, Florida, hawking gizmos, gadgets, new clubs, shirts, books — you name it. Club professionals from across North America come to see the new lines and to place orders.

In the 1960s, sales reps would drop in almost daily on golf pros in Florida during the winter. Irv Schloss, the pro at Dunedin Country Club, got tired of the countless sales calls so he asked all the reps to come to Dunedin on the same day. The first year, they showed their wares on card tables in the parking lot. The next year, they put up tents, and every year since the show has grown.

Schloss was a man of many talents. He gave seminars to young pros in the U.S. PGA, he was a pioneer in the use of high-speed film to study golf swings, he was an expert in club repair and he was a big believer in the mental side of golf.

In the winter of 1973, Moe became an eager student of the philosophical and mental approach to the game advocated by Schloss. Moe hung on Schloss's every word. "He was the first guy I ever heard talk about the mind and golf," Moe says. "It fascinated me."

Schloss believed in the power of inspirational sayings championed by motivational speakers and pop psychologists. He believed that the mental part of the game was crucial to golf and many of the same kinds of messages could help golfers. These messages included:

"Believe in the truth, it will set you free."

"If you dream it, you can become it."

"You can only do what you believe."

"If the mind's ripe, the shots are ripe."

Moe says that he had never heard anything like this before. He was initially attracted to Schloss's psychological approach to golf as a tool to make him a better player and student of the game. But he was stunned to realize the optimism and cheerful counsel inherent in these messages could also help him "in life."

"It rang a bell. I could see things more clearly, not just in golf but in everything. I realized that life wasn't so hard. He gave me a look at the inward part of life. It explained a lot about life!"

Like Hank Williams, Moe proclaimed he'd seen the light. With the fervour of the newly reborn, Moe threw himself into this new world with his heart and soul. Never one to do anything by half measure, Moe began compiling his own list of inspirational sayings from every source and his collection now contains more than 200 messages. He memorized a 16-page booklet Schloss had written on the mind and golf. He gobbled up self-help and positive-thinking books such as The

Psychology of Winning, and The Power of the Subconscious Mind. He sought out sports medicine journals on the mind and performance, attended seminars and traded ideas with other golf pros such as Bob Toski and Paul Bertholy, who were interested in golf's mental side.

Moe considered people like Schloss and Toski to be "golf analysts," and he was determined to become one too. He spoke passionately to friends about the mind and golf, telling them that the two dirtiest words in the English language were "hope and fear."

"It's like when a cop pulls up behind you — he controls you," Moe told a Canadian reporter soon after his return from Florida in the spring of 1973. "Or when teams play the Montreal Canadiens — they figure they're beaten before the game even begins. Golf is the same. It's an inward game. You putt with the mind — not with the club. Sometimes, you just know that the damn putt ain't gonna drop. Inside, you're burning up, burning up."

At tournaments, Moe was now spending more time preaching what some people called his "missionary work" than hitting practice balls. "If only I'd found out 25 years sooner. I'd have been a $100,000 winner on the tour every year. Now it's too late for that."

Today, his enthusiasm for the power of positive thinking and the role of the mind in golf hasn't diminished one iota. "This doesn't shoot 65," he'll say, touching his chest. "This shoots 65," he says, touching his temple.

"Hitting the ball is just 13 per cent of the game. The mind accounts for the other 87 per cent.

"Winners expect it. They have positive self-expectancy. They expect to do well. They expect to win every day."

Moe still spends two to three hours a day — often in his car pulled off on a quiet country road — studying his books. "I'm the only golf analyst in Canada. Nobody understands the mind and golf like I do." Ask him what he knows about the mind and golf and he'll launch into a list: "Kinesiology, mannerisms, unity, manoeuvrability, gross energy, key energy, orientation, administration, learned attitude of indifference..."

Many people have put Moe down for his obsession with the mind, saying he's just memorized a bunch of high-minded claptrap that he doesn't understand. Moe understands it all very well, although he's unable to put it into practice to the same degree that he preaches. Nevertheless, his studies have helped him take pride in his uniqueness, to trust his feelings and to think positively. "I feel more at home wherever I go. I don't feel out of place anymore. Now I know how to handle myself and what to say. I understand myself better."

Moe also arrived at a jarring conclusion. "I thought that I was dumb, and that everyone else was smart. I was so wrong. People don't even know themselves. I was so wrong." He finally realized what his friends had known for years — that he was very intelligent and bright. This realization fired up his intellectual curiosity and shot him full of pride.

His friends and fellow competitors on the Canadian Tour noticed a difference in Moe; besides his tendency to launch into zealous dissertations, he was a tad more open to strangers, less prone to confrontations and more sure of himself. Instead of blowing up at people who ticked him off, he was more apt to walk away or ignore them. He was, and still is, exceedingly shy, but he doesn't seem so fragile or combustible.

At tournaments and other events, Moe was now asking if he could give a speech, which he would often pepper with poems from a seemingly unlimited repertoire that related to golf or religion. Moe has a spiritual side that few people see — and he rarely talks about — but it accounts somewhat for his earnest belief that the meek shall inherit the earth, and for his rigid sense of right and wrong. "His speeches were excellent," said player Gary Menaul. "He'd get standing ovations, but the people were applauding his achievements, not his speaking prowess. He couldn't understand that."

Moe's mouth still worked as fast as his hands, and during a few speeches he said some ill-considered things about the quality of Canadian pros and teachers that got him in hot water. Most people forgave these few indiscretions, sloughing it off as "That's just Moe." On one particularly excruciating night, however, an official actually took a microphone out of Moe's hands. It convinced him the CPGA and U.S. PGA "didn't want to hear the truth" and that they undervalued his skill and knowledge.

Feeling more comfortable in front of crowds, Moe gave his first clinic in which he was paid a fee during the summer of 1974 at Toronto's Bayview Club for Gary Slatter, the head pro. In the past, Moe would just be hitting balls, a crowd would gather, he'd perform and a hat would be passed around. But Slatter offered Moe $200 to put on a clinic for his members. Many people thought there was a risk that Moe, in a moment of characteristic candour, might offend some outspoken members of the crowd, but everyone got along famously. Moe began to put on more clinics in short order.

He didn't hurl himself into practice anymore, hitting a relatively few 100 balls a day. "When I golf now, it's just a walk in the park." In that summer of 1974, he finished tied with Bob Panasiuk in the Quebec Open, but refused to go into a playoff. "I don't need the money. Give it to Bob," he said. If he didn't play, Moe was threatened with suspension from the tour's next stop, the CPGA Championship at his beloved Willow Park in Calgary. Moe relented and lost to Panasiuk after three holes. After the tournament, Moe was told that he had been exempted into the Canadian Open in Toronto.

He stunned everyone, however, when he said "my sticks aren't good enough" to play in the $200,000 Open. Moe went to Willow Park and, using the same clubs, managed to fire rounds of 69-66-68-68 for a two-shot victory and $6,500. Again, he told the RCGA his clubs weren't good enough to play in the upcoming Open. The next week he equalled the course record at the St. Charles Club in Winnipeg with a 65 at the Manitoba Open.

Moe finished second on the Canadian Tour money list for the 1974 season with $11,500, but pocketed about $17,000 overall from three months of golf. In Moe's remaining years on the Canadian Tour, he was the avuncular veteran, dispensing sage advice to his proteges, helping them with their swings and preaching his theories of positive thinking. Dan Halldorson said Moe encouraged the younger players, telling them that they could win if they believed in themselves — and quite often it appeared that Moe would let them win.

Moe found himself in a playoff in the 1976 Alberta Open with Halldorson and Tom Irwin. On the tee of the first extra hole, Halldorson and Irwin both sniped atrocious drives into bear country. Moe quipped, "Gee guys, I'm going to have to five- or six-putt for you to win this hole."

Moe won, albeit reluctantly. "I think he was embarrassed to win because Tom and I were such young kids," Halldorson said. "He really didn't want to win. Moe usually gave young guys tournaments. If he liked you and if you had a chance to win, it seemed he wanted you to win. He wouldn't give you the tournament outright, but he wouldn't play to the best of his ability."

Moe closed out his last Canadian Tour event in 1977, capturing the Atlantic Open six days after his 48th birthday. At the end of the season, Peter Jackson dropped its sponsorship of the tour. Purses plummeted in the next few years and so did the quality of the fields. It was unfortunate for Canada's professional golfers, but disastrous for Moe.

Chapter Twenty
Hitting the Rough on the Back Nine of Life

By 1985 Moe had ballooned to about 220 pounds, the vibrant red in his cheeks — a trademark — had drained out of his face, the fire in his blue eyes snuffed out. His shoulders were often flaked with dandruff and he often went unshaven. He looked sick and acted depressed. "He was pretty wrung out," said Gus Maue, who was the pro at Westmount at the time.

Moe was slipping further into debt, and making ends meet only by borrowing money from friends. He had few prospects to turn things around. He wasn't playing much golf; Moe was spending more and more time visiting friends at clubs around southern Ontario. A man of rigid routine, he'd always arrive at the same time — you could almost set your watch to the appearance of Moe's car in the parking lot.

Moe would talk golf, but with little enthusiasm. He was sullen and mopy. Friends tried to cheer him up, telling him that he was so talented he could be making lots of money, but Moe always had plenty of reasons why he couldn't. They also lectured him to eat better. He appeared to be subsisting all day on nothing but Coke, although he'd cap every day at Westmount with a free dinner from Gus and Audrey Maue.

Moe still talked the talk about "positive self expectancy" and "dream it and become it," but he wasn't walking the walk. Moe's lack of interest in competitive golf concerned friends such as Tim Wharnsby, who had caddied for him as a teenager. "It's like army generals who are forced to retire at 55 and die at 56 because they have nothing to live for," said Wharnsby, now a Toronto sports reporter. "That's what I was afraid of with Moe."

Moe's friends were also worried about how Moe would make ends meet. For about 30 years, he had made a living from golf, living hand-to-mouth, staying one step ahead of the game. Those days were over. He didn't have any other skill besides hitting a golf ball, and though he did that as well as anyone had ever seen, he still couldn't make a living. Most older pros latch on to a club and teach, or even act as a starter or ring in green fees. Heck, it's a living around golf. That wasn't Moe's way, and no clubs were coming forward with job offers.

He didn't trust banks, so he certainly hadn't been making his maximum retirement savings contribution every year. What would happen to an old Moe? Would he whither away a poor old man, alone and forgotten? "We always thought there'd be a day when we'd go to his rooming house in Daytona Beach and find him dead," Maue said.

In 1985, Moe won his sixth straight CPGA Seniors Championship and the $3,500 cheque. It was a remarkable achievement, but tournament golf yielded little joy. Other than the seniors championship, he hadn't won a two-day event in five or six years, and therefore few good cheques. He'd win the occasional one-day tourney here and there for $500 or so, but this was pocket change. There was little money to be won on the Canadian Tour; it was in shambles without a sponsor.

Moe had his chance at the emerging Senior PGA Tour. Led by honourary chairman Sam Snead, a group of six prominent former PGA Tour pros tested the waters for a tour with two events in 1980, when Moe was 51. Liking what they saw, the group expanded the circuit to five events in 1981. With a roster sporting names like Palmer, Snead and Boros — their considerable skills still intact — and the discovery of a huge audience hungry to see their heroes live out a middle-aged fantasy, the tour was on its way to becoming the sports success story of the 1980s.

From 1981 to '85, the tour made an annual stop in Canada. Moe played in a couple events, driving alone to Winnipeg in 1982. He also made the trip to Calgary in '83 after borrowing some money from Nick Weslock. Then, as now, the old pros put on quite a show for the folks with pro-ams, shootouts and clinics. "You'd have the likes of Billy Casper, Palmer, Miller Barber and Don January," said Dick Grimm, the former RCGA president who ran the Canadian events. "Invariably, someone would spot Moe standing by the edge of crowd and one of them would say, 'Hey Moe, come up here and show us how it's done.'"

Moe, ever bashful, would wave them off, saying "No, no, you don't want a duffer like me." Eventually, Moe would relent and bounce on to the range, often in his street shoes. "Casper or Barber or somebody would grab the mike and say, 'Now you're going to see someone who can really hit a shot.' And he'd hit these incredible shots — one-irons straight-as-a-die and land them all in a hat. That illustrates how he was regarded — as one of the best ball-strikers. And these guys didn't lavish praise on just anyone," Grimm said.

At St. Charles in Winnipeg, Moe's inferiority complex seemed ancient history. He played well from the tee and into the cup, firing rounds of 70-69-69-69, 11-under par. He finished a very respectable third behind winner Bob Goalby at 15-under. Despite his excellent finish, Moe was miffed to learn he'd have to qualify if he wanted to play two weeks later in Portland, Oregon. Moe headed home. He was already angry that with his record, they didn't invite him to play. He was exempted into the annual Canadian stop due to winning the CPGA seniors, but it was the principle of the thing — he wanted the recognition of an invitation. Moe was exempted to play the PGA seniors' stop in Vancouver in 1985, but refused to go, complaining that the number of spots for Canadian players had been reduced from the original 12 to just two. Besides, it was a long drive to Vancouver and Moe couldn't afford the trip.

Moe never played in another Senior PGA Tour event, once again dashing the hopes of his many friends that Moe could finally earn some big bucks. "With his skill and talent and the way he performs, he'd draw thousands on the senior tour," said John Czarny, echoing what hundreds have said. "He could make millions."

Whether it was the prospect of feeling lonely on the road again, memories of getting the freeze from many of the big-names the way he had 30 years earlier, fear, all or none of the above, Moe wouldn't go despite repeated overtures. He says it's very simple: he didn't have any sponsors and couldn't afford it.

Maue, a successful sports retailer and a partner in a couple of Kitchener golf courses, says he knows at least 10 people who offered to back Moe on the senior circuit. Sponsors of senior events in both Las Vegas and Hawaii thought enough of Moe to invite him to play, offering to pay his expenses and have someone act as his travelling assistant. "He turned them down," Maue said. "I don't know why."

Asked for his side, Moe responds: "Talk, talk, talk. When it came down to the nitty gritty, I never saw a cheque."

A rumour floated for years that Wayne Gretzky offered to back Moe on the seniors circuit after the pair played together in 1987, but The

Great One says "no offer was made nor requested."

Moe picked up a few hundred dollars here and there giving the occasional clinic around southern Ontario, but he was limited in the number he could do. Too shy to address the crowd, Moe needed an MC like Ken Venning or George Clifton. If someone wasn't available, Moe couldn't give his clinic. He didn't have a phone either; it was almost impossible to reach him. The best place to track down Moe was by calling the pro shop at Westmount. If he didn't know you, he wouldn't talk to you and Moe didn't return messages.

Moe couldn't collect money for lessons or clinics in Florida either. He didn't have a working visa. He was terrified that if the authorities caught him taking money, he'd be sent back to Canada in a heartbeat — never able to return. The thought of spending winters in Canada for the rest of his life was Moe's idea of hell, frozen over no less.

On top of his financial woes, Moe was also stung by the induction of George Knudson and Al Balding into the Canadian Golf Hall of Fame in 1985. He'd been passed over yet again. Marlene Stewart Streit was a charter member when the hall opened in 1971, and Nick Weslock and Gary Cowan were inducted the next year. Moe was certainly in the same league on any golf course, but they had three things he did not: money, respect and official recognition.

As if things couldn't get worse, Moe heard that his aged mother was dying of cancer. His sister Marie said the siblings tried to get hold of him, but received no response. "She wanted to see Moe so bad," Marie said. While he hadn't talked to his brothers or sisters in years, possibly not since his father's death 14 years earlier, Moe loved his mother despite his conviction that she didn't take pride in his golf.

Mary was in a hospital in London, Ontario, pumped with pain-killing morphine. Marie said that one day when she and Doreen arrived for a visit, 85-year-old Mary was ecstatic. "Her face was lit up. She said, 'Girls! Moe's been here! He was here to see me.'

"I don't know if it was true. She was so doped up. I hope it was true. I'm sure she lived to see him. She fought a long time to see him before it was time."

***

Moe hit rock bottom the next year. He lost the CPGA Seniors Championship — his annuity — for the first time in seven years. The days of the big wad in his pocket, loaning money, buying $300 shoes and driving Cadillacs were over. He was driving a Chevrolet Caprice and was way behind on his payments. He was almost penniless and about $20,000 in debt. "I'm getting back to where I was 30 years ago," he told the Kitchener-Waterloo Record. "I don't have two nickels to rub together. It's been a nice recess for 30 years, but now it's over. And it doesn't look like it's going to get any better."

Once again, Moe railed at the injustice of a world that seemed to parcel out good breaks with miserly reluctance, but threw roadblocks and potholes in front of him at nearly every turn. "Here I am, a better man than I used to be. I dress better than I used to. I'm the smartest in Canada in knowledge and insight into golf. I'm the best striker of the ball in the world, not just by my saying, yet I can't make a living."

The wind was gone from Moe's sails. The pressure of playing to eat, the weight of his financial troubles, the threat of losing his car — his lifeline — was killing his golf game. "He lost his competitive edge," Maue said. "He had nothing financially going for him and it affected his golf. He had no cash. He was really down."

It was late September. With his Florida trip in jeopardy, Moe's friends came to the rescue. Spearheaded by Gus and Audrey Maue, they organized a fund-raising dinner and tournament. They contacted many of Moe's friends and supporters from the last 30 years to take part in a "Tribute to Moe Norman." The cost was $100 or whatever you could spare. The response was overwhelming.

In three weeks, 200 people were confirmed to attend, the maximum number that would fit into Westmount's regal dining room. People from across North America who couldn't come sent cheques. Nick Weslock, Lloyd Tucker, Gary Cowan, and all the others who'd stuck by the side of this unpredictable but endearing enigma were there to pay tribute to him. Speaker after speaker lauded him, and Moe responded with a wave. "If you've seen Fred Astaire," Tucker told the crowd, "you've seen the best dancer. If you've seen Peggy Fleming, you've seen the best skater. And when you've seen Moe Norman hit a golf ball, you know you've seen the best who ever hit a golf ball."

When Moe got up to speak, he was met with a thunderous ovation. Many in the crowd had misty eyes and lumps in their throats. It was hard to believe this was the man who had been so afraid to speak before a crowd for decades. He was among friends. Polished, thoughtfully constructed, poetic and heartfelt, Moe's speech had the crowd howling with laughter and reaching for their handkerchiefs. "There had to be 50 people crying in the front row," Ernie Hauser said. "We all knew he could do it. All those years, you had to lie for him or go get his prize and then he gives this wonderful speech."

The event raised about $26,000 for Moe. The money helped pay his bills and got his car paid up. Just knowing that many people cared for him was a huge boost. "It got Moe on a roll," Maue said. "It seemed Moe was kicking around again."

Butch Martin, a friend at Stedelbauer Motors where he bought his cars, opened Moe's first bank account. Gus Maue's son Danny began to coordinate booking Moe's clinics through the Westmount pro shop. Word spread about his clinics and demand for Moe increased steadily.

When Moe returned from Florida in the spring of 1987, he was still flying high. "Moe's hitting the ball as well as any pro golfer could today," said pro Doug Bruton. He destroyed the field in the CPGA's Senior Championship, winning by a whopping eight shots — his largest margin of victory as a senior. It was his seventh victory in the event in eight years. The $9,000 first-place cheque was pretty impressive too.

Moe had successfully negotiated this tricky stretch in his life with plenty of help from his friends, but the road ahead was still very foggy. He was giving more clinics, but he wasn't making enough to live off them. After Moe's debts had been paid off, there was nothing left over to put away for the days when age or sickness would rob him of his ability to hit a golf ball. Then what?

It's a tired cliche, but one that makes Moe's case all the more tragic — he had a lifetime of great memories, hundreds of friends and the status of a legend. But without a nest egg, the world's best ball-striker appeared destined to fade away.

Chapter Twenty-One
The Rain Man and the Hall of Fame

For 30 years, Moe's closest friends have complained they never really understood the man. They've searched in vain for something that would explain his quirky personality. Some thought the car accident was partly to blame, others didn't think it ever happened.

Some thought they finally had the answer with the release of The Rain Man in 1988. Dustin Hoffman won an Oscar for his portrayal of an autistic man who blurts out words rapidly in short clipped bursts and lives according to obsessively strict routine in isolation from the rest of the world. But the character is also enormously gifted, capable of computing complex equations and counting vast sums with astounding speed and accuracy. He has a photographic memory — as Tom Cruise's character discovers to his pleasant surprise while playing cards in Las Vegas — that enables him to recall minute details after only a fleeting glance.

"When the Rain Man came out," Tim Wharnsby said, "a bunch of us said: 'That's Moe Norman!'"

"We never realized it until we saw that movie," Gus Maue said. "We're sure he's autistic. Positive. He has all the traits. He wasn't socialized, but he has an unbelievable mind. At cribbage or gin, you can't beat him because he remembers all the cards. In his late 20s, he was making a living in union halls playing cards. You can't beat him."

A number of other people linked Moe with autism after reading the bestselling book, Nobody Nowhere, by Britain's Linda Williams, an autistic.

Many of Moe's friends have latched on to the autism theory, but few ask him about it. How would he react? Would he be hurt? Or angry? Or sufficiently upset to terminate a friendship?

John Czarny raised the issue in June of 1994, albeit unintentionally.

After a game of golf at Brantford, Czarny, Moe and friends were having lunch in the grill room. Moe was complaining that many people don't respect him, that they can get very rude — often interrupting him when he's hitting balls or talking to friends. "Would you go up to Jack Nicklaus and say 'Hi Jack' and hit him on the back? You'd be on the floor."

Czarny looked over his bifocals at Moe, then at the others. "See, that's autism." People at the table were a little stunned at first. But given that the issue had been brought out in the open by one of Moe's best friends, the question of autism was put directly to Moe. He didn't blanch and answered directly, Moe's way. "I don't know. I've had people say it. Maybe. It's OK. It's hurt me in a lot of ways, but it's one reason I can hit a golf ball so well. It doesn't bother me if people talk about it, as long as they're friends."

On another occasion, however, Moe said that he's never heard any talk about autism. And Moe has never been to a psychologist to find out whether he is indeed autistic. Why should he? He's muddled through into his mid-60s. What good would it do?

***

Close friends and admirers have thought the issue worth pursuing. With so many people voicing the same opinion, it has seemed important to determine if it's just conjecture. Moe has been dogged by embellished tales most of his life.

Also, if he was indeed autistic, wouldn't it be something to be able to say, "Look what this man has accomplished despite a challenge such as autism." For an autistic man to be recognized as one of the best ball-strikers of all time would contribute greatly to society's understanding of the condition, and would provide inspiration to families struggling to cope with raising autistic children.

According to Uta Frith's book Autism: Explaining the Enigma, the character in The Rain Man could be said to display the features of classic autism: "autistic aloneness, desire for sameness and islets of ability." Autistic children often have difficulty looking others in the eye and scream when they are touched. They also flap their arms almost uncontrollably and spin to comfort themselves. For people with this kind of autism, it is nearly impossible to live independently.

There is a subgroup, however, of autistics who can manage their lives with a high degree of independence and productivity. These people are known as "high-functioning" autistics. One such person is American Temple Gradin, who received her PhD in 1988 in Animal Science. An author of more than 100 scholarly papers, Gradin is an expert in the design and construction of livestock facilities. Another is Britain's Stephen Wiltshire, who as a child refused to talk or play with other children but could do remarkably detailed drawings of buildings and landmarks with a quick look. Now in his early 20s, Wiltshire is a renowned artist.

According to medical literature on childhood autism, the "high-functioner" label is reserved for the rare, intelligent and highly verbal autistic child. Dr. Susan Bryson, a Toronto psychologist and an expert in autism, cautions that this group still has major difficulties in socializing. "They have an inability to relate to people in a reciprocal way. People with autism have problems understanding human behaviour. It's easier to deal with the physical world because the rules of logic are fixed. But social problems are so complex and so variable.

"People with autism find it harder to know what other people are thinking. We socialize with other people by making inferences about what they're thinking. We act differently with an older person than with a younger person. It's not easy for an autistic person to get a handle on relating to other people.

"There's a lot of social anxiety. They don't know what to say or do in social situations and the more aware they are of their anxiety, the more anxious they get. There's a social naivete. There's something I find beautiful, innocent and refreshing about many of the people I know who have autism."

These qualities certainly describe Moe, but to prove he has autism would require a battery of tests by a doctor, and there's no way Moe would submit to such a thing. Nor is there any need to prove it. The only purpose it would serve would be to show that there's an explanation for some of Moe's often quirky behaviour.

People, however, shouldn't need scientific proof to make them compassionate. Just knowing someone is different should be enough to make people more understanding and tolerant of eccentricities.

Dr. Richard Keefe is a clinical psychologist and assistant professor of psychiatry at the Mount Sinai School of Medicine in New York. He's the author of Understanding Schizophrenia, and an eight-handicapper with a big interest in the mental side of golf. He doesn't believe Moe is autistic. "Autism is a childhood disorder. It's almost impossible with autism to have a normal childhood." As Moe, his siblings and friends have attested, Moe had his quirks, but he was a pretty normal boy who liked to play games, run with a group of kids and horse around. While he hesitates to make a long-distance diagnosis, Keefe believes that it's more likely Moe suffered damage to the frontal lobes of his brain in the car accident.

Keefe thinks it would be a good idea to determine whether Moe suffered a brain injury — more than just to satisfy mere curiosity. As Moe gets older, his brain might age differently and cause him psychological and social problems that could be improved with professional help. There's simply no way to know without proper testing by a neurosurgeon.

The frontal lobes are responsible for major cerebral functions, such as speech and working memory, and abilities such as planning and imagining. "The frontal lobes are like the CEO of the brain," Keefe said. "The brain does all kinds of things at the same time and the frontal lobes act as an executive that takes charge and tells the brain what it should be doing."

Keefe says people who have suffered damage to their frontal lobes have many of the characteristics of autism: they tend to be socially isolated and inflexible; they find it's almost impossible to generate new ideas or develop alternate strategies. Keefe believes that Moe, instead of being autistic, was an exceptionally bright child with extraordinary powers of concentration. This observation would explain Moe's phenomenal memory and ability with numbers. After he was hurt, he began to rely more on his best skills, according to Keefe. "When you're young, if one part of the brain is injured, other parts will take over. But as you get older, your brain isn't as flexible; older cells die and your weaknesses reveal themselves more."

He says this might explain why Moe had a relatively happy childhood, but as he got older he found it more and more difficult to deal with rules and people in authority, and to co-exist comfortably with strangers.

Keefe believes Moe's difficulty with blind shots is the most plausible evidence of frontal lobe damage. Through Moe's golf career, he's relied on seeing the target. His swing reacts to the target. But when he can't see the target, such as a blind shot to a green or a dogleg that he's never played before, Moe has trouble. He sometimes appears confused — reluctant to commit to the shot and unable to focus. His shot is often off line or simply the wrong choice.

***

While playing at Brantford several years ago, Moe seemed to have difficulty with No. 9, a 308-yard par-four. There was a valley in front of the green. Most players hit a mid-iron so they could see the pin on their approach and hit a full wedge. Even so, Moe hit his driver. He always hits the longest club he can. Why? He's trying to hole every shot.

But a driver left Moe down in the valley with a wedge about 40 yards from the pin. He couldn't see the pin. Without a visual cue, Moe seemed unable to commit to the shot. He made a quick swing and pitched too far to the back of the green, leaving himself about 30 feet from the flagstick. It was very poor shot for a player of his ability.

Based on this and other examples, Keefe said Moe would appear to have a problem with working memory, which is in the frontal lobes. This mental facility allows a person to look at an object, look away and still have a vivid image of the object for a matter of seconds. Golfers need working memory because they don't — or, at least, they shouldn't — look at the target as they strike the ball. Without an image in the working memory, specific neurons in the brain will not fire. This might explain why Moe has trouble in situations where he can't see the target, and why he is so visually oriented in his golf game.

However, this leads to questions about Moe's ability to see his swing in his mind's eye. Teaching professional Craig Shankland, an authority on Moe's swing and a trusted friend, believes Moe's extraordinary ability to repeat his swing is entirely mental. "You cannot do that by feel," Shankland says. "You have to have a wonderfully clear picture of what you're going to do to."

Since Moe has repeated his swing so many times in his life, it would appear to be the result of long-term memory. Shankland tells a story that he believes demonstrates how Moe's golf game is "picture oriented". Moe envisions that his divots are always in front of the ball. "I once put a ball down behind a line and Moe hit one foot behind the ball. It went 10 feet. It screwed up his mental picture. It told me how picture oriented he was. If you interrupt his picture you scramble his on-off switch." This observation might also explain why Moe plays so quickly. He looks at the target and reacts to it.

Whether Moe lives with a mild brain injury, autism or is just a quirky guy, it is all the more reason to appreciate that he became one of the best ball-strikers who ever lived.

***

By the early '90s, Moe had largely disappeared from the public eye, but people were still telling stories about him and marvelling at his legend.

Amazingly, however, he was not in the Canadian Golf Hall of Fame. Why? One clue. The hall is run by the Royal Canadian Golf Association.

As one wag said, "What part of the word fame doesn't the RCGA understand?"

That Moe wasn't inducted years ago was regarded as an absolute travesty by his friends, many fans and golf writers. With Moe in his sixties, it was to the point of absurdity. Moe had many run-ins with the authority figures, but to be excluded from the hall of fame made no sense.

"What are they going to do? Give it to him posthumously," asked Nick Weslock, himself a hall of famer.

Moe's record spoke for itself: 54 victories (in tournaments two days or longer), two Canadian Amateurs championships, two CPGA titles and seven out of eight Senior CPGA crowns.

Moe always felt unappreciated by the Canadian golf establishment. Exclusion from the hall of fame added to the sting. In 1993, Moe said he didn't care if he ever got in, but Weslock said he cared a lot. "It's (the RCGA's) their loss," Moe said. "If I got in now, I'd thank the public. They'd be the reason."

Bob Weeks, editor of Score, Canada's golf magazine, began the debate about Moe's exclusion with an editorial in 1992. Weeks noted that Moe's exclusion was all the more ridiculous considering that 1991 inductee was Dorothy Campbell Hurd Howe. The Scottish-born Howe won the 1909 U.S. and British amateur championship. She emigrated to Canada in 1910 where she lived for three years. She won the Canadian amateur three times and moved to Pittsburgh.

It's doubtful Howe ever became a Canadian citizen. For a deceased, unknown foreigner who lived in Canada for 36 months to get picked over Moe was bizarre. The only conclusion was that there was a conscious effort to keep Moe out.

The controversy grew. And it diminished the glory of the moment for those who were enshrined. In 1993, the RCGA announced the induction of Bob Wylie and Cathy Sherk. Wylie won the national senior amateur title six times, while Sherk captured the U.S. Amateur in 1978 and two Canadian amateur titles. Both Wylie and Sherk deserved to be there. No question. But ahead of Moe? No way. Globe and Mail columnist Lorne Rubenstein wrote there was "a concentrated uproar" that Moe had been slighted again.

Sherk was amazed Moe wasn't in before her. "He should definitely been in, for goodness sake. Moe Norman has done all kinds of things for golf in Canada and promoted it outside the country. He's designated as the best ball-striker in the world. That deserves some recognition."

Although it's since been expanded, the hall of fame committee that selected the inductees usually consisted of five or six honorary life governors, including past presidents of the RCGA. One source close to the RCGA said a handful of RCGA governors essentially took a stance on Moe and the Hall of Fame akin to over-my-dead-body. He said members of the hall of fame committee included "guys Moe ticked off when they were running the RCGA and now they're saying 'Screw you.' Moe's career didn't reflect what the RCGA sees as its ideal."

Indeed, Moe had flouted the RCGA's rules of amateur status. That shouldn't be rewarded, but according to many players, including Weslock and Doug Sanders, the rules of amateur status were enforced very unevenly in Moe's day. In playing the game Moe never broke rules or did anything that gave him even the appearance of trying to gain an advantage. When Pete Rose bet on his own baseball team, there was the possibility for compromising the result. The same could not be argued of Moe.

Moe had run into problems with fans, CPGA officials, and turned down invitations into Canadian Opens. But he also had entertained thousands of golf fans through the years. And he was an inspiration that you didn't have to have a textbook swing, dress like a dandy, be born into the elite and take all day to play the game well.

The RCGA applied the same standards to Moe as everyone else, but he merited some compassion and understanding. For despite the confrontations, the lack of polish and his many indiscretions, it was obvious that Moe had done far more good for Canadian golf than harm.

Stephen Ross, executive director of the RCGA, acknowledged the controversy didn't make the RCGA any friends. "Yes, we look bad. But I can't say or defend why Moe's not in. It's a committee and a board and they're a strong group of people. They are very picky about the people they allow in. If we feel we've done the right thing, we don't get defensive."

Ralph Costello chaired the hall of fame committee in 1993 and he denied the committee snubbed Moe. "I don't share that view. I think he's a nominee worthy of consideration and he will be given due consideration. A number of people have been elected late in life."

John Marshall, chairman of the hall of fame committee in 1992, said that by 1992 Moe had not been nominated. That was a surprise. The nominating criteria is simple enough: anyone can send a nomination letter to the RCGA that details the candidate's accomplishments. The nomination stays active for five years.

That Moe had not been nominated could have been viewed as an indication his contributions to golf weren't that valued after all. But that didn't wash. The hall of fame itself wasn't that well known until the controversy over Moe began. And only a few people outside a small circle of a RCGA insiders knew the nominating criteria.

It was naive, however, to think it never occured to someone within or close to the RCGA to quietly mention that Moe had never been nominated and get it done.

A letter from Nick Weslock was accepted in June 1993 as Moe's nomination.

The voices that commented on Moe's exclusion from the hall were many:

Doug Ford, winner of 19 PGA Tour events in the '50s and '60s, member of PGA Hall of Fame: "The only reason Moe's not in the Canadian Golf Hall of Fame is politics. I've seen it here (U.S.). If you were a public links player, the associations, the blue-coats, discriminated against you, the real players like Moe. He was his own man. If you go along with them and kowtow, you're a great guy. If you're your own man and do things your own way, they take offence."

Richard Zokol, two-time winner on PGA Tour in the '90s: "I think the people that are responsible for it are viewing Moe negatively. They're looking at his eccentricities that may be not seen as normal, but more important are his strengths. Anyone who views his strengths first would recognize what an icon in golf he is. If they could look into his heart and understand the man, they could put the pieces together and he would also be in the hall of fame."

Stan Leonard, three-time winner on PGA Tour from 1957 to '60, winner of eight CPGA championships, inducted in Canadian Golf Hall of Fame in 1972: "If you think of the ability of the man, he should have been in there 10 or 15 years ago. It probably takes an all-round person to be inducted to have all that respect. I think it's unfortunate as hell. There were things that were detrimental to the man, but from the standpoint of ability to play golf, there were never any doubts he could play the game."

Dawn Coe-Jones, three-time winner on LPGA Tour in the '90s: "Maybe he's had his run-ins as a number players in all sports have had troubles with upper management, but yet what is a hall of fame? Is it being an all-round person as well as being a good athlete or do you look at the skill level? I believe it should be on the skill level."

Dick Grimm, former RCGA president and executive director, currently commissioner of the Canadian Tour, inducted in 1993: "I think halls of fame are based on the ability of the man in the sport. I don't think it has anything to do with the man outside the sport. What does Moe's behaviour have to do with his golf abilities? I think he definitely should be in the hall of fame."

Wally Uihlein, CEO and President of Titleist and Foot-Joy: "Hall of Fame criteria have to do with the contribution a person made and at the end of the day how do the majority of people feel about it. It's not the RCGA's hall of fame. The last I checked it was the people's game. If a majority of people want Moe in the hall who are they to disregard them?"

Chapter Twenty-Two
Moe's Repeating Swing

Moe Norman's golf swing is regarded by many teachers as the simplest and most repeatable golf swing in the history of the game. Yet it strikes many golfers as an amateurish abomination when they first see it. Moe appears to contravene almost every sacred tenet of golf instruction handed down through the ages, but at impact — the moment of truth — it's immaculate.

He certainly thinks so. "I've got the best move in golf. My move is way simpler than Hogan's. I have fewer moving parts. No one hits it as pure."

Whether you agree with him or not, the key is that Moe knows that his swing works for him every time. Even when the world's best players get "in the zone," they never know what the next swing will bring. "The key thing is that Moe totally believes in his swing," says Chuck Cook, whose students include Tom Kite, Payne Stewart and Ben Crenshaw. "That's the secret.

"I'd say there's a lot of genius in that swing. It's probably the most efficient way to hit a golf ball."

Moe's swing is definitely unorthodox, but as any tour player will tell you, the key to winning is a repeating swing. It doesn't matter a lick what the swing looks like — thousands of frustrated also-rans would gladly trade in their textbook swing for a motion that puts the ball on target every time. "I'm the only golfer who can hit the ball day in, day out where I want," Moe says.

The epitome of smoothness and simplicity, Sam Snead was gifted with one of the classic swings of the game. Snead acknowledged that Moe's swing was a "little different," but looks don't count for anything. "It's what you can repeat. It's what you can do with what you've got.

That's the whole ingredient.

"A lot of people experiment and they're constantly tinkering. Then they don't know what to do and what not to do. And pretty soon they lose it all together. Moe was quite accurate. He believed in himself and that's the name of the game. He had his own way of doing it, stayed with it and I thought that was just great."

David Leadbetter's vision of the ideal swing has been accepted by many tour players, including his celebrated students Nick Faldo and Nick Price. Golf's most famous teacher in the early 1990s is a big admirer of Moe's offbeat swing. "It's whatever works," Leadbetter says. "Moe's swing is very repetitive, very simple. There's no wasted motion. He uses the big muscles well and he's strong, and having hit millions of golf balls, it repeats. If you practice enough and you have a lot of talent, you can have success."

It's far from a consensus, but a number of teachers believe that Moe's swing is the better way to hit a golf ball. However, it's so unconventional, few people understand or appreciate it. "Technically, it's far more advanced and better than what's taught today," says teacher Jim Suttie, who has worked with tour players Loren Roberts, David Ogrin, Robert Wrenn and Vicki Fergon. "A lot of people say it's ugly, but they don't understand what Moe does. It's difficult to teach because so many others are teaching the opposite way and students don't want to look different."

"Different" describes the approach of physicist Jack Kuykendall, founder of Natural Golf, a club manufacturer in Bartlett, Illinois. He argues Moe's swing is the only scientifically perfect golf swing developed in the last 50 years. The swing method Kuykendall teaches is similar, but not identical, to Moe's. Kuykendall says most conventional theories of the swing are "scientific nonsense." He contends the traditional swing is nearly impossible to perform, requiring perfect timing to execute five simultaneous rotary movements while moving the spine upwards and downwards.

The most striking difference in Moe's swing — and its greatest advantage — is barely perceptible: Moe swings the club on the same plane on both the backswing and downswing. This is the key reason for Moe's consistency. He is the only successful player known to have mastered this ability.

Most players swing on two planes, increasing the chances for error. They take the club back on one path, but as their weight shifts forward on the downswing the shaft follows a shallower path back to the ball. "Moe is closer to a mechanical hitting machine than any human golfer," Cook says. "On a machine, the arm and club are all in one plane, and that one facet makes him very consistent and accurate. Most players have a double shift."

Moe's swing is closely related to the equipment he uses: the irons must be very upright, have thick grips and be heavy. Even for those who are not interested in changing their equipment, there are many insights that can be learned by studying Moe's swing.

Grip:

Moe has a neutral left-hand grip. He holds the club in the fingers and the back of his left hand faces the target. The right hand is under the shaft with the V pointing right of the right shoulder.

Moe uses a 10-finger or baseball grip instead of the standard Vardon grip. The biggest break from convention is that Moe places the grip in the palm of his right hand along the lifeline instead of in the fingers. "When the club is in your fingers, your hands are more mobile," says Craig Shankland, who has worked with Beth Daniel and Jane Geddes. "With Moe's grip, there's more chance for the club to stay in the same plane because there's less rotation and lift. They're more apt to work as a unit rather than in pieces."

With the club in the palm of his right hand, Moe says the club does not twist or turn away from the target. "It's always aiming at the flag — square."

Moe holds the club so tight with the left hand that he says, "I'm trying to draw blood." However, he applies light pressure with the right hand. His firm hold on extra-thick grips and very heavy clubs allows Moe to accomplish two important things. Firstly, his hands remain passive, which takes those small, twitchy muscles out of play. Secondly, he finds it easier to keep the club on line.

Another dramatic difference is that his irons all have the same upright lie. (The lie is the degree of bend between the shaft and clubhead.) The uniform lie allows Moe to place every club at the same angle, which means that he's the same distance from the ball every time. "Here you see the genius of the man," says Canadian teaching pro Mark Evershed. "With conventional clubs, our visual centre changes for each club because of the different lies, but Moe's visual centre stays constant."

Moe also chokes up on his clubs, which gives him added control by shortening the shaft.

Address:

Moe's set-up departs from convention in four major ways: his stance is wide; his legs and arms are ramrod straight; he stands a long way from the ball; and he places the clubhead about 12 inches behind the ball. It looks strange at first but after you've studied it for a while, it looks incredible — a balanced, cohesive and powerful platform.

How wide is Moe's stance? With his woods, a line drawn upward from his right instep would meet the outside of his right shoulder. A line drawn from his left instep would be about eight inches outside his left shoulder. That's very wide.

His left foot is turned about 25 degrees open toward the target, while the right foot is perpendicular to the target line. Moe's stance is square to the target, as are his hips. At address, Moe's knees are locked. There's no flex.

The positioning of his arms, however, really sets Moe's swing apart. Moe reaches out to the ball so far that his arms are straight and the end of the grip is 18 inches away from his stomach. Along with his grip, this positioning makes his arms and club shaft form a straight line. Put another way, they are on the same plane. Moe's long reach to the ball makes him appear awkwardly tipped over from the hips, but his wide stance ensures that he's extremely stable.

By placing the clubhead 12 inches behind the ball, the club shaft and his left arm form a straight line, which looks very powerful. With his right hand turned well under the shaft and the grip in his palm, the right arm is also straight and sits on the club like a support beam.

All of this makes a dramatic difference to the positioning of Moe's wrists. In the conventional address, the back of each wrist is concave or bent, while the sides of the wrists are hinged upwards as if you were trying to bring your thumbs toward your biceps.

In Moe's set-up, the backs of both wrists are flat. Along with his locked elbows there's no break from his shoulders through to his fingers. The side of his left wrist is hinged downward while the right is flat.

The way Moe positions his hands on the club also puts his head well back of the ball — about 18 inches with a driver. The majority of weight is already on his right side, so he doesn't have to shift his weight. It also puts his shoulders on a steep angle, with the left shoulder bisecting his ear and the right well below his chin.

By placing the clubhead so far behind the ball, Moe has reduced his margin for error in the takeaway: it prevents him from taking the club away too quickly, and ensures the club is taken back low from the ball. Evershed says it's also interesting to note that the club is not only behind the ball, it's also slightly inside the target line. Looking through Moe's eyes from address, you'd see the clubface square with the inside rear quadrant of the ball. This set-up also pre-turns his left shoulder, so he's already well into his turn.

For added consistency, Moe plays every shot — from wedge to driver — off his left instep. "It helps with your eye-hand-body co-ordination," Moe says. "My muscles are always on the same angle at address."

Backswing:

Moe's backswing is simple because his ingenious set-up removes many extra movements. He's already well into his turn, so he just sweeps the club back in one piece. "This gives him a very wide arc and a good turn," Shankland says. "It's easy to turn the shoulders from there."

Moe's forearms rotate clockwise as he takes the club back, but the shaft remains on the same flat plane as at address. When the club is about three feet back of the ball, Moe's knees soften and bend just a little. The right leg is dead solid, and the left knee moves toward the ball marginally.

Although Moe is hanging on for dear life with his left hand, just past hip height his hands appear soft and the wrists begin to cock upward beautifully. His wide stance ensures there is no upward or lateral motion. His upper body is turning while the fixed base resists. Both feet remain on the ground. Therefore, Moe makes a pure rotation with his upper body around the spine — he remains centred over the shot. All this eliminates extra motion and keeps the club moving on a fixed plane.

"He creates power through leverage," Suttie says. "He really torques the upper body against the lower, and the angle of his left arm and shaft becomes very pronounced — like Hogan — at the top." Moe's shoulder turn is at least 90 degrees, which is huge considering his hip turn is minimal, perhaps only about 15 degrees. The large difference between the two stretches the big muscles in his back and upper body. When he starts his downswing, it's like releasing a rubber band stretched to its maximum. His arms rip through the ball.

When compared to conventional hitters who swing the club back close to a position parallel with the ground, Moe has a very short backswing. Moe's backswing is barely a three-quarter turn. His hands never get higher than his right shoulder. They can't go farther because of his minimal hip turn and his feet are still planted on the ground.

"His coil is beautiful," Suttie says. "He's so level."

Teacher Wally Armstrong says he learned a valuable lesson from Moe's address position that can help other golfers. "For years, I tried to get soft at address and stay soft, but I'd get rigid. What I learned from Moe is that if you start rigid you have no where else to go but soft. At the top of the swing, he's pliable — like a cat ready to spring, and that's what you want."

Downswing:

While Moe's address appears awkward, once he's in motion his swing is a thing of beauty. Like a powerful blues song comprising just three chords, Moe's swing is simple, flowing, forceful and hits the mark beautifully.

While Moe's club is still moving upward to complete the backswing, he's already beginning the downswing by moving his left knee laterally to the target. "The left knee is setting the angle of the downswing already," Moe says. "Everything flows with the left knee."

Although Moe's left knee moves forward, the right leg resists. As the knees separate, Moe appears to be squatting, or sitting down into the shot like Snead. His right foot remains on the ground, which helps keep the club on that same plane.

At the beginning of his downswing, Moe's upper body appears very quiet but his arms drop, bringing the right elbow down to the right hip joint. This is known as the "vertical drop," and many teachers believe Moe's is one of the best in the business.

While Moe's weight shifts left laterally, the cock in his wrists increases. This is what Moe means when he says "lead and lag." The clubhead lags way behind the grip. "He's lagging it so much the angle between his left wrist and the shaft is colossal," Shankland says. "Few people can be that late and still square the blade. The release of Moe's wrist cock is very late, perhaps more than any other player. He has a tremendous delayed hit." This gives Moe's short swing more power.

While Moe's upper body unwinds, his arms stay out ahead of him, extend to their fullest and move at their maximum velocity. There is no breakdown of the left wrist or arms. His extremely wide stance prevents his hips from over-turning to the target or tilting. They remain level. As his weight slides forward, his knees bend but he remains flat-footed, again perhaps longer than any player in the game.

Impact:

At the moment of truth, Moe is no longer unorthodox — he is perfection. Both feet are solidly on the ground. His left knee is way out in front of the ball and bent, while the right knee is bent toward the left. Remarkably, his hips are nearly square to the target, or perhaps open only slightly. The left arm is extended to its maximum and moving very fast.

The shaft and left arm have returned to their address position in a perfectly straight line running up to his left shoulder. The right elbow is bent only slightly, and points at the right hip.

The most striking thing about Moe at impact is his hands and wrists. Like Hogan, the back of his left hand is bowed; the wrist bone is definitely raised and points toward the target. The thumb-side of his left wrist is turned downward. The palm of the right hand faces the target directly and the right arm just pours on the power underneath the guiding left arm. His head is slightly lower than at address but hasn't moved forward laterally.

The byproduct of the wide stance and flat-footed positioning is that Moe has a long flat spot at the bottom of his swing. This keeps the club on line with the target even longer than Lee Trevino. It also means he has a very shallow angle of attack on the ball, which is why he takes bacon strip divots ahead of the ball.

"Most people are a little early opening their hips and shoulders at impact, but Moe is exactly square," Suttie says. "That makes his club stay on the target line longer than anyone." Moe says his hands are square to the target 22 inches past the ball but photographs show his right hand crosses over his left well before that, which is still much later than most players.

Suttie says Moe's swing is also helped because he's naturally left-handed but plays right-handed. "He moves faster with his left side than his right on the downswing. This imbalance is what causes his knees to widen and keep his right heel down through the shot for so long. Most players jump off their right sides too fast and their arms can't catch up with their bodies. Moe is the ultimate upper body player in the world, but he also has the best leg action in the world."

Cook picked up on one little nuance of Moe's swing just before impact. "Only a few players could do this — and Ben Hogan was one. The face of the club is 90 per cent open all the way to the ball. Coming down he bows his left wrist just before impact, squaring the blade. This has to do with the way he shifts to the left with his hips and the club lags behind so the release of his club is very late. The club never flips past his hands because of his bowed left wrist position. This happens the same way every time so he has the same loft on the club every time and the same trajectory."

Follow-Through:

Even as his hands approach shoulder height on the follow-through, Moe's right foot remains on the ground. His head is also well behind the ball. Not until his hands reach head height and his upper body moves over his left foot does Moe's right heel finally come off the ground. "I let my swing balance me," Moe says.

His right side stays underneath the left side well past impact. Moe wants to avoid the feeling that the toe of the club is passing the heel. The result is that Moe's club never works around and behind him during the follow-through. As Moe says, "the club never goes out of bounds." The club shaft goes up dramatically and stays in front of him.

During clinics, Suttie has stood about a foot behind Moe while he took full swings with a driver. Moe's club hasn't come anywhere near Suttie.

When the swing is exhausted, Moe finishes beautifully with both arms and the club extended in a straight line pointed at the sky. Moe finishes in full height with his head, chest and hips facing the target. His weight is 100 per cent on his left foot and his right foot is straight up on the toe. Moe releases his upper body entirely into the shot so there is no reverse C, and therefore no pressure on the lower back.

His finish is so good, you could draw a straight line from the tips of his right toes through the leg, spine and through the arms and club.

Moe's ball flight:

The ultimate test for the effectiveness of a golf swing is ball flight. As CEO and president of Titleist, Wally Uihlein is an expert. He says that Moe has no equal in hitting a perfect shot.

"The ideal golf shot is stroked like it was hit by a ferris wheel. It would have perfect backspin and no sidespin. Of all the players we've ever seen, Moe comes as close to hitting the ball perfectly on a vertical axis.

"Since there is an angle and plane in the golf swing, most players have both sidespin and backspin. Sidespin contributes to a loss of accuracy as much as it does to a loss of velocity. Moe is as close to pure backspin with little or no sidespin. When you see Moe's shots, you can see the ball spinning. You think, 'Wow!' that's how a ball should be struck.

"As engineers and technicians, our analysis of Moe's swing tells us that he's approached the pure, efficient launch condition better than any other ball-striker. The golfer's trajectory is like a fingerprint and Moe's is as pure as it gets. Particularly with his irons, the ball climbs, peaks over the target, runs out of backspin and falls straight down.

"Moe understood long ago that golf was a target game."

***

For Moe's swing to become popular, a touring pro who emulates his swing would likely have to win some big tournaments. However, there are a number of lessons golfers can learn from Moe's swing:

If you have trouble making a smooth take-away, try putting the clubhead 12 to 18 inches behind the ball at address;

If you spin your hips toward the target too fast, Moe's wide stance will retard the "exploding" feeling;

If you tend to come up over the top and pull or slice shots, try keeping your right heel down well into the shot.

Some teachers such as John Redman believe that only Moe can use this swing motion because he's so strong and flexible, but Cook and Kuykendall believe Moe is a trailblazer who will change the game. "My feeling is that Moe's swing will become more of the swing of the future," Cook says. "It makes sense to me. I don't see any drawbacks to it."

Chapter Twenty-Three
The Feeling of Greatness

Despite a head of uniform grey, Moe is hitting the ball so far he's clearing trees at the back of the range, about 270 yards away. His broad face is rubbery and soft, the chin doubled and the jaw jowly, but the shoulders and arms are still thick and muscular. Moe the senior citizen is pounding drivers off the turf at a range near Burlington, Ontario — and hitting them farther than young bucks 45 years his junior. His meaty hands rip through shot after shot, the balls exploding off the clubface with the rocketing "phew" sound of a purely hit ball.

Many of the 50 onlookers at Carlisle Golf and Country Club gasp in awe, others shake their heads with permanent smiles plastered across their faces. Some laugh incredulously. The younger Moe may have blown his stack, but now he understands why people laugh and good naturedly chides the offending party: "Don't laugh. Don't laugh. You'd cry if you could hit it this good."

The man known for his excruciating shyness chats and kibitz's with the crowd, answering questions and dispensing concise pearls of wisdom, known as "Moe-isms," in his sing-songy voice.

On grip pressure: "I'm trying to draw blood with the left hand, but my arms are like cooked spaghetti."

On his thoughts during the swing: "I'm trying to get the iron in the hole, that's what I'm aiming at. I'm hole oriented, not green oriented."

On target awareness off the tee: "I see the word 'accuracy' across the fairway and I'm putting it right over the 'u.'"

On how to prevent a hook: "Don't excite the toe."

On balance: "I want both feet on the ground when I hit the ball. Most guys are way up on their right foot. I want my swing to balance me."

On footwork: "Roll the ankles, don't lift. You'll never see a spike on my left shoe back or through."

On preventing flippy hands: "Pretend there's no clubhead there. Hit with the handle. Where's the handle? If the handle is not in position, neither is the clubhead.

On the role of the right arm on the downswing: "Play softball, not hardball."

On hazards: "I don't see bad things. They don't exist on Moe Norman's golf course. I see only good things."

***

The crowd at the range includes several knowledgeable golfers. They're asking intelligent questions, so Moe's answering most of them. At many clinics he'll ignore a question that doesn't sound like something a golfer would ask, or if it's a leading question and the person is just fishing for an unusual answer.

On this day, Moe's calling his shots and hitting each one dead perfect as promised, even calling the number of bounces. "There's your Sunday paper. Same spot, same spot every time. There's a running hook, ha ha, run you little critter! OK here's the hardest shot in golf — dead straight." With a driver, he begins hitting shots by height. "There's 10 feet, 20 feet, 30 feet..."

Moe loves it when people watch him hit balls. He craves the attention. He likes nothing better than to captivate a crowd by launching rockets into the sky. All the while, he's doing a running commentary: "Is that pure? Oh man. Hoo boy. Is that pure? Hoo hoo. Never off plane. Watch again. Even a miss is dead straight. Watch again. Oh, it's so simple. Like falling off a log. Here's the purity of technique. Hoo man. Here's my feeling of greatness."

When he's hitting balls, he's on stage, freewheeling, improvising. He's like a virtuoso musician in absolute command of his instrument, playing out of his mind. He's the master and he knows people are in absolute awe. He feeds off their enthusiasm.

Moe's on a roll. Preaching his swing theories at clinics is now the driving force in his life. He's not interested in playing golf much anymore. He regards himself as the world's greatest ball-striker and he's on a mission to share his knowledge of the golf swing. Moe wants to make people aware of his heartfelt belief that his unique motion is the easiest, most repeatable swing going. "My move is the best in golf. You can learn from me because I'm poetry in motion."

Moe's also making some pretty good dough. Just around the time that people were becoming aware of Moe's exclusion from the Hall of Fame, demand was going up for his clinics. The CPGA books most of the exhibitions, and Moe drives alone from club to club across Canada, collecting about $900 per show. But after giving 70 clinics in 1993, demand fell to 53 in '94. Nonetheless, the clinics and some of Moe's other activities are finally generating some decent money. It wasn't until about 1992 that he was breaking even, said Gus Maue, who helps Moe with his business affairs. Moe was finally building up some savings. Moe's old-age pension — $907 a month — began to come in July of 1994.

Bob Dale Gloves, a small importer in Edmonton, signed him to a deal for a Moe Norman line of golf balls, a bag and a wedge. Moe was starting to get more media coverage in North America — even in Japan, where he's cult hero.

After more than 40 years in the business, Moe also finally landed a sponsor: Natural Golf. Jack Kuykendall, the physicist turned clubmaker, was giving a seminar on his unique hammer-action swing when Mark Evershed told him his swing was similar to Moe's — right down to the right-hand palm grip, upright clubs and thicker grips.

Kuykendall is committed to changing the way the world swings a golf club. Like Moe, he argues that swinging on a single-axis is far easier than the traditional swing. Kuykendall has been getting more media attention, but his greatest challenge is convincing people that changing their equipment and even looking a little strange is the only way they'll ever improve. "People say, 'I'll do anything to improve,' but what they mean is 'I'll do anything as long as I look like Jack Nicklaus.'"

***

Naturally enough, Moe's favourite song is Frank Sinatra's My Way.

Moe's way on the golf course was puzzling, illuminating, the stuff of genius. Some observers believe Moe's overwhelming insecurity may be the source of his remarkable talent and speed. One could argue the opposite. For Moe loved nothing more than to be the centre of attention when holding a golf club. But trying to figure out Moe is to wade into a minefield. Suffice to say, Moe played according to instinct.

"I played fast since the first time I picked up a golf stick. It suited me." Moe needed to keep moving to feel comfortable, like a nervous teenager who babbles to fill in the awkward gaps in conversation. Getting it over with quick was the key to his brilliant long game. The mechanics of the golf swing are hard enough to master, but the mind's tendency to sabotage the physical side makes the game even more difficult. The problem with golf is there's too much time to think. That darn ball just sits there until you somehow get it airborne. And the more you think about it, the more difficult the task becomes.

Moe's zippy style neutralized the psychological difficulty of golf. He didn't give mental gremlins any time to undermine his shots. Moe has made golf into a reaction sport. In most sports, you don't have time to think, you just react. When Moe swung, he reacted to his target like a goaltender snaring a slapshot with his glove.

Most players are fixated on their swing. All the mental energy is focused inwardly, and like a dog chasing his tail, the result can become frustrating. Golfers consistently forget that the goal in golf is to hit the target. Weslock says, "Even if the fairway is a mile wide, I'd ask him 'What are you thinking about here Moe?' He'd say 'Same old thing — target. That branch or that tree. That's all I'm interested in. Swinging through to that target.'"

It was easy for Moe to focus on the target because he had such complete confidence in his swing. "He knew he wouldn't make a bad swing, so that wouldn't happen," Ernie Hauser said. The confidence, along with Moe's sense of logic and desire to keep moving, inspired him to do things more effectively. Most people thought Moe never lined up his shots, but as Moe walked up a fairway, he would be analyzing the conditions, plotting his strategy and choosing the club. When he got to the ball, the only thing left to do was hit it.

"He'd be walking and talking and bouncing a ball on his club and be thinking about his next shot," Rockway buddy Ed Woroch said. "I've never met anyone like Moe who can carry on a conversation with attention to detail and think about something else at the same time."

Moe says he did everything according to his "mental pictures." While most players bark instructions at themselves throughout a game of golf, Moe pays attention to his pictures. "When I'm walking up the fairway, I look at the hole. I see the target in my mind and how I'll swing to the target. I memorize it so I'm set when I get to the ball. I just swing at the hole."

It never appeared that Moe lined up his putts either because he didn't

crouch down behind the ball. That's because Moe read the green well
before he got there. Moe knew far more about the science of the game
— notably design — than most people gave him credit. "It's the whole
picture, not just six feet behind the hole," Moe used to say to Ken
Tucker, Moe's Pleasure Park protege. "His mind was like a computer,"
Tucker said. "As he approached the green he was reading his putt. He'd
look at the surrounding landscape. Where did the rain run off the green?
How has the architect used mounds to create an optical illusion? He
didn't need to get behind the ball."

Moe also knew the conscious mind could complicate putting. If you
think too much about a putt, you're prone to read too much into it. "The
longer you look, the more you see," he says. Moe trusts what he sees on
the first glance. If he's not sure about the break, he'll just hit it at the hole.
This may well be the best advice any golfer will ever get on putting.

***

At the Royal Oak Golf Club in Titusville, Florida, Moe stands by the
putting green talking with friends. He's holding an ever-present driver in
the crook of his elbow, periodically grasping the shaft and smacking a
ball into the clubface with his other hand. This is how Moe spends his
days: talking with the young Canadian pros trying to take their game on
tour, club pros who try to keep their games in shape and older guys who
just want to bash the ball around with their buddies in the warm Florida
sunshine. Moe rarely plays, just talks, reads his psychology books and
hangs out.

In November of 1994, Royal Oak was buzzing with news that
Shankland would be showing a video of Moe's swing in front of 1,500
North American pros at the PGA of America Teaching Summit in New
Orleans in December. Moe was scheduled to speak after the video. "I
thought this would be dynamite," Irv Lightstone said. "This was a mind-
blower. It was about time the PGA took a good look at Moe."

There was one predictable problem: Moe wouldn't go. "I'm not
going to say 'Hi people and goodbye.' To hell with that noise. If I could
hit balls, OK, let's go."

There wasn't room nor time in the Super Dome. Up until the last
minute, Shankland tried to tell Moe that people wanted to learn from
him and pay tribute. It didn't change his mind.

Moe isn't just shy and afraid of crowds, he also appears to be afraid of himself. For many years, the PGA and CPGA have not called upon Moe to share his expertise, and his unique swing has been given short shrift by the gurus of the game. Perhaps he's afraid his bitterness might boil over. A man of deep emotions, Moe knows his feelings can run away on him on occasion so he avoids situations where he might lose control.

Later in the Royal Oak restaurant, when the subject of the teaching summit comes up, Moe blurts out to a reporter: "I'd love to go and grab that microphone. I'd ask 'When are you guys going to learn how simple the swing is.' I'd tell them things they've never heard before. I'd tell them they're making golf too difficult. They're giving people too many moving parts. No one hits it as pure as me."

Moe gets up from the table without saying a word, walks out of the restaurant and down the path to his Caprice parked behind the range. It's dusk. The reporter follows. It's obvious that discussing the summit has touched a deep nerve in Moe. Once again, circumstances, well-meaning friends and expectations have all appeared to gang up on him, leaving him angry and frustrated. The reporter asks him if he's felt frustrated throughout his life. "I couldn't reach many of my goals. I couldn't do what I wanted to do. Now I'm finally getting recognized at 65, that's what pisses me off. The Senior tour won't let me on. I'm not in the Hall of Fame. To hell with it!"

It's suggested to Moe he shares a lot in common with Trevino, who also felt like an outsider many times in his career. "Yeah, sure, I could relate to him." From a pile of papers in the backseat, Moe digs out an old Golf Digest magazine that he's saved from the early 1970s showing Trevino at impact. He looks at it admiringly, pointing out its beauty like a connoisseur of a treasured masterpiece. He gets out another clipping, a foldout picture of the 18th hole at Pebble Beach. He doesn't say anything, just waves his hand over the page as if to say, "behold."

The sadness of the moment disappears.

It is striking just how the game touches his heart and soul. He loves the game through and through. Golf has been his companion. In a life filled with anxiety and turmoil, golf has given him pleasure and security. He could put his trust in the game. The periphery of the game that caused him untold grief — rules, tournaments, officials, strangers — is far away. Hitting a golf ball never hurt him or frustrated him. It is perhaps the only thing he can trust in his entire life. Just the sensation of hitting a golf ball is a comfort.

What does Moe love about hitting a golf ball? "The thrill of feeling it," he says. 'Ah, that felt great. Now I did want I wanted to do. Every muscle enjoyed that shot. Oh that was nice.' That's what I get a kick out of. The feeling of greatness."

He takes a breath and continues: "Here's 40 million people, 40 million people who would love to be able to do what I can do. Isn't that a wonderful feeling. Only two things money can't buy — knowledge and talent. And I have more of these things than anybody in this world. Boy what a great world.

"I'm the richest person in the world by far — in feelings. I'm doing things everyone would love to do, and I know why. What a great feeling. Oh, you can take the money. I'll take knowledge and talent any day."

He's positively beaming. He gets in his car, backs up, drives down the road and disappears over the top of the hill.

Postscript

Moe was on a roll in early 1995, but his savings were meagre and his future was far from secure.

In February, however, Wally Uihlein, CEO and president of Titleist, announced the company would pay Moe Norman $5,000 a month (U.S.) for the rest of his life and make a video of his swing for posterity.

"To my mind, Moe Norman is in the same league as Ben Hogan, Bobby Jones and Byron Nelson as a ball-striker and deserves the same kind of respect," Uihlein said.

Moe's obligation in the deal?

"Moe just has to be himself," Uihlein said. Titleist has no commercial plans for Moe. It was strictly a humanitarian gesture.

"This Titleist deal is the only thing that gives him security," said Moe's lawyer Frank Genesee. "It is so important for Moe. This was sport at its noblest, to see golf look after its own."

It took nearly 45 years, but Moe's talent finally paid off.

***

On February 20, 1995, the Royal Canadian Golf Association announced Moe Norman had been finally elected to the Canadian Golf Hall of Fame.

At the same time it was also announced that Jack Nicklaus was elected to the hall in the Builder's category. Moe was elected on his playing record.

"We know that all Canadians will be thrilled by the selection of these outstanding golfers," said Keith Rever, chairman of the Hall of Fame selection committee and a RCGA past-president.

The election stems from the nomination letter sent by Nick Weslock in 1993.

"It's good news," Moe said. "But I should have been in years ago. I shouldn't have had to wait until now, when I'm 65. I owe a lot of thanks to the public. The public and the press put a lot of pressure on (the RCGA) to induct me. But overall, yes, I'm pleased."

The ceremony for Moe's induction was held on Aug. 24, 1995, at Foxwood Golf Club, a public course near Kitchener. It was fitting that Moe was inducted at a public course — the kind of course where average people play and he has always felt most comfortable. He felt at home. Heeding Moe's request, the RCGA invited only 50 people — most of whom were close friends.

A source within the RCGA said it was a great relief to many members to finally have Moe inducted. "It was way overdue. It took a lot of people and a lot of time to get it done. There was a lot of internal turmoil over it. Moe has a lot of allies in the RCGA." Many people criticized the entire RCGA, but it was only a few people who held up Moe's election. "Moe has a lot more friends in the RCGA than he knows," Rever said.

"I hope we can convince him it's an honour."

The Author

Tim O'Connor lives in Toronto with his wife Sandy and young son Corey, whom he did not name after Corey Pavin. He writes a golf column in The Financial Post daily and is Contributing Editor of Score, Canada's golf magazine.

He was named Magazine Writer of 1994 by the International Network of Golf. He has twice won first place in the writing contest of the Golf Course Superintendents Association of America, in 1990 and 1993. This is his first book.